THE
DEMOCRACY
PROMOTION
PARADOX

THE
DEMOCRACY
PROMOTION
PARADOX

LINCOLN A. MITCHELL

BROOKINGS INSTITUTION PRESS
Washington, D.C.

Copyright © 2016
THE BROOKINGS INSTITUTION
1775 Massachusetts Avenue, N.W., Washington, D.C. 20036
www.brookings.edu

The Brookings Institution is a private nonprofit organization devoted to research, education, and publication on important issues of
domestic and foreign policy. Its principal purpose is to bring the
highest quality independent research and analysis to bear on current and emerging policy problems. Interpretations or conclusions in
Brookings publications should be understood to be solely those of the
authors.

Library of Congress Cataloging-in-Publication data

Names: Mitchell, Lincoln A., author.
Title: The democracy promotion paradox / Lincoln A. Mitchell.
Description: Washington, D.C. : Brookings Institution Press,
    2016. | Includes bibliographical references and index.
Identifiers: LCCN 2015046469 (print) | LCCN 2016005723 (ebook) |
    ISBN 9780815727026 (paperback) | ISBN 9780815727033 (epub) |
    ISBN 9780815727040 (pdf)
Subjects: LCSH: Democratization—Government policy—
    United States. | United States—Foreign relations. |
    BISAC: POLITICAL SCIENCE / Political Ideologies /
    Democracy. | POLITICAL SCIENCE / International
    Relations / Diplomacy. | POLITICAL SCIENCE / Political
    Freedom & Security / General.
Classification: LCC JZ1480.A55 M58 2016 (print) | LCC JZ1480.A55
    (ebook) | DDC 327.1/1—dc23
LC record available at http://lccn.loc.gov/2015046469

9 8 7 6 5 4 3 2 1

Typeset in Janson

Composition by Westchester Publishing Services

CONTENTS

PREFACE

I STARTED WORKING IN DEMOCRACY PROMOTION in 2000. At that time, when I would leave my New York home to work in the Balkans, the former Soviet Union, or elsewhere, friends and acquaintances, on hearing where I was going and what I was doing, would express surprise that the United States was involved in that kind of work and would encourage me. Those were the last days of the Clinton administration and what still felt like the 1990s. Five years later other friends and acquaintances, when learning what I did for a living or that I was preparing to go to Kinshasa, Bishkek, or Baku to do democracy promotion work, would roll their eyes and sarcastically mutter "Just like in Iraq." By 2009 or so, the response I encountered was generally to the effect of "Why don't we use some of that money to build schools or something here?" (in the United States). These changing reactions capture the evolution of American opinion about democracy promotion as well as the changing environment in which that work has been pursued in the last quarter century. By 2012, I rarely bothered to explain to people why I was going away, but just told them it was for work.

In *The Democracy Promotion Paradox*, I draw on over a decade of experience implementing, evaluating, and advising on democracy promotion work. During most of those years, I was also a scholar studying and writing about democracy promotion. Working as a scholar and practitioner has brought a good synergy to both areas of work and, I hope, to this book as well. It has also created challenges for me in both the democracy promotion and scholarly communities. The former has often considered me too critical of democracy work, while the latter has occasionally seen me as too sympathetic to the work of democracy promotion. That tension is also reflected in this work.

This book is intended as an analysis of democracy promotion, emphasizing the paradoxes that can make democracy work simultaneously puzzling, frustrating, exciting, rewarding, and, occasionally, even effective. This approach leads to analysis that focuses on the shortcomings and problems of democracy promotion, while often appearing to overlook the positive aspects and successes of the work. Had I written a book called *The Democracy Promotion Synergy*, it probably would have had a different tone, but that approach would also have missed some of the most important points of the analysis. These paradoxes are real and important. Ignoring them or seeking to push them away through platitudes and assumptions will only create greater problems for democracy promotion and indeed for U.S. foreign policy more broadly.

Nonetheless, I struggled with the tone throughout the work. I sought a balance, identifying and exploring the paradoxes while avoiding simply reciting lists of the problems of political development or democracy work. My goal was to strike a tone of critical analysis, not hostility. A paradox of my own is that while I have written critically of U.S. democracy promotion, I have tremendous personal and professional respect for many working in the field and the work that has been done, and believe in the overall aim of trying to make it possible for more people to live in democratic and free states. I am a critic of some aspects of democracy promotion, but for many years have also been a member in relatively good standing of the democracy promotion community. This is my own democracy promotion paradox that also lies at the heart of this book.

A tendency to focus on the difficulties of democracy promotion while quickly brushing over the successes of democracy work is difficult to avoid. There are, however, many successes. The transformation of postwar Germany and Japan into democracies, the spread of elections and democracy as the norm (albeit one still too often honored in the breach) to almost every corner of the world, and consolidation of democracy in much of postcommunist Eastern Europe and in parts of Asia and South America are all among the major global developments in which

U.S. supported democracy promotion has played a role. The work of U.S. democracy promotion should not be overlooked, however, in other less visible or dramatic areas. All over the world, local civil society organizations that would not exist absent American support are fighting for free media, against corruption, and for women's rights; parliaments and other legislatures are more responsive because of U.S.-backed programs; and authoritarian leaders are a little more wary of stealing the next election because they know local organizations, trained and supported with help from the United States, will be watching. All this has been achieved despite the paradoxes that surround democracy promotion.

Democracy promotion is associated with the United States more than with any other country—especially among Americans—but many other countries, mainly in Europe, also seek to promote democracy abroad. This work is done sometimes in collaboration with U.S. efforts and sometimes independently. Tsveta Petrova and Laurynas Jonavicius are among those who have written about democracy promotion work by newer democracies, specifically postcommunist countries in Eastern Europe.[1] Gerd Schonwalder and Sarah Repucci have studied the efforts of non-European democracies such as India and South Africa to promote democracy.[2] Andrew Youngs and others such as Frank Schimmelfennig and Hanno Scholtz have written about European democracy promotion as well as the challenges of U.S. and European collaboration on democracy work.[3]

This book, however, focuses on American democracy promotion efforts and the relationship between that and broader American foreign policy. A larger, more global examination of democracy promotion would raise, and perhaps answer, different and important questions, but Poland's efforts to promote democracy or the question of whether or not India is meaningfully contributing to global democracy have little bearing on the paradoxes and challenges confronting U.S. democracy promotion.

REGIME TYPES AND TERMS

The terms "democracy promotion" and "democracy assistance" are used interchangeably throughout this book. The term "democracy work" is also used occasionally, but usually refers to a broader definition of democracy promotion.

Most of the countries in which the United States seeks to encourage democracy, and in fact most of the world, exist in a gray area between democracy and authoritarianism. While some of these countries may appear democratic, few are vibrant consolidated democracies such as those of Europe and North America. Similarly, while many countries in which the United States supports democracy promotion are not free, they are not totalitarian regimes like Stalin's Soviet Union, fascist Germany, or contemporary North Korea. Instead, almost all these countries have elements of democracy, however imperfect, and elements of authoritarianism, however flimsy.

Numerous terms are used to describe these in-between countries, including "transitional," "semi-democratic," "new democracies," "semi-authoritarian," "democratic," "authoritarian," and a bevy of modified terms such as "competitive authoritarian," and "illiberal democracy."[4] The study of these kinds of regimes and their taxonomies is important, but it is not the subject of this book. Nonetheless, it is important to use terms accurately when discussing political systems.

Accordingly, I use three main terms to describe regimes that are neither democratic nor authoritarian. I largely eschew the term "transitional," because it implies something—that the country in question is in a state of transition—that is frequently no longer the case. Instead, I use the term "nondemocratic" as a broad and general term for all countries that are not democratic. This range of countries can include consolidated authoritarian regimes such as North Korea, postconflict governments such as those in Afghanistan and Iraq, regimes with strong elements of democracy such as Moldova, and regimes that employ various forms of authoritarianism such as Azerbaijan or Vietnam.

I also use the terms "semi-democratic" and "semi-authoritarian" to describe various regimes at various times. Semi-democratic draws on the work of Thomas Carothers and refers to several different kinds of flawed or modified democracies. These are countries that have enough contestation, participation, and accountability that election outcomes are uncertain and where there is a reasonable amount of media and civic freedom. However, these countries may be plagued with corruption, occasional government excesses, flawed elections, and the like. Carothers describes two types of semi-democratic regimes. The first is "feckless pluralism," characterized by significant amounts of political freedom, regular elections, and alternation of power between genuinely different political groupings. Despite these positive features, however, democracy remains shallow and troubled. Political participation, though broad at election time, extends little beyond voting. Political elites from all the major parties or groupings are widely perceived as corrupt, self-interested, and ineffective. The alternation of power seems only to trade the country's problems back and forth from one hapless side to the other.[5]

The second regime type is "dominant power," characterized by

> limited but still real political space, some political contestation by opposition groups, and at least most of the basic institutional forms of democracy. Yet one political grouping—whether it is a movement, a party, an extended family, or a single leader—dominates the system in such a way that there appears to be little prospect of alternation of power in the foreseeable future.[6]

In this book, "semi-democratic" refers to regimes characterized by "feckless pluralism."

The term "semi-authoritarian" is best described by analyst Marina Ottaway, as

> ambiguous systems that combine rhetorical acceptance of liberal democracy, the existence of some formal democratic institutions, and respect for a limited sphere of civil and political liberties with essentially illiberal or even authoritarian traits. This ambiguous character, furthermore, is deliberate. Semi-authoritarian systems are not imperfect democracies struggling toward improvement and consolidation but regimes determined to maintain the appearance of democracy without exposing themselves to the political risks that free competition entails.[7]

Semi-authoritarian regimes may look from the outside like semi-democratic regimes, as both have some of the elements of democracy, but there are critical differences. While semi-democratic regimes are flawed democracies that have the potential to consolidate, semi-authoritarian regimes are flawed authoritarian regimes that for one reason or another cannot or will not consolidate into fully formed authoritarian regimes. Thus, semi-authoritarian regimes usually have less uncertainty around election outcomes and less media and civic freedom. They can also have less corruption, however, and election days are often smoother than those in semi-democratic regimes. The key difference in semi-authoritarian regimes is that institutions such as elections and legislatures exist to keep the nondemocratic regime in place and rarely present a possible opening for democracy.

This discussion of regime types is not an entirely academic exercise, since democracy promotion has different impacts on semi-democratic and semi-authoritarian regimes, and many of the paradoxes explored in this book are exacerbated by the difficulty, and political stakes involved, in determining which country fits which regime type.

CONFRONTING THE PARADOXES

The paradoxes of democracy promotion described in this work are unlikely to surprise people experienced in the field of democracy work or even those who have considered the complexity of this multitiered and often misunderstood policy. Nonetheless, for many in the field of democracy work, and even in foreign policy more generally, it has long been easier to look past the paradoxes of democracy work. This approach is a plausible short-term strategy, but ultimately it has contributed to democracy promotion policies that have grown more stagnant and less effective over time.

Drawing attention to these paradoxes can lead to a better scholarly understanding of both democracy promotion and its relationship to U.S. foreign policy, as well to a democracy promotion policy more grounded in nuance than in cutting intellectual corners, which has become too common in democracy promotion. However, the future of democracy promotion with regard to challenges ranging from domestic U.S. politics to the increasingly multipolar world is far less certain than many in the field care to recognize. Democracy promotion is unlikely to succeed in the future if the major paradoxes hamstringing its success continue to be overlooked.

THE
DEMOCRACY
PROMOTION
PARADOX

CHAPTER ONE
INTRODUCTION

IN EARLY 2012, NINETEEN EMPLOYEES of U.S. based democracy assistance organizations, including the National Democratic Institute (NDI), the International Republican Institute (IRI), and Freedom House were arrested by Egypt's post-Mubarak military regime. In the twelve to eighteen months before those arrests, several semi-authoritarian regimes from Bishkek to Tunis had collapsed, but unlike a similar wave of regime transitions a few years earlier, these events occurred with the official democracy assistance community most emphatically on the sidelines. If the Color Revolutions, the peaceful uprisings that overthrew corrupt regimes in Georgia in 2003, Ukraine in 2004, and Kyrgyzstan in 2005, were nurtured and encouraged by democracy assistance policy, the Arab Spring and its preamble, in Kyrgyzstan in mid-2010, were something very different.

In a related event, as the Arab Spring was just getting into full swing in early 2011, fully 165 members of the U.S. House of Representatives, almost all of them Republicans, including many serving their first terms in Congress, signed a statement calling for the abolition of the U.S. Agency for International Development (USAID), the donor agency responsible for funding most U.S. backed democracy assistance work.

The year 2011 ended with fraudulent Russian elections followed by widespread demonstrations, calls for Russian prime minister Vladimir

Putin's resignation, and a strong sense that the authoritarian regime that Putin had so carefully constructed over a decade was beginning to crack. Russia under Putin had been hostile to Western democracy assistance efforts for years: it had passed numerous laws defanging NGOs (nongovernmental organizations) working on democracy issues and, in 2011, had not allowed the Organization for Security and Cooperation in Europe (OSCE), the most visible and professional election observation group in the region, to even send observers. Nonetheless, when the demonstrations started Putin did not hesitate to point the finger at the United States generally and Secretary of State Hillary Clinton specifically.

Those demonstrations have done little to weaken Putin, Russia's president again since May 2012, or the increasingly authoritarian regime he has put in place. A Freedom House report, "Contending with Putin's Russia: A Call for American Leadership," describes how, since that election, Putin has

> step by step . . . pushed through measures to deter public demonstrations, smear and limit funding for nongovernmental organizations, and place restrictions on the internet. He has also made anti-Americanism a central part of his political message. He has accused the United States of fomenting demonstrations against election fraud, shut down all U.S. Agency for International Development (USAID) programs in Russia, withdrawn from a series of cooperative agreements with the United States, and signed a vindictive law that prohibits the adoption of Russian children by citizens of the United States.[1]

This despite years of U.S. democracy promotion activity in Russia, although by 2012 or so Russian policy on foreign support for NGOs had caused many of these programs to be reduced or shut down.

Roughly a year after the demonstrations, a major upset victory in Georgia saw the defeat of President Mikheil Saakashvili's United National Movement Party (UNM) at the hands of the Georgian Dream (GD) coalition. This upset occurred despite efforts by the ruling party to restrict the opposition by arresting its activists, stripping its leader of his citizenship, and limiting the opposition's access to the media. More significant, the GD won its victory despite very little support, or even recognition of the increasingly authoritarian nature of the UNM, by the West.

The relative absence of the democracy assistance community in helping to bring about the GD victory, which represented yet another potential democratic breakthrough for Georgia, stood in stark contrast to the Rose Revolution nine years before. In 2003, the democracy promotion NGOs had been very close to the events, helping draw attention to election fraud, develop coalitions between opposition forces, and support a vibrant civil society. In 2012, the role of those organizations was substantially less. The election was still monitored, but election observers close to the campaign, foreign consultants, and powerful lobbyists on both sides were much more central to the developments than any U.S. or other foreign-backed democracy organizations.

As the wars in Iraq and Afghanistan moved into their second decades, elections in those countries were no longer analyzed or discussed as having any bearing on democratic development because most in the West no longer took the possibility of those countries becoming democratic, or of the West contributing to that outcome, seriously. These elections functioned more as grim reminders of the failures of American military and political development policies in those two countries.

THE PARADOXES OF DEMOCRACY PROMOTION AND FOREIGN POLICY

Thus, although during the Bush administration democracy assistance had become associated with the neoconservative movement, the Republican Party, and the controversial and aggressive foreign policy of President George W. Bush, by a few years into the Obama administration it was becoming apparent that democracy assistance faced a new but equally serious set of challenges. These challenges were not simply the result of failed and unpopular military adventures in Iraq and Afghanistan, but were the product of the coming of age of many of the deep paradoxes that have long characterized U.S. backed democracy assistance. These paradoxes also raise important but often complex questions about the role and place of democracy assistance in U.S. foreign policy.

These paradoxes, which frame our understanding of democracy assistance and are addressed in greater depth throughout this book, are briefly introduced here. The first major paradox is inherent in democracy assistance in a larger political and historical context. U.S. efforts to develop democracy have been linked to military intervention and massive postwar reconstruction efforts going back to at least the end of World War II and, according to many, even further. Political scientist Tony Smith describes efforts by the United States to support democracy in the Philippines and throughout Latin America in the late nineteenth and early twentieth centuries following the Spanish-American War and other conflicts.[2]

The long pedigree of democracy promotion is often overlooked. The attention paid to democracy promotion from about 2003 to 2007, in no small part because of the connection made by the Bush administration between the wars in Afghanistan and Iraq and efforts to create democracy in those countries, was considerably greater than at any time before or since. Observers of American foreign policy could have come to mistakenly believe that democracy promotion was an idea cooked up by the same neoconservatives who pushed for the war in Iraq. They would have been wrong, however. Democracy promotion has been, in one form or another and with varying degrees of success, part of American foreign policy for a long time. This reflects the importance of democracy to American policymakers as well as the deeply, and to a large extent, uniquely, American view that remaking the world in our image is not only our right, but our duty.

The broadly ambitious mission of democracy promotion, however, often manifests itself in less dramatic, even ordinary, ways. Today, democracy assistance funding often goes to benign and even mundane-sounding projects such as capacity building for local civil society organizations, strengthening legislatures, training political party activists, and similar programs. For example, in fiscal year 2012, USAID spent only $2.8 billion of its almost $34 billion budget on democracy and governance.[3] Over two-thirds of that went to rule of law and human rights and good governance. The remainder went to political competition and consensus building and civil society. If our understanding of democracy promotion is limited to this kind of direct funding, it is hard to see it as anything other than a modest, even harmless, policy.

In some respects, however, democracy assistance encompasses both groups of activities: military intervention, diplomatic statements, and positioning on one hand, and programmatic activities on the other. But democracy assistance is often considered primarily the former by the media and the public, and as the latter by people working in the field. This paradox naturally and inevitably leads to a disconnect between practitioners and the public when talking about democracy assistance.

CAN NONDEMOCRATIC REGIMES HELP BRING DEMOCRACY?

A second, similar paradox arises from the disconnect between how democracy assistance is seen by those on the outside and how it is seen by those on the inside. Democracy assistance seeks to change the very nature of governance, but programs are often crafted based on the implicit assumption that nondemocratic governments are partners in this effort and that these governments will be supportive and are seeking to become more democratic.

For example, the executive summary of a USAID strategic document on Azerbaijan for the years 2011–16 states,

> Azerbaijan has demonstrated political will in some areas to embrace reform and has taken steps to improve the socio-economic conditions for its people. In other areas, change has moved at a slower pace. . . . USAID aims to support the following objectives over the five year strategy period . . . increasing the effective participation of diverse actors and institutions in the democratic development of the country. . . . To implement these objectives, we will partner with the private sector, NGOs, regional governments and with the Government of Azerbaijan (GOAJ). . . . The U.S. government's longstanding development partnership with the GOAJ has evolved. . . . Today the partnership is one of equals, and focused on long-term development. In the coming years, we will build on the strong foundations of our relationship with our partners to broaden and deepen our collaboration, and strive to leave behind a sustainable legacy of our joint efforts.[4]

By 2010, however, Azerbaijan was no longer a transitional country by most measures. Freedom House reports from 2004 to 2011, drawing on information from 2003 to 2010, describe Azerbaijan as "not free," with a combined score of eleven on political and civil liberties.[5] The score of eleven was particularly low, as Freedom House scores range from a combined two to fourteen, with two being the most democratic. While the governments of Azerbaijan and the United States enjoyed a partnership in the years preceding the report, it was not one where any progress had been made on democratic development. Beginning in 2014, Azerbaijan's human rights record went from bad to worse, as NGOs were harassed more and prominent journalists and NGO activists were arrested. This not unpredictable development highlights the contrast between the wishful strategy document and the political reality in Azerbaijan.

Thus, programs have been implemented in countries such as Azerbaijan, and many others, that rely on cooperation with the governments of these semi-authoritarian countries, implicitly assuming that the host governments share the U.S. interest in greater democracy. Not surprisingly, these assumptions are frequently wrong; and working closely with nondemocratic governments all but assures failure for democracy assistance programs or limits them to, at best, improving governance. However, in many nondemocratic countries, U.S.-supported democracy assistance programs that challenge the government too strongly are restricted, harassed, or expelled. Those charged with crafting programs are therefore forced into these unrealistic and paradoxical assumptions, because programs that do not rest on these assumptions cannot function at all.

POLITICAL VERSUS TECHNICAL APPROACHES

The conflict between political and technical approaches creates a paradox that permeates both the implementation of democracy assistance projects and U.S. strategies for promoting democratic development in many countries. It should be obvious that in most cases helping countries move from authoritarianism to democracy is a profoundly political project. It involves changing how leaders and ordinary citizens think about government, power, and the state. It also inevitably requires some people to give up power and the wealth and perks that accompany that power. The obstacles to greater democracy in countries ranging from Tajikistan to Tanzania are there largely because the people in power simply do not want democracy, yet the approaches to building democracy in these kinds of places are often heavily focused on the technical side.

The idea that better trained parliamentary staff or more comprehensive voter lists will lead to fundamental political change, absent political pressure on the country's leadership, is almost absurd, but that is how most democracy assistance programs are structured, reflecting the assumptions on which the programs are based.

Twenty years ago, these technical programs were effective because many countries genuinely were in a period of transition and were led by governments seeking to become more democratic. In those countries, such as Poland or Hungary in the early 1990s, technical programs were good ways to transfer needed skills, expertise, and knowledge. While the context has changed, it remains true that technically oriented programs align more consistently with the approaches and structures within most funding agencies, notably USAID. It is much easier to secure funding for a program aimed at, for example, providing political party activists with campaign skills than one aimed at providing useful strategic guidance to those same political parties. In many cases these technical programs are useful, but not highly so, and not focused on the major problems of democracy in the countries in which they are implemented.

DEMOCRACY PROMOTION AND THE U.S. GOVERNMENT

The relationship between democracy assistance programs and organizations and the U.S. government is also fraught with complexity and paradoxes. For example, in many countries with active and well-funded democracy assistance programs, the United States is also providing ample foreign assistance to the governments. For example, between fiscal years 2005 and 2010, the United States gave approximately $9.9 billion in assistance to Egypt; roughly $7.8 billion was in the form of military assistance.[6] Democracy assistance support during this period never reached even $60 million per year; and in most years it was considerably less.[7]

In Cambodia, a country that has historically received significantly less assistance than Egypt, the United States contributed $3.4 billion between FY2008 and FY2012. However, during those years, a total of only about $60 million was allocated for democracy assistance.[8] Cambodia is not as big or strategically important to the United States as Egypt is, but that may be why the numbers there are particularly illustrative. In a country such as Cambodia, a lesser U.S. priority, about 1.6 percent of U.S. assistance went to democracy promotion.

In most cases, democracy assistance resources are dwarfed by other foreign assistance, as seen in the data from Egypt and Cambodia. This equation is rarely lost on the government in question. Governments that enjoy close and, frequently, lucrative relationships with the U.S. government despite their shortcomings on democracy find it difficult to take seriously U.S. claims that democracy is important. Democracy programs in this context have very little leverage with the governments they seek to democratize.

In addition to this split in U.S. resources, which makes democracy work difficult in many cases, a similar paradox exists in how foreign assistance programs are implemented. Democracy assistance is often earnestly pursued by one branch of the U.S. government in a given country while another branch is working to support the incumbent authoritarian regime. This most often takes the form of substantial military assistance from the United States going to a regime that relies heavily on the military to stay in power. It is also not unusual, for example, for a country to receive U.S. assistance for fair elections and also equipment for their interior ministry, or money to buy the equipment. These dynamics create situations where the tools used by troops to put down protests are paid for from the same foreign assistance package as the training provided to the demonstrators being beaten. If this example is dramatic, less extreme cases occur all the time, as when assistance from the United States makes it possible for an embattled government to dole out key preelection patronage and thereby, often in tandem with election fraud, help secure reelection.

Moreover, in bilateral discussions it is usually made clear that democracy, despite official rhetoric, is not America's top priority. USAID country strategies usually list democracy promotion as the third or fourth most important priority; and it is very rare, except perhaps when a visit to a foreign country coincides with an election, to hear a U.S. president, cabinet member, or other highly visible American visitor mention democracy as a top priority. Even when there are legitimate and reasonable explanations for these strategies, they obviously make democracy promotion more difficult for those working in the field.

THE PARADOXES OF AMERICAN NGOS

The role of American NGOs is central to the implementation of democracy assistance, but these organizations are not without their own paradoxes. Many working in the field of democracy assistance stress that this work is done by NGOs, but these organizations receive the overwhelming majority of their funding from the U.S. government. In mid-2014, the "welcome" section of the website of the International Republican Institute (IRI), one of the most prominent NGOs working in democracy assistance, said, "IRI works with multilateral organizations like the Organization for Security and Cooperation in Europe and the United Nations, with partners like Australia's Liberals and the European People's Party, and with institutions in newer democracies, such as India, Mexico, Lithuania, Slovakia and Indonesia, who bring recent, relevant democracy building experiences to bear."[9]

No mention was made, however, of USAID, by far IRI's biggest donor, or the U.S. government more generally, in that section. When the general media covers democracy organizations they almost always refer to them as NGOs. A story in the *Washington Post* on June 4, 2013, about the trials of NDI and IRI workers in Egypt was headlined "NGO Workers Convicted in Egypt."[10] A more colorful headline that same day in the *Christian Science Monitor* read "Egypt to Global Democracy NGOs: Drop Dead."[11] Similar coverage and language is used to describe organizations such as NDI, IRI, and Freedom House whenever they are in the news. Although these organizations are NGOs, using this language and not providing other details often obscures the dependence of these NGOs on the U.S. government.

For example, in 2012 Freedom House received 88 percent of its funding from the U.S. government.[12] Although specific data for NDI and IRI are more difficult to find because annual reports with this information are not easily available, the consensus among scholars and activists, including current and former NDI and IRI staff, is that these organizations each receive roughly 80 percent or more of their funding from various branches of the U.S. government. Numerous local NGOs in foreign countries are equally dependent on U.S. or European money. NGOs funded by their governments and working closely with those governments in crafting and implementing programs cannot be called fully nongovernmental. Although democracy assistance NGOs do not necessarily do exactly what they are told by the U.S. government, the relationship is too close for these organizations to be independent of U.S. government influence in a meaningful sense. Moreover, the close relationships between democracy NGOs and the U.S. government are understood by governments and others in the countries where they work, rendering the notion that they are distinct from the U.S. government one that is largely believed only by the NGOs. The question of whether or not the United States should fund democracy work is a separate one, and is not the point here. Instead, the point is that NGOs can be distinct from the U.S. government or heavily dependent on the U.S. government for financial survival, but probably not both.

Many American NGOs that operate only domestically are supported by local, state, or federal governments. Service-oriented NGOs such as senior centers, youth programs, and the like frequently get most of their funding from various levels of government. Moreover, many European NGOs are dependent on government money to a greater degree than those in the United States. Nonetheless, to American audiences, the term "NGO" suggests that funding is not dependent on the government and comes either from individual members or through donations from wealthy individuals or foundations. Organizations like NDI and IRI seek and receive this kind of funding as well, but it generally constitutes a very small proportion of their overall budgets. The failure of these organizations to secure substantial nongovernmental sources of funding very much blurs the line between a genuinely nongovernmental organization and an instrument of American foreign policy.

DEMOCRACY PROMOTION AND THE MILITARY

Several paradoxes permeate most academic and policy debates around democracy assistance and its value, efficacy, and impact. The first revolves around the role of the military in democracy assistance. During the Bush administration, democracy assistance became linked, in the view of many, to U.S. military intervention in Iraq and Afghanistan. It therefore became an article of faith among critics of the Bush administration and of democracy assistance more generally that democracy could not be linked to military intervention. This makes a lot of intuitive sense, as it seems apparent that democracy needs to come from people's own desires and cannot be simply imposed following military defeat. This idea also appeals to progressive political sensibilities, as it weakens arguments in favor of military intervention.

For example, a 2003 article by Chris Patten, called "Democracy Doesn't Flow from the Barrel of a Gun," is a well-thought-out overview of U.S. democracy promotion strategies, but the title probably originated with an editor at *Foreign Policy* seeking more clicks on the website. Also possible is that, because the piece focused somewhat on Hong Kong, the title was a riff on Mao Zedong's famous thought on political power and gun barrels. A similar 2006 article by Jeffrey Pickering and Mark Peceny exploring Western democracy promotion was titled "Forging Democracy at Gunpoint."[13] Between 2002 and 2005, publications as diverse as *The Economist*, the *San Francisco Chronicle*,[14] *The Progressive*,[15] and (in an article by then Rep. Jesse Jackson Jr.) *Common Dreams* all published articles about Iraq using the words "gunpoint" and "democracy" in the titles.[16]

Unfortunately for the advocates of the view that democracy and military intervention cannot go hand in hand, this view is demonstrably false. Some of the most impressive successes of democracy assistance have occurred as a result of military actions. The most obvious and high profile examples of this are Germany and Japan where, following defeat at the hands of the United States and its allies in World War II, democracy was very successfully imposed. In other countries, including in eastern Europe and the Baltic states, democratic development was only possible following the Western, and substantially American, victory in the Cold War.

The lure of NATO membership has been and continues to be an important strategic tool of democracy promotion. Fifteen to twenty years ago, the promise of NATO membership, and thus a guarantee of membership in and protection by the world's most powerful military alliance, helped nudge many countries of the former communist bloc toward democracy. Similar incentives exist today for Georgia and Moldova. Although this is not quite democracy promotion through military intervention, it demonstrates the role American and allied military strength can play in encouraging democracy.

LEFT CRITICISM OF DEMOCRACY PROMOTION

Left-of-center critics of democracy promotion often frame their concerns around two mutually exclusive arguments. These critics argue that this assistance is not driven by a U.S. desire to see democracy at all, but rather about ensuring that foreign countries have leaders that the United States wants. Proponents of this view suggest that democracy assistance is the latest iteration of American imperialism, with NGOs and the National Endowment for Democracy (NED) replacing the CIA and covert operations. Tom Hayden, writing in the pages of *The Nation* in 2014, referred to

> the growing US pattern of ignoring democratic electoral outcomes where they are inconvenient, in the name of "promoting democracy." Ultimately this process of "democracy through intervention" reinforces bureaucratic authoritarian trends in both East and West. The thrust of this US foreign policy mirrors conservatives' efforts at home to limit and divide the ascending multicultural American political majority.[17]

A blog post by independent foreign policy analyst Stephen Gowans also captures the nature of left critiques of democracy promotion. Gowans refers to Freedom House as "a CIA-interlocked think-tank that promotes free markets, free enterprise and free trade. . . . Peter Ackerman has been at the forefront of efforts to topple foreign governments that place more emphasis on promoting the welfare of their citizens (and often their own bourgeoisie) than providing export and investment opportunities to US corporations, banks, and investors."[18]

The paradox of this assertion is that it is not consistent with the previous argument that democracy assistance "at gunpoint" is useless, which is often made by the same people. If, after all, democracy assistance cannot work, it can hardly be compared to imperialism. Twenty-first-century democracy assistance can either be a nefarious imperialist plot masquerading as an effort to bring democracy to people, or it can be ineffective with no possibility of success, but it cannot be both.

DEMOCRACY PROMOTION–THE BIGGER PICTURE

Together, these paradoxes capture the complex and often confusing nature of democracy promotion, a nuanced policy that exists in various shades of gray but is often understood by those closest to it in absolute terms. It is a policy that has roots in American imperialism and militarism but that also has an altruistic side. Many Americans involved in democracy work are true believers in democracy, even if it is not in the immediate interests of the United States, and believe deeply in the value and goodness of their work. And democracy promotion NGOs, despite their rather precarious independence from government, are an important voice in U.S. foreign policy.

In many countries where I have worked, I have seen representatives from democracy organizations argue with the official U.S. representatives passionately and persuasively, although not always successfully, in support of greater U.S. emphasis on democracy, or for the United States to be more critical of the nondemocratic host government. Many working in the field of democracy assistance are progressives drawing on their own experiences in various left-of-center movements in the United States, but the origins of democracy assistance are found in the rise of postwar conservatism in both major political parties.

It is ironic that while many in the progressive media portray democracy promotion as a conservative, neoconservative, or even imperialist project, many Americans working in the field would be horrified and offended to hear themselves described in any of those ways. Many of the best and most dedicated people I have worked with in democracy assistance have their roots not just in Democratic Party politics, but in the labor, women's, LGBT, or civil rights movements. Many others are ardent critics of American foreign policy, including recent U.S.-led wars in both Iraq and Afghanistan.

Democracy assistance is additionally perplexing because it is both a major theme of American policy, often central to bilateral discussions and U.S. strategy, and a discrete set of programs implemented by a relatively small number of organizations. A 2007 State Department strategic plan lists "governing justly and democratically" as the second goal of U.S. foreign policy, noting in the introduction, "In today's world, it is impossible to draw clear lines between our security interests, our development efforts, and our democratic ideals." The strategy document later goes on to state, "Finally, U.S. support for anti-corruption, good governance, and democratization reinforces our development and transformational diplomacy goals of working with partners to help them build their own sustainable institutions of democratic governance. The U.S. Government goal is to promote and strengthen effective democracies and move them along a continuum toward democratic consolidation."[19]

A State Department strategic plan for fiscal years 2014–17, created and released during the Obama presidency, drops "Protect[ing] Core U.S. Interests by Advancing Democracy and Human Rights and Strengthening Civil Society" to the fourth strategic priority for the country. This strategy also stressed that "the National Security Strategy makes clear that in order to advance our common security, we must address the underlying political and economic deficits that foster instability, enable radicalization and extremism, and ultimately undermine the ability of governments to manage threats within their borders and to be our partners in addressing common challenges."[20] This document demonstrates that democracy promotion is central to U.S. foreign policy generally and cannot be fully disaggregated from the larger foreign policy goals and aspirations of the United States.

Democracy assistance also encompasses a very broad array of activities, including statements made by American diplomats and government officials, military intervention, various exercises of soft power such as exchange programs, incentives regarding organizations like NATO, and democracy assistance activities such as legislative support or election monitoring. Different people speaking about democracy assistance are therefore often speaking of very different things. An educated American who pays attention to foreign policy might think of democracy assistance in Iraq or Afghanistan as something involving war, platitudinous statements by American leaders, and long and costly entanglements in various countries. This view arises directly from the media coverage of democracy assistance and its relationships to the U.S. presence in Iraq and Afghanistan. However, someone working in the democracy assistance field in one of those countries or elsewhere might define democracy assistance more narrowly as the programs funded by USAID's democracy and governance division. For many Americans, democracy promotion is closely linked to elections, so they view democracy promotion as, at worst, about forcing elections on other countries and, at best, about observing those elections. Many civil society activists in

nondemocratic countries see U.S. democracy promotion efforts as integral to the struggles for freedom and democracy in their countries. They
see the efforts as essential, but often do not have a broader sense of U.S.
goals and priorities in their countries, leading to frustration when democracy work takes a backseat to other less savory priorities. Others,
notably authoritarian governments and their backers, see democracy
work as CIA wine in more modern NGO bottles. Clearly, these very
different visions of what constitutes democracy assistance make it difficult to have a mutually understandable discussion about the issue.

Democracy promotion is both deeply embedded in U.S. foreign
policy and a subset of that policy, both part of and distinct from it. Democracy promotion, moreover, is not always consistent with the rest
of U.S. policy toward a given country. The United States tends to view
stability, access to markets, and cooperation on security issues as the
foundations of most bilateral relations. These things can be consistent
with democracy, but they can also exist in nondemocratic countries.
Thus, U.S. democracy assistance goals are often secondary to other more
immediate, and important, considerations. In countries where the government has little interest in being democratic, the United States is in a
difficult position: it can either reduce its commitment to democracy or
seek to change, or even overthrow, a regime that is generally supportive and helpful to U.S. interests. Too often, the United States resolves
this problem by overstating the democratic accomplishments and aspirations of the regime in question. Amy McDonough argues,

> The degree to which the United States Government holds coun-
> tries in the former Soviet Union publicly accountable for respecting
> human rights and democracy depends on each country's relative
> strategic importance to the United States, not the human rights
> conditions in each country. U.S. officials publicly laud countries
> such as Kazakhstan and Uzbekistan that are vital to the U.S. mis-
> sion in Afghanistan or other key interests, while saying as little
> as possible about these countries' failings in the areas of human
> rights and democracy.[21]

McDonough contrasts U.S. policy in Kazakhstan and Uzbekistan
with that toward Belarus, arguing that the three countries have similar
regimes and similar levels of democracy, but the United States is much

more critical of Lukashenko's regime because Belarus does not support
the United States in Afghanistan or in a number of other U.S. foreign
policy endeavors. Elsewhere in the region, the United States diligently
ignored the deterioration of democracy in Georgia during the later years
of President Saakashvili's term, most likely because of Georgia's strong
support for the United States in Afghanistan and Iraq.

Democracy then loses much of its meaning as it becomes at least partially defined by the positioning of a particular country toward the
United States. Many regimes have elements of democracy and elements
of authoritarianism existing side by side. Many countries have decent
elections but an absence of freedom that precludes competition in those
elections, or they have ample media freedom but state institutions that
are either very weak or respond to only one leader and are not held accountable through legal or constitutional organs. Georgia under Saakashvili is a good example of the former, Pakistan of the latter. Many
countries can be seen as either democratic or authoritarian, but too frequently this distinction is based on relationships with the United States
above everything else. Over time this becomes clear even to those local
activists working with, and often with the support of, U.S. democracy
promotion organizations or donors. Working on democracy-related projects in recent years, I have encountered activists from places such as
Pakistan, Azerbaijan, and Georgia who have expressed their frustration
with a U.S. government that supports democracy, but only to a degree,
and is too unwilling to challenge an undemocratic government with
whom it is cooperating on other issues.

Therefore, disaggregating democracy assistance from broader U.S.
policy in a country or region is extremely difficult. U.S. government actors are, on some level, able to do this by distinguishing between NGO
and government personnel, funds, and projects, and by separating out the
democracy-related goals. However, to people inside the country, these
distinctions are frequently without differences. This is particularly
true in countries where Americans are viewed with suspicion or even disdain. In these places, Americans who are paid, even in a roundabout way,
by the U.S. government and answer to official U.S. government representatives like USAID or the U.S. embassy are generally viewed as part
of the government, not as independent simply because they work for an
NGO. Therefore, despite what are often both good works and good
intentions on the part of the NGOs, the work they do is rarely viewed

as being unambiguously about democracy. Moreover, these organizations are easily portrayed as fronts for various nasty American plans by the local government.

These and other paradoxes frame almost everything about U.S.-supported democracy promotion, making the policy confusing for observers, policymakers, and ordinary citizens. Not surprisingly, this confusion is often expressed in conflicting statements about democracy promotion from supporters or opponents. It is not unusual to hear opponents, for example, describe the policy as both unworkable and an abuse of American power. Writer and analyst David Reiff argues both these points in a strong and persuasive critique of democracy promotion, writing, "To put the matter even more pointedly, after all the harm the United States has done in the Arab Middle East over the course of the past decade . . . the only sensible thing to conclude is that in fact Washington is very bad at promoting democracy," and "Only the belief that in fact democracy is what the world wants already, and thus, morally speaking, we are pushing on an open door, could justify such a swollen ambition. . . . We have been down this road before, and its name is empire."[22]

Understanding, or at least recognizing, this complexity is essential for fully understanding democracy assistance. Moreover, it is likely that as the world becomes more multipolar, questions about the efficacy and wisdom of democracy assistance will become more acute. These paradoxes will be highlighted by regimes opposed to the United States. Russia, for example, has used its soft media power to undermine and counter the American position in much of the former Soviet Union, largely for pointedly attacking the United States as hypocritical at virtually every turn. Russia has many motivations for this kind of propaganda; countering American influence is only one of them. Misrepresenting their own aggressive and militaristic behaviors to the rest of the world is also an increasingly significant motivator for Russian propagandists.

DEMOCRACY PROMOTION IN CONTEXT

In the context of the national budget, or even of foreign policy, democracy promotion is a very minor expenditure. According to a 2014 Chatham House report, between FY2006 and FY2014, the total U.S.

budget for democracy promotion ranged from $1.6 billion to $3.4 billion. Those numbers may seem like a lot, but the budget for democracy work is generally between 5 and 10 percent of the foreign assistance budget, which, in turn, is around 1 to 1.5 percent of the overall budget.[23] Kenneth Wollack, the longtime president of NDI, estimates that "the entire democracy promotion budget of the United States government reflects about three percent of our total foreign assistance budget."[24] The military budget, for example, obviously dwarfs the democracy assistance budget by a factor of several thousand. The United States also spends more money on direct foreign assistance, supporting embassies, economic development, health, and other issues, than it does on democracy work, as demonstrated by the small proportion of the foreign assistance and international affairs budget earmarked for democracy promotion. Moreover, the USAID budget line for democracy assistance includes programs that look a lot more like service provision or even educational programs than genuine democracy work. Civil society programs that mobilize people to demand basic services or media programs that provide very basic training to journalists are examples of programs that are several steps removed from direct democracy work but are frequently part of democracy and governance budget lines. The amount of money that goes to the higher profile work of democracy assistance organizations in areas such as political party work, civil society development, or election monitoring is, in relative terms, miniscule.

The relative size of the democracy assistance budget is small, but measuring democracy assistance, and its role and place in American foreign policy, by looking only at the amount of money spent directly on democracy assistance is misleading. Democracy assistance includes many things that do not turn up when analyzing budgets. Statements by policymakers, the nature of the relationship between the United States and another country, and even the extent to which assistance is given or withheld are all only part of the democracy assistance equation. More significant, democracy assistance, or the spread of democracy more generally, is one of the macro-ideas that frames the more expensive parts of U.S. foreign policy, including military expenditures, bases, and the like. Because democracy promotion is one of the major strategic goals of U.S. foreign policy, it can be argued that all of American foreign policy is, to some extent, related to it. The biggest part of the U.S. budget that has direct bearing on democracy work is defense. Wars in

Afghanistan and Iraq are very expensive and have, at times, been linked to democracy promotion. In a more quotidian way, the promise of security agreements with the United States has been an important incentive for countries where democracy promotion projects have been pursued.

Because the spread of democracy has been one of the core pillars of U.S. foreign policy for roughly two decades, it is reasonable to consider democracy assistance as being bigger than just the few programs, and the few dollars, that fund those programs that are explicitly about democracy. However, it is also necessary not to err too far in the other direction and expand the definition and role of democracy promotion so much that it includes virtually every aspect of foreign policy. Although the dollar impact of democracy assistance, viewed holistically, cannot be fully determined, it is apparent that if the United States no longer sought to help countries become more democratic, the overall picture of U.S. foreign policy would look very different and probably cost markedly less money.

Understanding where democracy promotion ends and the rest of foreign policy begins is rarely easy. The most obvious example is that although recent American wars in Afghanistan and Iraq were not explicitly about democracy, the promotion of democracy was an important post facto justification for both wars and became an objective that was clearly more than just peripheral to the U.S. project in those two countries. Thus the wars in Afghanistan and Iraq were, in some respects, both about and not about democracy assistance.

Democracy promotion also reflects the larger vision of the U.S. role in the world, which for much of the post–Cold War era has enjoyed a virtual consensus among the American foreign policy elite. The vision of the United States as being both able and obliged to attempt political outcomes in more or less every corner of the world has been shared across partisan and ideological lines and has played a major role in some of the most significant foreign policy successes and failures of recent decades.

This consensus exists at the elite level and is generally bipartisan. Although Democrats and Republicans may disagree on some specific policy recommendations, foreign policy establishment elites from both parties generally agree that the United States should pursue an internationalist, indeed interventionist, approach to foreign policy. Thus, whenever a foreign policy crisis arises, the debate in Congress and inside the beltway is almost always about what the United States should do, not about whether or not it should become involved.

The Russian invasion of Crimea in 2014, for example, was met by a bipartisan consensus that the United States should do something, although there was some disagreement about what that something should be. Hawks such as John McCain argued for a more military and confrontational approach with Russia,[25] while the Obama administration urged applying sanctions and moving military assets closer to Russia. The difference between policy recommendations on this issue was much narrower than the rhetoric in Washington might have suggested, but the general agreement that a strong response was needed was clear. The view that the United States should not do much in Ukraine was simply not entertained by policy elites in Washington,[26] despite it being the view held by most Americans. The policy at which the United States finally arrived, a combination of sanctions, strong rhetoric, and moving military resources to NATO's eastern border, demonstrated both the limits of U.S. foreign policy and the persistent need to remain involved in much of the world.

A corollary to this view is the idea that events anywhere around the world are caused by some U.S. action or mistake. Again, the specifics differ between the parties, as Republicans generally attribute events like the Russian invasion of Crimea to a policy of weakness by a Democratic president, while Democrats often blame excessive aggression by Republican presidents for the nefarious actions of other countries. Crimea in 2014 is only one example: others include the Arab Spring of 2010, Iran for much of the last thirty-five years, and numerous other cases. The fundamental problem is that if any event around the world is attributed, at least in some significant part, to American action or mistakes, then the solution will always lie in more American action seeking to either right the mistake, finish the job, or something else. This is the circular yet powerful logic that underpins the internationalist consensus of the foreign policy elite. Democracy promotion is, of course, only a part of this.

Democracy assistance in its current incarnation is a battery of programs in areas such as civil society development, political party support, legislative strengthening, and election monitoring that is implemented in almost every country where the United States provides assistance. With only a few exceptions, it took shape in the 1990s in the wake of the Cold War, a period when American hegemony was at its height. During these years U.S. foreign policy transitioned from being locked in a global competition with another superpower to assuming the role of lone superpower, resulting in an unprecedented rise in American influence and reach; the United States was able to have an impact on almost every corner of the world. This did not mean that the 1990s was simply an unbroken string of American foreign policy successes, but that it saw a more or less consistent increase in the American role in international relations and the internal politics of foreign countries.

Throughout the 1990s, these ideas were not strongly challenged, as bipartisan agreement on America's role in the world made it possible for the United States to take on more responsibilities and pursue ever more ambitious foreign policies. By the second decade of the twenty-first century, however, this had changed. The combination of the downturn in the global economy and the ensuing increased awareness of the problem of the national debt (addressed in the 1990s but ignored in the new century), the rise of China as a global power, and the seemingly never-ending wars in Afghanistan and Iraq contributed to a growing feeling, both domestically and overseas, that the United States was overextended internationally and unable to effectively pursue such global policy goals.

Determining the precise number of countries where the United States is doing democracy work at any one time is difficult: the data is not easily available, and many different agencies support democracy work. The available data show that NDI has worked in 110 countries since its founding in 1983,[27] and in 2014 the NED reported that it was working in 90 countries.[28] Regardless of the precise number, by the turn of the century democracy promotion had evolved from a policy pursued in specific countries for strategic reasons to being simply what the United States does in most poor countries.

This sentiment is expressed on the intellectual level in a spate of books and essays analyzing the imminent end of American hegemony.[29] Politically, isolationist politicians, not just in the antiwar wing of the Democratic Party but also in the deficit hawk and Libertarian wings of the Republican Party, began to question the logic of continuing U.S. involvement in every part of the world. Gradually, the ability to influence outcomes in any corner in the world, an obvious demonstration of American power, morphed into the need to be concerned about events in any corner of the world, a less obvious demonstration of American vulnerability. This transition took place in the first years of the new century, and democracy promotion was at its center.

Democracy promotion rests on assumptions, and even an atmosphere, of ample U.S. influence and resources. Only if America believes itself to have both the best model for governance, and the means, ability, and right to spread this model globally, is the democracy promotion premise possible. As the triumphalism and relative hegemony of the immediate post–Cold War period gave way to the self-doubt, hyper-partisanship, increased multipolarity, and rising debt of the years defined first by 9/11 and the global war on terror and then by the global economic downturn, these beliefs weakened, and so did the rationale and support for democracy promotion. This contributed to a climate of uncertainty, beginning in the later years of the Bush presidency and continuing into the Obama presidency, regarding America's ability to influence outcomes globally and to execute what the political elite viewed as the country's unique mission in the world.

The uncertain climate was exacerbated by a growing sense that U.S. democracy itself was flawed combined with a technological environment making it easier for people around the world to see these flaws. The 2000 election, years of extremely rancorous partisan politics, government shutdowns, and consistent legislative gridlock in Washington have framed U.S. democracy in a less-than-great light for much of the twenty-first century. There have also been moments of hope and triumph for U.S. democracy, not least the election of Barack Obama in 2008. Both the good and the ugly aspects have been made more visible more quickly than ever before with the new technology that has swept the world.

If the U.S. fiscal situation remains unchanged, it is likely that calls for a reduced American role in the world—which, as late as the 2008, 2012, and 2016 presidential elections were still expressed only on the fringes of the political establishment by people like Ron Paul, Dennis Kucinich, and Rand Paul—will grow. Today, while these views are still absent from mainstream political life, they are represented on the left by anti-interventionists such as Noam Chomsky: "What are termed 'national security interests' have only an incidental relation to the security of the nation, though they have a very close relation to the interests of dominant sectors within the imperial state."[30] These views can also be found on the Libertarian right. Senator Rand Paul, the most prominent Libertarian in Congress, argued against intervention in Syria in 2013 by writing simply, "War should occur only when America is attacked, when it is threatened or when American interests are attacked or threatened.

I don't think the situation in Syria passes that test."[31] Politician and author Patrick Buchanan, more a social conservative and American-style fascist than Paul, argued, "Is it not understandable to patriots of the original 'Don't Tread on Me' republic that foreigners might resent paid U.S. agents operating inside their countries to alter the direction of their politics?"[32]

Calls for a reduced U.S. role in the world will probably originate with ordinary Americans, but it is only a matter of time before entrepreneurial thinking politicians begin to realize their potential political gain from championing these positions, moving the idea from the fringe into the mainstream of American political debate. Moreover, if the current trends in the United States toward a growing deficit and, internationally, toward increased multipolarity continue, the rationale for these calls, and ultimately the inevitability of reducing American involvement in the rest of the world, will become clearer in the not too distant future. It is possible that these decisions will be foisted on the United States by larger circumstances, thus leading to a debate not about the role of the United States in the world, but about how to manage the shrinking of that role.

Democracy assistance will be a clear target for those seeking less U.S. involvement in the rest of the world, not because the programs are expensive—they are not—but because of the political nature of these programs, the difficulty of successfully implementing these policies, and the tenuous benefits to the United States even when democracy is strengthened in a given country. The centrality of democracy assistance to a U.S. foreign policy that is concerned about domestic political outcomes and conflict resolution in every part of the world is reasonably self-evident, but if foreign policy begins to embrace a more modest set of goals focusing on, for example, keeping America safe from terrorism or other enemies and only taking a position regarding the domestic politics of other lands when the most egregious human rights violations are occurring, democracy assistance would be relegated to a significantly smaller role.

During the last two decades, the high-profile stories involving democracy work, most notably in Afghanistan, Iraq, the Color Revolutions, and similar cases, have overshadowed the more mundane side of democracy work, which occurs in lower-profile countries and involves lower-profile activities. Millions of U.S. dollars in democracy work in countries such as Armenia, Cambodia, Mexico, and elsewhere, while not significant expenditures, are harder to rationalize in a political climate moving away from unquestioned commitment to global involvement. It is easier to explain the value of supporting democracy during critical times in particular countries than it is to explain why democracy assistance should be the default relationship between the United States and any nondemocratic or semi-democratic country that will allow it.

In addition, the excitement around democracy has waned substantially in recent years. The climate of 2003–05, when the Color Revolutions caught the imagination of policymakers in Washington and Europe, no longer exists. The time between the initial democratic breakthrough and the recognition in Washington of the perils facing nascent democracies has also decreased substantially. In recent years the celebrations around, for example, the Arab Spring or the Euromaidan movement in Ukraine in 2013–14 that brought down the corrupt President Viktor Yanukovych have barely ended before the democracies ushered in by those events begin to falter.

It is not at all evident what U.S. foreign policy would look like if it were to phase out democracy promotion. Despite its modest size, democracy promotion reflects and is integrated into many broader trends in U.S. foreign policy, so it would be difficult to simply extricate it from foreign policy and expect other policies to continue more or less unchanged. Phasing out democracy promotion would be part of a process suggesting that the United States views itself as no longer interested in or able to effect political outcomes in much of the world. If this were to happen, the rationale for much foreign assistance would soon be brought into question as well. The humanitarian side of foreign assistance—providing food to people suffering from hunger caused by famine or war, fighting disease, or helping with responses to natural disasters—would be easy to continue. But programs aimed at fighting corruption, or strengthening rule of law or even human rights, would be harder to maintain, and quite limited, if not supported by democracy work.

In the short run, however, democracy promotion, despite the current challenges it faces, is likely to remain an integral, if perhaps not central, component of foreign policy. It is difficult to know the direction it will take or how democracy advocates will rise to the challenges presented by the nondemocratic regimes increasingly entrenched in countries such as Belarus or Kazakhstan that, ten or fifteen years ago, could still be described as transitional. A similar challenge has been raised by countries such as Egypt and others in North Africa, where nondemocratic regimes have come to power in countries before the West was done celebrating the fall of the previous authoritarian regime. However, it is clear that democracy will continue to be a goal of American foreign policy, and that building democracy will be a rationale for involvement in the domestic politics of many countries for at least the next few years.

From a policy angle, it is therefore still important to find ways to sharpen democracy promotion programs while making them more effective and more attuned to the political realities and environments of today. It is also important to confront the paradoxes that characterize this work and to recognize that things may not always be as they seem, or as the American position might suggest. Sometimes, in other words, an NGO is not just an NGO; and democracy promotion is sometimes not just benign capacity building. In addition, if democracy promotion is still framed by platitudes that democracy cannot be imposed or brought through military force while the United States continues to use the military, with varying degrees of success, as an agent of political change, or if democracy programs continue to view powerful nondemocratic governments as allies or partners in efforts to strengthen democracy, the democracy promotion project will be exposed to more criticism from different angles.

To address this it is necessary to examine democracy promotion holistically, looking at its programmatic side, its place in foreign policy, and even its historical development from the late nineteenth century to the present. This approach grounds democracy promotion in the evolution of foreign policy and of the U.S. role in the world and makes it a little easier to think about how this policy might evolve as the United States transitions into being something other than a global hyper-power.

Without this holistic approach, democracy promotion policy will simply reflect the domestic political moods and pressures of the time. We have already seen this during the years of the Obama administration, when democracy promotion was a reminder to many of the excesses of the Bush administration, thus leading the new administration to downgrade its importance, based largely on minor domestic political issues. Significant also, the change with regard to democracy promotion from the Bush to the Obama administrations was primarily one of rhetoric: the latter administration spoke about it less, but the programs did not change very much.

It is also important to recognize that democracy promotion has evolved, as has the political context around the world. Projects aimed at promoting freedom in the communist world were not appropriate for helping postcommunist countries evolve toward becoming stronger democracies. Programs that helped transitional countries move toward becoming democracies, or that successfully helped get rid of weak kleptocratic regimes, are also increasingly less useful in an era in which fewer regimes are transitional and many semi-authoritarian or authoritarian regimes are becoming stronger.

The democracy assistance approach and programs of the last twenty years are only the latest iterations in a long-standing American policy. For democracy promotion to remain relevant, it will have to move beyond this iteration and possibly beyond the institutions and agencies that have become driving forces in democracy promotion policy, and may also need to be reconfigured to fit the mood of a less confident and less affluent America.

CHAPTER TWO
DEMOCRACY PROMOTION BEFORE AND DURING THE COLD WAR

DEMOCRACY ASSISTANCE HAS BECOME AN increasingly significant part of the foreign policy discussion during the last decade or so, partially because of the unprecedented—if substantially rhetorical and partisan—use of the term during George W. Bush's administration and partially because of increased questioning of the U.S. role in the world on the heels of the long wars in Afghanistan and Iraq that coincided with the economic downturn in 2008.

In his 2005 inauguration speech beginning his second term as president, Bush stated, "The survival of liberty in our land increasingly depends on the success of liberty in other lands. The best hope for peace in our world is the expansion of freedom in all the world. . . . The concerted effort of free nations to promote democracy is a prelude to our enemies' defeat."[1] Similar sentiments have been expressed by other administrations, but rarely in such a high-profile setting.

Despite its emphasis during the Bush administration, democracy assistance in its current form has strong roots in the late Cold War and immediate post–Cold War era. During that time organizations such as the National Endowment for Democracy (NED), the International Republican Institute (IRI), and the National Democratic Institute (NDI) were formed; USAID missions began to expand and bureaucratize the democracy and governance portions of their portfolios; and the community of people and organizations working in the field began to grow rapidly.

Casual observers of American foreign policy over the last twenty-five years or so could come to the incorrect conclusion that democracy assistance began at the end of the Cold War, accelerated during the George W. Bush administration, and wound down during the Obama administration. This simple and straightforward explanation is largely consistent with the story most people read and see in the media. It is also almost completely wrong. Democracy assistance has roots that go much deeper than the post–Cold War period, or even than the Cold War itself. It has been part of American foreign policy, in one form or another, for at least a century.

Bush's immediate predecessor, Bill Clinton, for example, created policies that shared Bush's focus on democracy, but he rarely placed them at the rhetorical center of his presidency. The 1995 national security strategy listed "To promote democracy abroad" as one of its "three central goals." That document continues,

> While democracy will not soon take hold everywhere, we know that the larger the pool of democracies, the better off we, and the entire community of nations, will be. Democracies create free markets that offer economic opportunity, make for more reliable trading partners, and are far less likely to wage war on one another. It is in our interest to do all that we can to enlarge the community of free and open societies, especially in areas of greatest strategic interest, as in the former Soviet Union.[2]

If the words "former Soviet Union" were replaced with "Middle East," that statement would have fit in well with President Bush's comments on democracy promotion throughout much of his presidency.

To understand democracy assistance fully, and to appreciate the perspectives and positions that underlie many of the assumptions on which democracy work is based, it is necessary to be familiar with the history of democracy assistance and its role in American foreign policy. Political scientist and democracy scholar Jonathan Monten argues,

Although a radical departure in many other respects, the current U.S. grand strategy's privileging of liberalism and democracy falls squarely within the mainstream of American diplomatic traditions. For reasons unique to the American political experience, U.S. nationalism—that is, the factors that define and differentiate the United States as a self-contained political community—has historically been defined in terms of both adherence to a set of liberal, universal political ideals and a perceived obligation to spread those norms internationally. The concept of the United States as agent of historical transformation and liberal change in the international system therefore informs almost the entire history of U.S. foreign policy.[3]

Political scientist Tony Smith captures the role of perceived morality in the historical foundations of U.S. democracy promotion, asserting, with regard to the Philippines, "Ultimately, therefore, the democratization of the Philippines came to be the principal reason the Americans were there; now the United States had a moral purpose to its imperialism and could rest more easily."[4]

Democracy assistance, however, has not been applied consistently over the last century. Different organizations have played important roles in implementing policies, a range of theories and rationales have guided the work, varying amounts of resources have been put into developing democracies, different countries and different numbers of countries have received U.S. democracy assistance, and, of course, success has been intermittent. Nonetheless, the idea that the United States should be helping other countries become more democratic, and that becoming involved in the domestic political life of those countries was an important element of that process, has been relatively constant.

Ignorance of democracy assistance's long history is not, as Thomas Carothers, the leading American scholar on democracy promotion, points out, limited to journalists and pundits: "They [democracy promoters] rarely have much sense of history about what they do, either in regards to the countries in which they are working or to the enterprise of using aid to promote democracy."[5] It seems that those involved in democracy assistance are at least partly hamstrung by not looking at history, or enough history, to find useful precedents and guidelines.

One clear example of this is the consensus, at least on the political center and left, that democracy cannot be exported through military means or, according to the more popular parlance, "at the barrel of a gun."

This consensus arises because many people either do not remember America's role in postwar Germany and Japan or choose to ignore it, perhaps because it was so successful; many therefore miss the bigger, more relevant, lesson offered by that history. Democracy development in Germany and Japan was successful because of the enormous investment of time, money, and human resources that the United States made in both those countries, and because of urgency of the task, particularly as the Cold War intensified beginning in the late 1940s. Takashi Inoguchi argues that following World War II, the United States "step by step . . . helped to craft a small, conservative pro-American force in Japan . . . and in doing so successfully brought democracy to the island nation."[6] The United States also understood and was able to become involved very deeply in Germany and Japan precisely because they were utterly defeated former foes.

Alexander Downes and Jonathan Monten argue that the successes in Japan and Germany cannot be explained simply by pointing to a greater U.S. effort, noting that "Iraq has received comparable levels of aid to Germany and twice the amount of aid that Japan received from 1946 to 1952, and it was the largest recipient of U.S. of development assistance from 2004 to 2008."[7] While there are clearly numerous possible explanations for the strength of democracy in Japan and Germany, these data do not capture the level of commitment and military involvement applied in Germany and Japan and, equally important, the degree of planning, compared with Iraq and Afghanistan.

In the early years after the fall of Saddam Hussein, the stories of U.S. unpreparedness for the collapse of the Baathist regime were, by contrast, appalling. Larry Diamond notes, "As has been documented in a number of excellent investigative reports, the United States invaded Iraq without a coherent viable plan to win the peace."[8] One of these reports, "After Saddam: Prewar Planning and the Occupation of Iraq," points out,

Although many agencies and individuals sought to plan for post-Saddam Iraq, senior policy makers throughout the government held to a set of fairly optimistic assumptions about the conditions that would emerge after major combat and what would be required thereafter. These assumptions tended to override counter-arguments elsewhere in the government. Meanwhile, senior military commanders assumed that civilian authorities would be responsible for the postwar period. Hence they focused the vast majority of their attention on preparations for and the execution of major combat operations.[9]

Historian Stanley Nider Katz summarizes the contrast between the two eras well:

> In 1943, arguably before it was even clear that the Allies would defeat Japan and Germany, the U.S. government set up training programs at the University of Virginia and at Yale to equip (with the language and administrative skills that they would require) those who might later have to oversee transitions from authoritarianism to democracy. Sixty years later, we read in the *New York Times* of a senior U.S. staff officer noting that, on entering Baghdad, his division had no further orders whatsoever—no instructions about where to go, who to see, how or what to occupy, what to do.[10]

It would have been valuable to remember the complex and multiple variables contributing to U.S. success in postwar Japan and Germany in 2002–04, when the United States was making, or not making, plans for what kind of work and commitment would be needed in Iraq and Afghanistan following the defeat of the incumbent regimes. Instead, the administration gave in to wishful thinking, such as the belief that the Iraqi civil service would step in and govern effectively after Hussein was ousted. It is hard to imagine that officials in the Bush administration were unaware of the breadth and extent of the democracy promotion effort following World War II, and of how their cavalier and unprepared approach might be compared so unfavorably to that. The more likely case was that decisionmakers in the Bush administration did not see why Germany and Japan were relevant precedents for Iraq or that they were committed to ideological views that precluded, for whatever reason, looking to the German and Japanese cases for guidance.

ORIGINS OF DEMOCRACY PROMOTION

The theoretical foundations for U.S. democracy promotion are usually traced back to Woodrow Wilson, the first American president who sought to place the expansion of democracy at or near the center of American foreign policy. Wilson's comments on the eve of entry into World War I are often cited as the primal drumbeat of U.S. democracy promotion:

> The world must be made safe for democracy. Its peace must be planted upon the tested foundations of political liberty. We have no selfish ends to serve. We desire no conquest, no dominion. We seek no indemnities for ourselves, no material compensation for the sacrifices we shall freely make. We are but one of the champions of the rights of mankind. We shall be satisfied when those rights have been made as secure as the faith and the freedom of nations can make them.

Historian Lloyd E. Ambrosius draws a direct parallel between Wilson and George W. Bush, asserting that both "appealed to historic American ideals to justify their new foreign policy. . . . They both led the nation into war for the avowed purpose of protecting traditional values and institutions at home . . . promising to make freedom and democracy the foundations of peace."[11] Tony Smith argues that the true origins of democracy assistance as a centerpiece of American foreign policy go back to Thomas Jefferson. Jefferson, according to Smith, believed the spread of democracy was important because it would ensure a safer world for the United States. This is an early appearance of the democratic peace theory, which asserts that democratic countries are less likely to go to war with each other and has become one of the principal arguments in support of democracy assistance.[12]

In addition, although Wilson provided the theoretical underpinning and policy rationale for U.S. efforts to promote democracy, only after the Spanish-American War did the United States first get its democracy promotion feet wet, as, following the defeat of Spain in 1898, the United States sought to establish democratic governments in Cuba and the Philippines. Not surprisingly, the Spanish-American War also marked the movement of the United States toward becoming a global power. Efforts to assist the democratic development of Cuba were unsophisticated, certainly by today's standards, but were significant because they marked the first time the United States became deeply involved in the domestic workings of another country in an enduring way. This initial iteration of democracy assistance was characterized by a strong focus on institutions, particularly elections and constitutions.

It is also worth remembering that efforts to establish democracy in Cuba were ultimately not successful, as the country grew into what could be described as, at best, a deeply flawed democracy for more than half a century before giving way to the totalitarian regime that has governed there for an additional half century or so. The U.S. experience in Cuba foreshadowed the results of many democracy assistance efforts in the twentieth and twenty-first centuries, as well as the difficulties inherent in democracy work and the blowback that often occurs when democracy assistance fails.

These early efforts at democracy promotion also marked the beginning of a strain of U.S. foreign policy reflecting the belief that democracy was the best form of government for all states and peoples, a belief reasserted by the United States, if at times only rhetorically, throughout the more than one hundred years that followed. But this belief, however central to the U.S. democracy promotion mission, has not always reflected American political thought. During various points in American history, certain types of countries have been seen as unready for democracy: for example, those that were largely Catholic, nonwhite, or Muslim.

Democracy promotion thus has its roots in American interests; the American perception of itself as a country with a unique mission, or even duty, toward the rest of the world; various American interests at different times; and America's early efforts to find a role for itself as a growing global power and, later, as a superpower and hegemon. Democracy promotion is therefore a reflection of American self-interest or, in the eyes of its critics, imperialism, but it is something else as well. It is a reflection of the unique role America has played in the world during the last century or more and the unique view Americans hold of their own country and its place in the world.

DEMOCRACY PROMOTION AFTER WORLD WAR II

The United States became considerably more engaged in seeking to expand democracy as World War II came to its end and ultimately gave way to the Cold War. World War II was not, of course, fought to defend abstract principles of democracy. Nor was victory in World War II immediately framed as a victory for democracy. Defeat of the fascist powers was the goal, and the primary achievement, of World War II. Nonetheless, by the last months of the war, questions of how the postwar world and Europe in particular would look after the war and of what to do about defeated Germany and Japan took on more urgency. These questions had to be examined in the context of an increasingly powerful Soviet Union that was seeking a role for itself in the postwar world. The United States therefore began planning for the postwar reconstruction and occupation before the war was over. Colonel Kenneth McCreedy notes, "The occupation was not an ad hoc, extemporaneous affair but the product of careful calculations and extensive preparation."[13] He concludes, "Arguably, if the West had failed to prepare adequately for post-conflict operations, it would not have been able to avert a humanitarian disaster in Germany, which would have had severe repercussions in the rest of Europe."[14]

In the decades since the war, frequent retelling of the story of how Germany and Japan became democracies has begun to form the narrative that, following the war, the United States and its noncommunist allies understood the value of democracy as a bulwark against future wars. A secondary part of this narrative is that Japan and, in particular, Germany were countries where there had been at least some previous experimentation and experience with democracy.[15] This, of course, made it easier to bring democracy to Japan and Germany.

The narrative provides the nucleus of two of the democracy promotion paradoxes. First, the preeminent concern in Washington in the last days of World War II was how to most effectively dismantle the German and Japanese war machines and how to make sure they would never be in a position to threaten the rest of the world again—not how to help Germany and Japan become democracies. The Morgenthau Plan, created in the final months of World War II, set out to destroy Germany's future ability to make war and function as a strong, prosperous state.[16] It would have also made it impossible for Germany to become an industrial power, apportioned some German territory to various allied powers, and put parts of the German economy under UN control for decades. Although the plan was never adopted and was quickly abandoned, it received strong support initially, demonstrating America's rancor toward Germany as World War II came to an end.

In the post–Cold War period a central rationale for the United States engaging in military adventures or wars has been to help the people in those countries where the wars occur. Thus, wars are presented to the American people as an effort to rid the world of a tyrant or to liberate the people living under the sway of a tyrant. These rationales imply that the United States views the people of the country in which they are waging a war as potential supporters, hearts and minds that need to be won, rather than enemies. This sets a different tone for democracy related efforts than the one that predominated in the United States during the last months of World War II.

This shift in rationale is also a reflection how post–World War II democracy promotion has changed foreign policy, and even war, for the United States. Virtually every post–World War II American military victory has been followed by an effort to assist and bring democracy to the vanquished country. This was most apparent in the aftermath of the Cold War, as well as after the defeat of the Baathist and Taliban regimes in Iraq and Afghanistan.

Since the efforts in Germany and Japan, the notion that the United States would limit intervention in a defeated country only to ensuring it could never make war again is almost unthinkable. Instead the United States has sought to bring democracy to defeated enemies following long conflicts lasting decades or short conflicts lasting days. This could be perceived as a reflection on the unique benevolence of American power, but that would be a simplistic and jingoistic interpretation. It is more accurately attributable to evolutions in international law, as well as to the new universality of democracy and democracy promotion.

But World War II was different. During World War II the American people viewed Germany and Japan as enemies, a view that extended to the citizens of those countries. Moreover, because of the duration and scope of the war, many Americans, whether or not they had served in the military, harbored genuine hatred for the Germans and Japanese. This is not the environment from which a desire to help a defeated power rebuild and become democratic evolves. GIs who were part of the initial occupying force were given "strict orders not to converse with or even smile at Germans, and grave punishments were meted out to those who violated this command. Treating Germans with humanity was seen as the surest way to bring about another saga in the Teutonic destruction."[17] Moreover, it created a political climate where, until 1948, American politicians who proposed trying to help the Germans or Japanese, at a time when America and its allies were also recovering from the war, would have faced angry voters at home.

In the second paradox, the inevitable success of democracy assistance in Germany and Japan only became apparent after these two countries had made clear strides toward democracy. This ex post facto inevitability contrasts sharply with the views held by many in the mid-1940s. Events of the years during and immediately preceding World War II were seen as evidence that Germany and Japan were places where democracy would be difficult to establish. Smith describes how the prospect of democracy in Germany and Japan looked to the United States at the end of the war:

> The American determination that postwar Germany and Japan be demilitarized, that their political orders be democratized . . . constitutes the most ambitious program American liberal democratic internationalism had ever undertaken. . . . Could the United States expect to foster basic developmental changes there where it had failed to do so in seemingly more malleable countries like the Philippines and the Dominican Republic?[18]

The lack of any real precedent of democracy and, in the German case, the weakness and ultimate failure of Weimar democracy were presented as reasons for this outlook.

The raison d'être for actively supporting democratic development, and for putting substantial resources behind this effort, was the Cold War. As Soviet power increased and became a greater threat, the value of Germany and Japan to the United States—not as defeated powers, but as strong and prosperous countries—also increased. Democracy was a part of that equation.

In the immediate aftermath of World War II, Japan and Germany were not the only countries where America sought to influence domestic politics and push toward liberal democracy and away from communism.

Throughout southern Europe, notably in Greece and Italy, the United States sought to weaken communism in favor of democratic regimes favorable to U.S. interests.

During this period many of the tools of contemporary democracy assistance were forged. Civil society development, working with political parties, and the use of American soft power were critical parts of U.S. efforts in Greece, Italy, and elsewhere. These tools were not always so-named, but the ideas were there. Moreover, the structures and language for using these tools differed from those that would be used in the post–Cold War era. Carothers notes that "political aid programs ranging from constitution writing to civic education were part of the successful efforts to help reconstruct and democratize Germany and Japan after World War II." Carothers also describes how, in the 1960s, political aid grew from public administration to include things like local governance and civic participation.[19]

U.S. democracy promotion during the Cold War was at times placed at the center of the fight against communism. For example, President John F. Kennedy's Alliance for Progress, which sought to strengthen ties between the United States and the developing world, placed a strong emphasis on democratic development. Despite the anticommunist roots of Cold War democracy promotion, the policies were often progressive. In much of the developing world, America pursued or facilitated land control policies as key components of democracy promotion. In many countries the anticommunist left was a central participant in the U.S.-supported fight against communism, so programs such as land reform helped keep them supporting U.S. policy. During this period democracy promotion was not necessarily known as such, as it was frequently part of overall assistance packages or development projects.[20]

Understanding the place of democracy promotion in American history is further complicated by language. In many discussions of democracy promotion, the terms "democracy building," "state building," and "nation building" are used, if not interchangeably, then at least interrelatedly. The last two terms are used interchangeably in the United States, but, although it may seem nitpicky to mention it, they are different. "State building" refers to attempts to build, or rebuild, institutions of governance, usually after a conflict, including developing a constitution, strengthening rule of law, and supporting the creation of legislatures, functioning government agencies, regulatory agencies, and the like. "Nation building," in American media, is generally used to mean the same thing but actually does not. "Nation building" should be used to refer to efforts to craft an identity for citizens of a country, because a nation is a people, whereas a state is a collection of institutions.

In some countries, nation building is important. For example, following the U.S. invasion of Iraq, it was important to build a national identity that the people of post–Saddam Hussein Iraq could share. These efforts were unsuccessful, but similar efforts to build a post-Nazi, and later a post–Cold War, German identity were considerably more successful.

Democracy building is related to both these terms. Some countries, such as post-invasion Afghanistan and Iraq, need both state and democracy building, but some, as in postwar Germany and Japan, did not need state building quite as much because the state already existed. This is significant because when looking at precedents it is worth noting that states where the United States needed to engage in only democracy promotion often got to democracy more quickly than countries where significant state building and sometimes nation building needed to be done as well.

DEMOCRACY PROMOTION AFTER THE COLD WAR

One of the most significant differences between democracy promotion work in the period before and the period after 1991 is the degree of openness about the goals and strategies of democracy promotion. Information of the kind that is today freely available on the websites of organizations such as the NED, NDI, IRI, or Freedom House was kept secret during most of the Cold War. Even critics of democracy promotion seeking evidence of U.S.-backed plots in foreign countries draw most of their information from sources that are today publicly available, primarily on the Internet.

In the twenty-first century, U.S. democracy promotion seeks to back political parties that are more or less democratic and pro-West, primarily through helping them develop relevant skills and tools, strengthening democratic (and implicitly) Western-leaning elements of civil society and the political elite, and leveraging American cultural capital and soft power to generate positive feelings toward the United

States from citizens in countries more or less across the globe. These tools are not new for the U.S. government, but during the last twenty years they have been used differently and more transparently than in the past.

Cold War historian Hugh Wilford describes the Cold War era CIA fighting on a range of cultural and informational fronts to win a battle of hearts and minds against communists supported by the Soviet Union. Wilford draws on the phrase "Mighty Wurlitzer," which Frank Wisner used to describe the array of tools the CIA had at its disposal, for the title of his book on the CIA during the Cold War. However, the things Wilford describes, including "organizations intended to provide a cover for émigrés and refugees," "a series of operations designed to shore up civil society," and "programs intended to ensure that 'developing nations' did not succumb to Communism," evolved to become the core functions of many post–Cold War democracy-oriented NGOs.[21] Wilford describes the efforts of the CIA to leverage American culture for Cold War advantage. Today these Western intellectuals, entertainers, and others would not be, knowingly or unknowingly, brought into CIA programs but would simply be funded by USAID or the NED to perform or lecture in nondemocratic countries.

In recent years these types of activities have been advertised and boasted about on websites, in glossy annual reports, and at conferences hosted by USAID or other government agencies, as well as by NGOs supported by the U.S. government. During the Cold War they would have been concealed, with few Americans aware of these activities. Moreover, during the Cold War when artists being supported by the CIA gave concerts or lectures in foreign countries, posters advertising the events would have displayed names and logos of front organizations, but today the name and logo would be USAID or NED. Understanding why this is the case can lead to a better understanding of the evolution of democracy promotion.

Some secrecy still surrounds democracy promotion work, on the periphery. For example, a program publicly described as being focused on political party development might really be more focused on helping one specific party win an election, or a legislative strengthening program might place emphasis on ensuring that some particular pieces of legislation are passed into law. These examples speak to the inevitably political slant of democracy promotion.

Democracy promotion in the contemporary era is not entirely transparent in other ways as well. For example, the term "NGO," referring to organizations that work closely with and receive much of their funding from their governments, may shed more shadow than light on the democracy promotion infrastructure. U.S. assertions that it never gets involved in foreign elections also do not withstand serious scrutiny; and the instruments and organizations of democracy promotion are sometimes complicit in this. On several occasions when working with democracy promotion organizations, it was made clear to me that I was supposed to help one side win and also that the U.S. embassy and other relevant officials working on that country were comfortable with that.

In other more benign cases it is essential to conceal, at least to a degree, the U.S. role in supporting local NGOs and other organizations simply because receiving American money or working closely with Americans would put local activists at risk. In these cases, the United States takes precautions to conceal the true sources of funding to help keep activists safe from harm.

DEMOCRACY PROMOTION AND COMPETING IDEOLOGIES

Several additional things have changed since the Cold War, most notably the collapse of the Soviet Union and the ideology that lay at its foundation. During the Cold War, capitalist democracy struggled against communism for influence throughout the world. Today no ideology rivals democratic capitalism with a global appeal comparable to the one communism enjoyed during the Cold War. In fact a few decades after the Cold War, most nondemocratic leaders, even in places as clearly nondemocratic as Russia, now present themselves as democrats. Thus the struggle in recent years has been about democracy and pseudo-democracy, or perhaps about interpretations of democracy.

A related point is that no global power can now compete with the United States and its allies economically, militarily, or ideologically. The American hegemony of the immediate post–Cold War era may no longer exist, resulting in a more multipolar world, but this multipolarity is not strongly grounded in competing ideologies. American power may be waning, but the power enjoyed by countries such as Russia, China, and Saudi Arabia is economic and military, not ideological. Even the soft power of a country like Russia is more cultural and linguistic than based on a popular model of governance.

It is striking that, while it certainly could be argued that the twenty-first century has been a difficult time for democracy generally and American democracy in particular, it has not been a great time for authoritarianism either. No powerful authoritarian model such as fascism in the 1930s or communism on and off during much of the twentieth century has emerged to challenge liberal democracy, even a liberal democracy in crisis. The strongman authoritarian regimes in places like Russia are appealing to other authoritarian leaders but have little grassroots appeal anywhere. China has made little effort to export its Confucian-Leninist form of governance.[22] The only cohesive ideological threat to liberal democracy comes from fundamentalist Islam, but that model has a naturally very limited resonance and is not relevant outside majority Muslim countries.

During the Cold War, U.S. efforts to strengthen democracy were met with counterefforts by the Soviet Union to increase its influence in various parts of the world. The United States felt compelled to conceal this work because it was understood to be part of a global struggle for power and influence between two powers. Even ardent cold warriors who believed deeply in the U.S. position understood the situation this way. It was therefore believed that these efforts would be more effective if the U.S. hand was at least a little bit hidden. Moreover, if the U.S. role had been more public in, for example, supporting noncommunist left-wing parties or labor unions in places such as Italy or Greece, this would have been exploited and used to the advantage of the Soviet Union and their allies in the countries in question.

In the post–Cold War era, democracy promotion has changed, at least in the eyes of American policymakers, from being part of a broader conflict and struggle for influence with the Soviet Union to an attempt to promote a universal good and human right that also aligns with U.S. interests. Human rights can be promoted transparently, while struggles for control of the globe cannot always be executed out in the open. In the twenty-first century there is still strong opposition to U.S. democracy promotion, both from nondemocratic countries and from other regional powers and patrons of nondemocratic regimes, most visibly Russia. However, this opposition to democracy promotion is based on opposing U.S. power rather than on an explicit ideological counter to democracy.

During the early days of the Cold War, democracy promotion was not the modest or limited policy it became, in some respects, in the years following the collapse of communism. In the late 1940s and the 1950s, democracy promotion was not left to NGOs and other organizations with only indirect ties to the U.S. government and relatively small budgets. Rather, particularly in Germany and Japan, democracy promotion was implemented primarily by the U.S. military and supported by enormous financial and human resources. The United States spent $40 billion in Germany and $30 billion in Japan in the seven years following the end of World War II.[23] During this period there were roughly 1.6 million U.S. troops in Germany and 350,000 in Japan.

Precisely because Germany and Japan were defeated military powers, there was no need for the United States to be particularly sensitive to the needs of the defeated regimes, limit the U.S. role, or restrict the visibility and work of the military. This probably contributed to the success of democracy in Germany and Japan, but it did not come without a cost and has never been replicable. Because of the total defeat of Germany and Japan, the United States did not need to hesitate, or even seek much local input, as it appointed local leaders, crafted new constitutions, adjudicated disputes, and rebuilt political institutions in these two countries. The United States therefore had relatively unchecked power, and because of the Cold War, the incentive for getting it right was extremely high. For Germany and Japan, the potential rewards were significant; cooperation with the United States meant affluence and a not unsubstantial amount of freedom. Moreover, the Soviet Union was not popular in Germany or Japan at the end of the war either.

Despite U.S. democracy promotion and, as Smith points out, a compulsion to turn the defeated enemy into democrats having preceded the end of World War II by roughly half a century, when World War II did end, the United States had not yet completed plans or programs for bringing democracy to Japan and Germany. At that time, this type of project was completely without precedent.

In addition, because of the scale of military defeat and the nature of the previous regimes, the United States did not hesitate to take on powerful interests or push for broad societal changes. As part of its attempt to bring democracy to Germany and Japan, the United States challenged powerful economic and political forces and, when necessary, dismantled them.

Smith identifies three key areas where the United States sought to reform the economic relationships in Japan and Germany and limit the
influence of powerful economic forces after the war. First, it ensured that
the rights of workers to organize and collectively bargain were respected.
Second, and in this case only in Japan, the United States implemented a
strong land reform program that weakened the power of large landown-
ers, who had been among the strongest supporters of Japanese fascism.
Last, it broke down the nationalist-based economies in favor of more
open and global systems.[24]

These American policies are the product of a post–World War II political climate in the United States that favored a broad, though not
universal, consensus around the New Deal policies of the 1930s and
1940s. Even the most stridently anticommunist American policymakers
were often either New Deal Democrats or Republicans who did not
challenge the basic tenets of the New Deal. This influenced the nature of
the democratic regimes the United States sought to nurture in Germany and Japan, as well as in southern Europe and other places contested between the Soviet Union and the United States immediately
following World War II. It was possible for democracy in many of these
countries to take on a social democratic slant, which helped bring the
anticommunist left, an absolutely key political force in the early Cold
War struggle, on to the side of the United States. This was fortunate
because economically ruined postwar Europe had little appetite for conservative economic policies. Right-wing democracy would have been a
much less appealing option for most of the European countries recovering
from World War II.

Post–Cold War democracy assistance differs starkly from that following World War II, when promoters of the New Deal brought a progressive economic vision to democracy assistance. In the triumphant spirit
following the Cold War,[25] democracy promotion was closely linked with
free markets and a limited role of the state in the economy. This was
particularly true during the presidency of George W. Bush, where neoconservatives were in the forefront of democracy assistance in Iraq and
elsewhere. Thus, as Smith points out, the nature of the democracy the
United States sought to promote differed over the course of the twentieth and early twenty-first centuries. Democracy obviously should be able
to encompass a reasonably broad array of economic arrangements. The
composition of democratic arrangements and structures within a given

country are, in fact, one of the primary subjects with which democracy should be concerned. Linking democracy inextricably with free market capitalism, or any other rigid economic system, undermines and limits democracy.

For much of the post–Cold War period, the conservative view of democracy, at least with regard to economics, has remained central to the form promoted by the democracy promoters. Philippe Schmitter noted that "absent . . . from the cases of attempted democratization in 1974 is experimentation beyond the basic institutions of liberal democracy."[26] Milja Kurki makes the same point, writing that "indeed, it is notable that the liberal democratic view of democracy has gone curiously unchallenged in the post–Cold War world, even among the political left."[27]

During the Cold War, it was considerably more difficult to separate democracy promotion from U.S. foreign policy, including U.S. military activity more broadly. This was obviously true in Germany and Japan where, immediately following World War II, military personnel were deeply involved in establishing democracy. It was true elsewhere as well. During these years, the advance of democracy was not viewed as a standalone goal of the United States, either rhetorically or otherwise. Rather, it was always subsumed under the broader struggle against communism.

Promoting democracy was therefore not part of U.S. policy in every possible country, as it came to be, in some ways, during the years following the end of the Cold War. Instead, in some cases the United States made little effort to promote democracy or to liberalize right-wing authoritarian regimes. As long as right-wing regimes in countries like South Korea, Taiwan, Chile, or Iran stayed in place and dutifully sided with America in the struggle against communism, the United States did little to try to change those regimes for most of the Cold War period. In some cases, as in Iran or during the early years of the Pinochet regime in Chile, the United States overtly supported nondemocratic regimes as part of a broader Cold War strategy. During the later years of the Cold War several of these countries, such as Taiwan and South Korea, as well as South American countries such as Chile and Brazil, began to move toward more democracy and were supported by the United States in these efforts.

This measured approach dovetailed well with the prevailing understanding in the Western democratic world at the time that democracy was not something that all countries could achieve. Today democracy is understood to be a global value, and something that all people can achieve, or at the very least to which all people can aspire. Of course, there are still those who argue that, in spite of the millions of Muslims who live in democratic states, Islam is somehow incompatible with democracy.[28] However, even as recently as fifty years ago, many in the West believed that democracy was a political system that only European Protestants could achieve.

Indeed, many Americans at the end of the nineteenth and beginning of the twentieth centuries believed that the large numbers of Catholic and Jewish and other non-Protestant immigrants would ultimately undermine U.S. democracy.[29] This belief underpinned the various nativist movements arising over decades of American history and continues to echo in the rhetoric of contemporary American politics, such as, for example, that of Donald Trump's 2016 presidential campaign. The so-called third wave of democracy was largely a Catholic wave, leading to the democratization of heavily Catholic countries in South America and southern Europe, but before that time many viewed Catholicism as incompatible with democracy.

Accordingly the democratic aspirations of the people in much of the non-European world were not taken seriously by the United States for most of the early post–World War II period. Cold War era democracy promotion was largely a phenomenon limited to Europe and a few other countries, such as Japan, in the years immediately following the conclusion of World War II. Even in countries that became democratic in the 1970s and early 1980s, such as Spain, Portugal, or Taiwan, U.S. democracy assistance was not a major impetus, nor did the United States seek to facilitate or encourage these transitions.

For these reasons, some of the paradoxes that characterize democracy assistance in the twenty-first century had not yet become part of democracy promotion in the early years of the Cold War. For example, most of the work was still done by governmental organizations such as the military or the CIA, rather than NGOs who asserted their independence, with varying degrees of credibility, from the U.S. government. Clearly, because much of the Cold War era work was done covertly, NGOs and an extensive network of people and firms working on democracy issues were not practical. Also, democracy promotion, from a programmatic angle, had not yet been translated into a battery of benign and modest sounding programs focusing on issues such as strengthening legislatures or funding civil society organizations. Even when these programs were pursued, they were presented not as part of an effort to have a modest but positive impact on the political development of a particularly country, but as an urgent tactic aimed at stopping communism.

During the Cold War, the language of democracy and democratic development was also indivisible from the language and terminology of the conflict between the United States and the Soviet Union. "Democracy" was frequently used as a synonym for "noncommunist," as the Cold War was often presented in the West as a struggle between communism and democracy. U.S. allies were almost axiomatically described by Washington as democratic, while democratic advance, if it came at the expense of U.S. positioning in the Cold War, was equally often dismissed as the advance, not of democracy, but of communism.

The Cold War lasted close to half a century. During these years American policy, including democracy promotion, naturally evolved. Thus, while democracy promotion in its current form did not exist during the Cold War, many of the institutions at the center of U.S. democracy promotion today have their roots in the later years of the Cold War.

In the 1980s, while competition with the Soviet Union was still intense, the third wave of democratization in southern Europe and, later, South America and East Asia had begun. This created a new set of challenges for the United States, because right-wing nondemocratic governments were giving way not to communist insurgencies but to democratic movements seeking not to align their countries with the Soviet Union but to liberalize or democratize without changing the Cold War alignments of their countries. The first countries where democracy promotion in its contemporary form was implemented were not in eastern Europe or Eurasia but in places like Chile, the Philippines, and Indonesia while the Cold War was still going relatively strong.

The NED, NDI, and IRI were founded in 1983, which was still, for the most part, the height of the Cold War. Although the Soviet Union had less than a decade of life remaining at that point, almost nobody foresaw that at the time. Instead these organizations were founded to provide both support to democratizing allies and also another tool in the struggle against communism. President Ronald Reagan's remarks at the founding of the NED, for example, capture this dual goal well:

The establishment of the National Endowment [for Democracy] goes right to the heart of America's faith in democratic ideals and institutions. It offers hope to people everywhere. Last year in London I spoke of the need and obligation to assist democratic development. My hope then was that America would make clear to those who cherish democracy throughout the world that we mean what we say.[30]

Reagan used very general language about democracy and freedom, but in alluding to his speech "last year in London," the famous Westminster speech in which he strongly attacked communism and spoke of its inevitable defeat, Reagan made clear that the NED would have a role in the Cold War as well.

One of the deepest paradoxes of democracy promotion today, one with strong roots in the Cold War, is that democracy and democracy promotion are tools and core beliefs of both the left and the right in American politics. The origins of this paradox are based in the Cold War because fighting for democracy, particularly when the most powerful nondemocratic force is communism (as was the case from the late 1940s through the early 1990s), has strong appeal to the left and the right. In this context, both ideological sides can see democracy as uniquely appealing to their worldview.

The idea that people should have the right to elect their own leaders, despite politically and financially powerful forces both inside and outside the country, is a basic value on the left; the right of people to rise up against a powerful state that seeks to strip them of their basic freedoms is a cherished value on the right. These values may not be identical, but they are similar, with a great deal of overlap. However, because of the political contexts in which these struggles occur, the left and right frequently disagree on the democratic nature of a regime or of the struggle to overthrow that regime.

During the Cold War, for example, those on the right saw democracy axiomatically as being a contrast to, and bulwark against, communism. People on the left, however, often understood movements against right-wing but pro-American authoritarian regimes as being about democracy as well. Reagan's Westminster speech, now remembered for the president's strong resolve against communism and eloquent expression of the universality of freedom and democracy, also drew on right-wing tropes that did not resonate well with progressives. Reagan's description in that speech of the 1982 election in El Salvador was a highly partisanized right-wing interpretation of an election that was viewed by many as fraught with fraud and terror: "Suddenly the freedom-fighters in the hills were exposed for what they really are—Cuban-backed guerrillas who want power for themselves, and their backers, not democracy for the people. But on election day, the people of El Salvador, an unprecedented 1.4 million of them, braved ambush and gunfire, and trudged for miles to vote for freedom."

The overthrow of Salvador Allende in Chile was seen as a blow to democracy by the left, but as an effort to protect Chilean democracy by the right. Similar opinions during the Cold War framed U.S. support for right-wing leaders in Indonesia, South Africa, and elsewhere. On the other hand, right-wing Americans tended to perceive any opposition to communism as driven by a desire for democracy. During the Cold War, one of the persistent challenges of the American left was to find a way to criticize right-wing authoritarian allies of the U.S. without being accused of being a communist or soft on the Soviet Union. Many, however, even while accepting the need to combat soviet communism, understood that American allies in Seoul, Johannesburg, or Santiago were very far from being democrats.

In the 1970s, 1980s, and 1990s, efforts to overthrow authoritarian regimes in Nicaragua, El Salvador, South Africa, and numerous other countries were highly partisanized in the United States. For example, the left supported the government in Nicaragua and the opposition forces in El Salvador, while the right held the opposite position. These regimes were comparable, however, in their levels of democracy and freedom. During the Cold War it was understood that democracy was an extremely politicized concept, susceptible to change depending on the context, and democracy remained a contested concept between the left and right.

In the years immediately following World War II, however, it was conservative political forces that first used democracy promotion as a means of stopping communism. Progressive supporters of democracy in foreign countries often found themselves supporting governments less hostile to the Soviet Union, and thus supporters became vulnerable to red-baiting and anticommunist rhetoric. In the language of the Cold War, an American who opposed the authoritarian regime in Poland was supporting freedom, while an American who opposed authoritarian regimes in South Africa or Chile was often considered subversive by conservatives.

The Cold War era approach led to a deception in which anticommunist and pro-American governments were treated and described as democracies by Washington almost regardless of their domestic political arrangements. Of course, there had to be a modicum of democracy for this charade to be maintained, so elections of varying quality, constitutions guaranteeing rights but honored only in the breach, and even Cold War related emergencies suspending democracy but promising its resumption at a later date were central elements of these regimes. U.S. policies in Chile, South Korea, and Indonesia during much of the regimes of Augusto Pinochet, Syngman Rhee, and Suharto, respectively, particularly the earlier years, are examples of this.

These issues, albeit in slightly different forms, carried over to the twenty-first century as well. The U.S. led invasion of Iraq was, to a significant if belated extent, presented to the American people as, at least partially, an effort to make Iraq a democracy. This cause was embraced by the right but not taken seriously by the left. Therefore, the left generally dismissed both the viability of the project and the legitimacy of the effort. For many on the left, the excesses of the war on terror, including the Iraq War, were frustrating, outrageous, and an enormous mistake for several reasons—for one, that it was all so familiar. U.S. efforts to present clearly nondemocratic leaders such as Pervez Musharraf in Pakistan as democrats, or corrupt mediocrities such as Nouri al-Maliki in Iraq as leading their country to democracy, did not seem at all unfamiliar to progressives old enough to remember or interested enough to read about the 1960s, 1970s, and 1980s.

CHAPTER THREE
DEMOCRACY PROMOTION SINCE THE COLD WAR

THE CHANGING RESPONSES OF MY friends and neighbors to my democracy promotion work grew almost directly out of the Iraq War and President Bush's efforts to link it to democracy promotion. By late 2003, President Bush described the Iraq War and the subsequent effort to democratize Iraq by saying, "We did not charge hundreds of miles into the heart of Iraq and pay a bitter cost of casualties and liberate 25 million people only to retreat before a band of thugs and assassins. We will help the Iraqi people establish a peaceful and democratic country in the heart of the Middle East."[1] This view may have resonated with the president's neo-conservative base but was viewed much more critically on the left of the political spectrum, where the predominant view was that oil and power, not democracy, were the foci of the Bush administration.

This rhetoric from a Republican president coexisted alongside another change in how democracy and democracy promotion were viewed globally between the last years of the Cold War and the beginning of the twenty-first century. During that time, democracy was transformed from an ideology, a system of government, or one of the poles in a global conflict to a universal human right. Article 8 of the "Vienna Declaration and Program of Action," adopted by the World Conference on Human Rights in 1993, in which 171 states participated, stated,

Democracy, development and respect for human rights and fundamental freedoms are interdependent and mutually reinforcing. Democracy is based on the freely expressed will of the people to determine their own political, economic, social and cultural systems and their full participation in all aspects of their lives. In the context of the above, the promotion and protection of human rights and fundamental freedoms at the national and international levels should be universal and conducted without conditions attached. The international community should support the strengthening and promoting of democracy, development and respect for human rights and fundamental freedoms in the entire world.

This document is not a legal commitment for the 171 participating countries, nor is it binding in any way, but it is nonetheless significant, not only because it treats democracy as a human right but also because it makes it clear that countries are allowed, actually obliged, to help nondemocratic countries become democratic.

Michael McFaul, a prominent scholar of democracy who later served in President Obama's National Security Council and as U.S. ambassador to Russia, responded to criticisms of U.S. democracy promotion policy during the Bush years, by arguing that

democracy promotion as a foreign policy goal has become increasingly acceptable throughout most of the international community. . . . Today, however, the United States no longer holds a monopoly on the business of democracy promotion. That development is a sign that such policy is not just a U.S. national interest (or camouflage for other U.S. national interests), but an international norm embraced by other states, transnational organizations, and international networks.[2]

The evolution of democracy and democracy promotion to the point they could be described as an "international norm" made it easier for the U.S. to delink the promotion of democracy from American interests. This represents a significant change in the way democracy promotion has been pursued during the post–Cold War era, but it has not changed the larger reality that, for Washington, democracy remains a tool that has never been completely distinct from the pursuit of American interests.

In the immediate aftermath of the Cold War, the impetus for a greater emphasis on democracy promotion did not come from the neoconservative right. As scholar and policy analyst Mark McLelland describes, "Neoconservatives began the 1990s by largely supporting the direction for U.S. foreign policy that had been charted by George H. W. Bush's realist foreign policy team . . . yet greeted the twenty-first century with calls for American hegemony in the cause of liberal democracy."[3]

During this period, democracy, as seen from Washington, has transformed from a tactic in a broader global struggle against Soviet communism to a universal good that the United States needed to promote because it was both in our interest and a collective good. In general, conflating U.S. interests with universal good has been one of the hallmarks of the evolution of American post–Cold War foreign policy. Increasingly, what America supports, such as democracy in specific countries and laws that inevitably are good for U.S. interests, are presented by Washington as universal goods. This then makes it possible to portray countries that oppose the United States as opposing universal good rather than as simply acting in their own interests, and for the United States to frame foreign policy as a moral struggle between the forces of good and evil, rather than as a struggle between U.S. interests and those of other countries.

In addition, as democracy and democracy promotion were treated more as universal goods, they grew to be applied more universally. This is not to say that democracy became universal, because obviously it did not. However, efforts to promote democracy became more universally recognized. By the beginning of the new century, democracy promotion was far removed from a specific policy applied, often with substantial resources, to a small handful of strategically important countries.

Instead, it grew into a policy pursued almost universally by the United States. This contributes to an asymmetry between the Cold War and post–Cold War eras of democracy promotion. During the Cold War, democracy promotion could be identified as a discrete phenomenon in a few countries, but by 2000 or so, it had permeated all of American foreign policy and was pursued in dozens of countries with varying degrees of intensity. Afghanistan and Iraq, along with countries like Ukraine and Egypt, continue as the sites for democracy work that is occasionally in the spotlight and most often discussed in the media and among politicians, but they are just a few among dozens of countries where America pursues democracy promotion, usually as a tertiary goal with very modest financial support.

The current approach lends itself to a similar but deeper deception and paradox. Democracy is often both in America's interest and a universal good, but the promotion of democracy is often driven by the former while presented as the latter. Much of the post–Cold War structures, rhetoric, and even programs of democracy promotion have been established substantially to obscure, either deliberately or not, this paradox.

The power of the paradox is its complexity. Describing democracy promotion as simply a sort of diplomatic sleight of hand, whereby the United States pursues its interests while claiming to support democracy, particularly in the post–Cold War era, is inaccurate. Activists, policymakers, and others involved in democracy promotion in many cases genuinely and deeply believe that democracy is the best form of government and that all countries and peoples would benefit from democratic systems. Much of the sleight of hand, however, occurs in determining what countries are democracies and what leaders are democrats. During the Cold War, anticommunists were more readily viewed as democrats; since the Cold War, political forces supportive of America and the West are more likely to be seen as democrats. Democracy, according to this approach, is almost always in the interest of the United States, because those who support the interests of the United States are more likely to be seen as democrats.

THE EVOLUTION OF DEMOCRACY PROMOTION STRUCTURES

Democracy promotion has been a durable and surprisingly flexible policy for much of American history. Since the Spanish-American War, the goal of making other countries more democratic has been part of American foreign policy. The United States, for most of this time, pursued this policy through a variety of means and for a variety reasons. Military intervention, efforts to make defeated countries more democratic, building democratic institutions to combat the spread of communism, and fighting poverty have all been part of the means and rationale for U.S. democracy promotion over the decades.

After the Cold War, democracy promotion remained an important part of U.S. foreign policy, but it took on a larger role. The collapse of communism in Eastern Europe and the Soviet Union created an opportunity for the United States to help spread, or reestablish, democracy in a large part of the world, and also to further vanquish its defeated ideological enemy. Sometime in the decade or so following the end of the Cold War, democracy promotion changed once again and became essentially the default setting in a significant number of U.S. bilateral relations. In almost every country of what had once been the communist bloc, America actively engaged in democracy promotion. Democracy and governance also became integrated into numerous USAID field offices throughout the world.

Democracy promotion, in this iteration, was no longer something America did following military victory or to pursue a particular strategic end but became simply the way the United States related to much of the world. It became, to some extent, something the United States did because it could. By the beginning of the twenty-first century, therefore, democracy assistance had evolved into the path of least resistance for U.S. policy toward most poor countries, even some, such as Mexico, that were already relatively democratic. Moreover, the substance and structure of this democracy promotion work, particularly on the programmatic side, looked very similar in all these countries.

On the surface, this appears a benign and natural development, which it may in fact be, as many democracy promotion programs are limited in scope and impact. For example, providing financial and technical help for a few civil society organizations in Mexico or facilitating some exchanges for political parties in the Baltic countries are relatively modest activities. Nonetheless, the evolution of democracy promotion, from a project driven by strategic goals and national security to something that America does because it can, reveals a fair amount about America in the post–Cold War era. It suggests that the United States sees its global role as ensuring, or at the very least facilitating, more freedom and democracy everywhere. This American conception is equal parts grandiose, admirable, unrealistic, and ambitious.

As democracy promotion became the norm of American foreign policy, democracy promotion itself became more homogeneous. A battery of domestic election monitoring, legislative strengthening, support for political parties, local governance, and programs seeking to empower women became the heart of democracy promotion programs virtually everywhere in the decade or so following the end of the Cold War. From a programmatic perspective, these topics are important in most countries, but beyond the big picture many differences remain regarding what is most appropriate for each country. For example, countries moving out of decades of communist rule tend to have specific and similar challenges related to building civil society, whereas countries emerging from weak-state kleptocratic nondemocratic regimes may already have stronger civil societies but greater challenges related to rule of law. Too often, at the programmatic level, these differences have not been taken into consideration. Instead, programs have evolved to a standard that is applied broadly, without consideration of different needs in different countries.

A major difference between democracy promotion strategies in the Cold War and post–Cold War eras has been the evolution of government agencies, semi-governmental organizations (NGOs), and private companies that implement democracy promotion. These organizations function largely like policy networks in other areas of domestic and foreign policy. Melia referred to this as the "democracy bureaucracy."[4] In some respects the evolution of this bureaucracy, despite its negative connotation, has made the policy stronger, bringing transparency and accountability to work that was once done mostly in secret with little input or accountability from elected officials or voters in the United States. It has also made possible the development of individual and organizational expertise, as well as institutional memory. Because of this we know a lot more today about how to help democracy develop than we did a half century ago. Much of this knowledge is shared throughout the industry by conferences, online databases, informal discussions, and the like.

The National Democratic Institute (NDI), International Republic Institute (IRI), National Endowment for Democracy (NED), and U.S. Agency for International Development (USAID), for example, all have searchable databases that make reports, public opinion polls, manuals, and evaluations going back for many years available to the public. These resources are extremely valuable to scholars, practitioners, and others, including those outside the United States. USAID and various Washington think tanks also hold periodic conferences to discuss lessons learned and future directions for democracy assistance. Private contractors frequently draw on consultants with years of experience doing democracy work in both the NGO and governmental sectors. All of this helps sharpen the programmatic side of the work and make it less necessary for practitioners to learn everything anew in the field.

Melia's so-called democracy bureaucracy is sprawling and encompasses numerous organizations and individuals both inside and outside government, including numerous government contractors that are private businesses. Many of these firms make most of their money from USAID contracts and have evolved largely to win and implement those contracts. These organizations, whether for-profit companies or NGOs, are primarily involved in funding and implementing various democracy assistance programs but are only part of the democracy assistance landscape that has evolved since the end of the Cold War. Democracy promotion includes a range of policies, government statements, diplomatic endeavors, and multilateral institutions, as well as other actors. Presidents and secretaries of state call for democratic reforms. Ambassadors address potential election fraud in advance of elections. Congress even occasionally passes sanctions or other punitive measures when the absence of democracy and the presence of human rights violations in a particular country becomes too severe. NATO observes elections. The military seeks to bring democracy on the spot to war-torn countries such as Afghanistan and Iraq.

A broad definition of democracy promotion is useful, but it is also important to be able to identify where democracy promotion ends. Democracy promotion is affected by activities throughout the foreign policy arena, but not everything in the foreign policy arena can be described as democracy promotion. Nonetheless, military actions, trade policies, and other U.S. government actions can affect democracy in ways that are not always foreseen.

Democracy promotion in the post–Cold War era can be divided into three general periods: the first from 1991 to 2001, the second from 2002 to 2009, and the third from 2010 to the present. The first period was characterized by a domestic consensus on the importance of democracy promotion and on the ability of the United States to succeed in this area. During these years, few people paid much attention to democracy promotion, but it was not a controversial or partisan policy. As scholar Thomas Carothers points out, "Democracy promotion achieved significant bipartisan support within the U.S. policy community and public from the late 1980s until the early years of this decade (the 2000s), but that consensus has shattered."[5] This was the period during and immediately following the conclusion of the Cold War, when American triumphalism was running high and there was broad support for a bigger American role in the world.

During this period strong American confidence was buoyed by the victory in the Cold War and the expanding economy of the 1990s. Americans and their leaders were confident in the country's ability to do, and pay for, almost anything. Russia was a defeated power that had still not found its post–Cold War footing, while China was viewed as a potential but not yet actual superpower, so there was no strong international backlash to democracy promotion either. Islamic fundamentalism was a threat, but did not yet dominate American foreign policy concerns as it would in the years following the attacks of September 11, 2001.

Before 1990, democracy promotion was still implemented sporadically through different methods and organizations. Organizations such as NDI, IRI, and the NED had not yet become the institutions they are today. Activities such as election monitoring were less routinized and structured, and the bevy of democracy-related programs that dominate the field today were in the process of being created. By 2000, however, democracy promotion was pursued, if not quite uniformly then certainly similarly, in many different countries. The lead organizations and programs became homogenized so, for example, almost every postcommunist country had legislative development, political party strengthening, civil society development, women's leadership, and a handful of other programs. These countries also had a substantial USAID democracy and governance presence, with visible offices of IRI, NDI, IFES (International Foundation for Electoral Systems), and a smattering of other American organizations.

In many respects these years marked a triumphant era for U.S. democracy promotion, during which democracy expanded not only to the former communist countries of Europe, but also to South America and Asia. Countries as diverse as Poland, South Africa, and Chile, which were authoritarian in 1980, were democratic or semi-democratic by the dawn of the new century. While U.S. democracy promotion, even according to its biggest advocates, likely played only a supporting role in those developments, these events contributed to a sense of confidence regarding democracy promotion and led people to believe that democracy promotion was a relatively straightforward activity that could be replicated with similar results in even more countries.

These triumphs also colored the perception of democracy promotion. In many parts of postcommunist Europe and elsewhere during these years, the primary project of democracy work was to help countries committed to becoming more democratic make that transition more smoothly and quickly. Of course, numerous postcommunist countries did not become democratic during these years, but for most of the 1990s, there was still a sense that the world was moving toward democracy. Carothers describes this attitude: "In the excitement of the early 1990s, many people both outside and inside Eastern Europe and the former Soviet Union thought that once launched, transition processes would unfold naturally, with their own internal logic and momentum. People imagined that transitions would be akin to placing a boat in a rapidly moving river and then simply steering it along."[6]

This approach was also bolstered by the incentive of EU membership, which played a major role in encouraging leaders to reform and democratize in eastern Europe and the Baltics. For countries like Hungary, Poland, or Estonia, the prospect of joining the EU, and being formally reconnected with Europe and enjoying the economic benefits of that connection, made democracy an easy choice, and one for which there was substantial public support.

DEMOCRACY PROMOTION AFTER SEPTEMBER 11

By the early years of the twenty-first century, much had unmistakably changed. A series of events, beginning with Vladimir Putin's ascendancy to the Russian presidency in May 2000, followed by the attacks on the United States on September 11, 2001, and the U.S.-led war in Iraq beginning in March 2003, dramatically altered the environment in which democracy promotion was pursued by the United States and ushered in the second period of post–Cold War democracy promotion.

The 2003 invasion of Iraq—more precisely, the aftermath of that invasion, as the United States sought to build a democracy there in the wake of Saddam Hussein's defeat—drew more attention to U.S. democracy promotion than anything had in many years. It also, not incidentally, reduced American soft power and gave rise to increases in global anti-American sentiment. In this environment it was very difficult for the United States to make a case that it was a model other countries should follow.

In addition, from roughly 2004 to 2008, democracy promotion was largely defined by U.S.-led efforts to establish democracy in post-invasion Afghanistan and Iraq. In that conflict, particularly in Iraq, democracy promotion occupied a different position than it had in previous conflicts. In World War II, for example, establishing democracy was a postconflict American activity. In the Iraq War, by contrast, the Bush administration presented the creation of democracy as one of the reasons America went to war.[7]

However, Vladimir Putin's rise to power in Russia and the reemergence of Russia as a major regional power were significant developments that also had a big effect on U.S. democracy promotion. In a related development, the Color Revolutions, both successful and unsuccessful, in several countries of the former Soviet Union also had an enormous impact on the politics of democracy promotion. This series of largely peaceful mass demonstrations overthrew corrupt semi-democratic regimes, replacing them with pro-Western governments with strong (although in some cases short-lived) democratic credentials in Georgia (2003), Ukraine (2004–05), and Kyrgyzstan (2005). They occurred at the height of the Bush administration's interest in democracy promotion and were heralded in the West, particularly in Washington, as major advances for democracy. Bush famously described Georgia in May 2005 as a "beacon of democracy." In the years following the Color Revolutions, the democratic credentials of regimes in Kyrgyzstan and Georgia faded quickly, while in Ukraine the ancienne regime returned with the 2010 election victory of Viktor Yanukovych. Yanukovych had been the candidate in 2004 who tried to steal the election, thus precipitating the mass protests that winter.[8] By the time of the Euromaidan movement of largely peaceful pro-Europe protests in Ukraine that ousted Yanukovych in early 2014, the Orange Revolution was sufficiently forgotten that it was rarely even mentioned in media analyses of events in Ukraine.

The Color Revolutions, while ultimately doing little to advance democracy in the former Soviet Union, are probably more appropriately understood as an early skirmish in the ongoing and deepening tension between the West and Vladimir Putin's Russia, described by some as a new Cold War.[9] Russia viewed the Color Revolutions as having little to do with democracy and a great deal to do with Western incursion into what Moscow viewed as Russia's sphere of influence—specifically, as U.S.-led plots to destabilize the region and put pro-American leaders into power. This led to a Russian pushback against Western- and U.S.-led democracy work in the former Soviet Union.

These years also marked the period when democracy promotion was the most aggressive overseas and the most partisan at home. Particularly in the heady days when Washington believed the Color Revolutions were poised to bring democracy to places like Georgia and Ukraine and when it looked, at least to some, that Iraq might end up democratic, the United States (more accurately, the Bush administration) considered democracy promoted through a combination of military intervention, NGO activism, and diplomacy as a potential tool for remaking the world. This view required an extraordinary combination of hopefulness, arrogance, and vision, but the Bush administration had ample supplies of all three.

A speech by President George W. Bush at the United Nations in September 2006 demonstrated the extent to which his Freedom Agenda linked democracy promotion and military intervention as complementary tools for advancing freedom and democracy:

Some of the changes in the Middle East have been dramatic, and we see the results in this chamber. Five years ago, Afghanistan was ruled by the brutal Taliban regime, and its seat in this body was contested. Now this seat is held by the freely elected government of Afghanistan, which is represented today by President [Hamid] Karzai. Five years ago, Iraq's seat in this body was held by a dictator who killed his citizens, invaded his neighbors and showed his contempt for the world by defying more than a dozen U.N. Security Council resolutions. Now Iraq's seat is held by a democratic government that embodies the aspirations of the Iraq people. It is represented today by President [Jalal] Talabani. With these changes, more than 50 million people have been given a voice in this chamber for the first time in decades.[10]

The language Bush used in this speech is a bit strange since the president recounted the advances of democracy in Iraq and Afghanistan without mentioning the U.S.-led invasions of those countries. Nonetheless, Bush is clearly claiming two victories for democracy and democracy promotion based on events in which the U.S. military played a very significant role. With the benefit of hindsight, it is now clear that Bush's assessment was somewhere between overly optimistic and delusional, but it is also clear that at the time, the president was deeply enthusiastic about what he perceived to be the boundless potential of democracy promotion.

This energy evolved into the Freedom Agenda, the name given to the Bush administration's goal of remaking the world, particularly the Middle East, in a new and more democratic form. The Freedom Agenda was a product of the extraordinary overconfidence and vision of the neo-conservatives who dominated foreign policy during the first six years of the Bush administration and was a uniquely American combination of hubris and a deep belief in democracy and freedom. Ultimately, the Freedom Agenda proved a failure and was more or less forgotten by the final two years of Bush's tenure in office. Needless to say, it was not revived by the Obama administration.[11]

The enthusiasm the Bush administration showed for democracy promotion occurred in the context of a very divisive political environment in America. In that environment, democracy promotion became a polarizing issue, with supporters of the Bush administration seeing it as central to American foreign policy while the activist antiwar left viewed it as a new form of imperialism.

DEMOCRACY PROMOTION AFTER THE "THUMPIN'"

It is easy to imagine the end of the second period coinciding with the election of Barack Obama in November 2008, but the beginning of the end was two years earlier, caused by a big Republican defeat in a midterm election that was a harbinger of 2008. In November 2006, Bush's Republican Party lost six Senate seats and thirty-one House seats. Bush, in one of the more eloquent turns of phrase of his presidency, referred to this defeat as the "thumpin'."[12] The "thumpin'" was a resounding rebuke of Bush's policies, leading to Democratic control of both houses of Congress and the resignation of Secretary of Defense Donald Rumsfeld, one of the administration members most associated with Bush's foreign policy. In a period of a few weeks, American politics had been shaken up and the groundwork for Barack Obama's election laid. At that moment it also looked like democracy promotion and, at the very least, the rhetorical emphasis on democracy promotion would be collateral damage from the "thumpin'." This has not entirely been the case, but in the years since 2006, enthusiasm for democracy promotion has not approached the levels it enjoyed during the middle years of the Bush administration.

In this context, Obama's election is better understood as the end point of a series of events that led to the third period of democracy promotion in post–Cold War America, rather than its cause. The other critically important event was the collapse of the global financial market in August 2008 that plunged America into recession, creating additional domestic political incentive for a less ambitious foreign policy.

By the time Obama took office in January 2009, the U.S. economy was in very bad shape, exacerbating the budget crisis created by President Bush. Americans were losing confidence in their ability to shape foreign policy outcomes, and powerful forces in Moscow and Beijing were able to combat the U.S. agenda overseas. This was a dramatically different environment from the one that George W. Bush found when he took office in January 2001. In addition, candidate Obama had run aggressively against the Iraq War and its legacy; included in that legacy was democracy promotion and President Bush's ill-fated Freedom Agenda.

The third period of post–Cold War democracy promotion therefore reflects a very different setting, both domestically and internationally, than the one that had characterized U.S. efforts less than two decades earlier. This is the period in which the United States now finds itself. In the early 1990s America was confident, without any challenge as the world's most powerful state, fresh from a victory of historic proportions in the Cold War, and beginning a period of solid economic growth. These conditions no longer existed by 2009 and had in most cases been replaced by their polar opposites. Despite this changing mood and context, the third period of democracy promotion is also characterized by important challenges remaining in precisely those countries and regions that have proven least amenable to democracy.

A report undertaken by the Pew Research Center in the waning months of the Bush administration, titled "Declining Public Support for Global Engagement," summarized the mood of the times with regard to overseas commitment: "The public . . . has a sharply diminished appetite for US efforts to deal with an array of global problems. . . . There is also decreased support for an assertive national security policy."[13] The data from that poll show that during Bush's second term, the proportion of Americans who thought America should prioritize "stopping genocide," and "promoting human rights," dropped by 11 percent and 8 percent, respectively. Falloffs were also seen in "reducing the spread of AIDS/disease," and "protecting against terror attacks," which dropped by 19 percent and 6 percent, respectively. According to this same poll, the margin of Americans who wanted "the next president to focus on domestic policy" outnumbered those who wanted a focus on foreign policy by a margin of three to one. This indicated a public that, by the end of the Bush years, was not confident about America's ability to accomplish much overseas and did not want an aggressive or particularly active foreign policy. This was the mood when Obama took office, and probably the mood that helped him get elected.[14] It also was a mood that would have an impact on democracy promotion.

The third period of democracy promotion has predictably been marked by very few cases of democratic advance, thus contributing to, but also reflecting, the changing mood in the United States toward the promotion and expansion of democracy. The Arab Spring of 2010–11 has not only led to much less democracy than initially was hoped in the days when peaceful demonstrators were bringing down authoritarian regimes in Egypt and Tunisia but has also generated less hope and optimism than the Color Revolutions, the equally unclear phenomenon of less than a decade earlier.

The Arab Spring and the Color Revolutions share some commonalities, at least in relation to cycles of democratic development. Both were democratic breakthroughs broadly mistaken in the West for democracy; both saw regimes come to power that proved less democratic than initially hoped. However, the West soured much more quickly on the Arab Spring, raising concerns almost immediately, and appropriately, about Islamic fundamentalism and threats to democracy and freedom in the region. This was partially because the undemocratic nature of successor regimes was more pronounced, in Egypt for example, but also because of a different feeling in the West regarding the prospects for democracy. By contrast the West, especially the United States, was reasonably comfortable with the state of democracy in Kyrgyzstan and Georgia as late as 2008, when the democratic glow from the Color Revolutions had distinctly faded.

By 2014, however, the Euromaidan in Ukraine was viewed by Western governments as an unambiguous advance for democracy, rather than as the more complex phenomenon that it was. In the Ukraine 2014 case, perceptions of the Euromaidan movement were framed largely by the subsequent Russian invasion of Crimea and incursion into other parts of southern and eastern Ukraine. The antipathy toward Russia in the West influenced the extent to which the anti-Russian Euromaidan movement was perceived as an important step forward for democracy.

The three periods of post–Cold War democracy promotion define the political context and outlook for democracy promotion rather than the practices of democracy promotion itself. Therefore while post–Cold War democracy promotion has evolved in a changing political environment, the programs and institutions at the heart of democracy promotion have grown and developed in ways that have not always responded to or recognized these changes. In the last twenty years, institutions like the NED, IRI, and NDI, as well as the IFES and the numerous private contractors that implement democracy programs have become bigger, better funded, and more numerous. They have also gained expertise and, presumably, become better at the nuts and bolts of helping develop democracy in different countries.

But in many cases, particularly with regard to programmatic developments, changes have been largely of degree, not of kind. The basic tools and programs of 2014 do not look very different from those of 2004 or even 2000. The battery of political party development, civil society programs, and the like remain common today, just as they were in the late 1990s, and many programs being implemented today are similar to the ones of twenty years ago. In some cases they have been implemented more or less continuously in the same country for more than a decade. It is still possible to go to many countries—including post-conflict countries like Afghanistan, but also the remaining nondemocratic countries of the former Soviet Union—and see organizations doing political party workshops or training new members of parliament as they would have done twenty years ago.

Training new members of parliament is very important when the parliament is the first freely elected legislature after years of authoritarian rule, but significantly less relevant in a consolidated nondemocratic regime where the executive holds all the power and the legislature is a hotbed of corruption. Helping political parties learn communication, organization, and campaign tactics is also very valuable in countries during their first few post-authoritarian elections, but more or less a waste of time if the election is stolen months in advance, as is the case in many authoritarian and semi-authoritarian regimes. In too many consolidated nondemocratic regimes, these programs persist because of bureaucratic incentives and logic on the part of funders and implementers of democracy programs rather than because of political need or effectiveness.

In addition, in consolidating democracies, governance programs that help new governments deliver services more efficiently are very important because they build confidence in democratic processes by linking them to better policy outcomes. In nondemocratic countries, helping governments govern better has nothing to do with democracy and generally makes nondemocratic governments stronger but not more democratic.

Technological advances have also effected changes in programs, but of a relatively minor nature, reflecting the need to learn new tools, rather than any groundbreaking advances in program impact. In the mid-1990s, for example, civil society activists were not trained on social media or blogging as they are now. In many cases new technology, innovative approaches building on years and even decades of experience, and a growing cadre of better and more appropriately trained professionals have made democracy promotion programs seem stronger, or at least relevant again. However, the work is still technical and program-based and not as well positioned as it might be to effect political change in the context of the second decade of the twenty-first century.

The basic assumptions—that democracy can best be built through technical programs and that the civil society/political party/judicial reform/legislative support construct is the best programmatic approach—therefore remain largely unchallenged. It is not clear why this is the case; the track record of these programs is deeply mixed, and even good programs do not always lead to greater democracy or significant outcomes. For people who work in democracy promotion, it is also hard not to notice that, increasingly, people in countries receiving democracy assistance are not interested in this kind of support. Some already have the expertise being offered, some can buy it elsewhere, and some have more pressing problems. The approach persists nevertheless and is unlikely to change anytime soon.

In many countries where I have worked, opposition political parties, for example, cooperate with American organizations such as NDI and IRI not because they expect to benefit from the workshops and seminars led by these organizations. Rather, they participate in these events as a way to signal to the West that they want to cooperate and be friendly to the United States. In some cases, the parties find themselves surprised that they benefit from the seminars, but it is more common that they partici-pate sporadically, send junior members, or otherwise act in a way that indicates that the substance of the workshops is not of great interest.

TECHNICAL ASSISTANCE AND REGIME CHANGE

Many democracy promotion programs remain substantially unchanged, but the world around them does not. Two central tenets of the early Cold War period of democracy assistance—that most countries in which pro-grams are implemented welcome democracy and simply need support and technical guidance, and that the Western model of liberal democracy is ascendant ideologically and politically—are much less clear than they were twenty or even ten years ago.

The 1990s and earliest years of the twenty-first century saw a spate of countries become democratic, notably in the western part of the former communist bloc. Almost all these countries, including Croatia, Poland, Hungary, and others, accomplished this with the support of Western democracy promotion. These countries all fit the early post–Cold War model well; they were seeking to become democratic and ben-efited significantly from Western support and guidance in that effort.

Fifteen years later, very few countries remained that resembled these postcommunist countries on the brink of democratic consolidation. Al-though the transition period was clearly winding down by 2005 or even earlier, the idea that governments were still in "transition" remained a central assumption in much of the democracy promotion community. By that time the remaining countries in the world that were not democratic had become a somewhat consolidated nondemocratic regime. This is significant, because it is a very different thing to help a transitional country such as Poland in the early 1990s or Chile after the fall of Pinochet move toward democracy than it is trying to make a consoli-dated nondemocratic regime such as twenty-first-century Kazakhstan democratic, or to liberalize a regime like the one in Cambodia. Each task requires different programs and approaches and carries different political implications.

This is also the political space wherein democracy promotion or assistance melds into its close relative, regime change. Helping a country that is clearly in a period of transition or uncertainty move toward a regime type, particularly if it has made that goal clear, is very different from trying to change the regime of a stable nontransitional country. The former is democracy promotion; the latter is regime change. The latter strategy is certainly appropriate at times, indeed sometimes needed, but recognizing the difference leads to a more honest and effective policy.

In addition, in the twenty years between 1990 and 2010, the U.S. position in the world changed a great deal. By 2010, unlike throughout the 1990s, other powerful states—notably China and Russia, but others as well—could provide material and political support to nondemocratic regimes. An effective counter to democracy promotion had evolved: by 2010, states from Africa to Central Asia and elsewhere could receive ample foreign assistance from China, and occasionally from regional powers as well, that was not at all linked to pressure to liberalize or democratize. These states could also receive technical guidance to help them stay in power and combat democracy movements. The clearest example of this was the spate of laws passed in Russia and other parts of the former Soviet Union limiting civil society and media freedom in the aftermath of the Color Revolutions beginning in 2004.

In Central Asia and the former Soviet Union, for example, organizations such as the Shanghai Cooperation Organization (SCO) and the Collective Security Treaty Organization (CSTO) formed to act as counters to Western organization such as NATO and the OSCE. These organizations allowed member countries to learn from each other and in some cases create mutual treaties to defend against potential domestic unrest.

Alexander Cooley, a political scientist at Barnard College, noted,

Soon after the Orange and Tulip Revolutions, a variety of Eurasian regimes, with strong backing from Moscow, adopted a series of measures to counter the activities of external democracy actors so as to avoid a replay of the sequence of events which led to the overthrow of these governments. This backlash has not only eroded basic civil liberties and media freedoms in many Eurasian countries, especially in Central Asia, but also challenged the authority of many international organizations and nongovernmental organizations in the region.[15]

Longtime democracy advocate Christopher Walker (2014) argued,

> Today's leading authoritarian regimes are turning "containment" on its head, using massive resources and coordinated political efforts to chip away at the rules-based institutions that have served as the glue for the post–Cold War liberal order, while checking the reform ambitions of aspiring democracies and reshaping the way the world thinks about democracy.[16]

Both Walker and Cooley describe a context where resistance to democracy promotion is coordinated and given ample resources. This clearly represents a major challenge for U.S. democracy promotion that did not exist at the turn of the century. This resistance is backed by powerful and wealthy countries, including China and Russia, lending credibility and strength.

It is ironic that these barriers that changed the nature and challenges of democracy promotion, raising grave and generally unanswered questions about the viability of these policies, arose during the time democracy promotion became firmly entrenched as a central part of American foreign policy.

Russia in particular has a great deal of soft power to use to support its anti-Western and anti-democratic agenda. "Soft power," a term first coined by Nye (1990), refers to the ability of a country to attract or win support based on means that are not financial or military.[17] The United States seeks to exercise its soft power globally. Russian soft power does not have a global reach, but in Central Asia and some other parts of the former Soviet Union, it is a significant resource. In these places the widespread use of the Russian language, and therefore access to Russian media that is largely in the service of the Kremlin, combined with Soviet nostalgia and suspicions of the West, particularly among the older generation, are employed by Russia to weaken support for democracy and raise questions about the motives of the United States and Europe. Strong economic ties, particularly in the form of labor moving from Central Asia to Russia, give Russia substantial leverage over the Central Asian states. While not exactly soft power, this leverage was exercised in the years preceding the Russia-Georgia war of 2008 when Russia passed a series of discriminatory laws against Georgians working and living in Russia as tensions between the two countries rose.[18]

DEMOCRACY PROMOTION AS A FOREIGN POLICY GOAL

As noted above, during the two decades following the Cold War, democracy promotion transitioned from a tool in the struggle against communism to a stand-alone pillar of American foreign policy. This significant transition should be recognized, but the absence of major policy discussion or debate over the question of the role of democracy promotion in U.S. foreign policy should not be overlooked. The transition occurred seamlessly as the Cold War wound down and America found itself in the position of the unquestioned global hegemon. The first debates about the wisdom and role of democracy promotion, which occurred outside the foreign policy elite, took place late in the George W. Bush presidency, but by that time it was way too late as the United States was already deeply committed to, and engaged in, democracy promotion. Therefore there was no substantial debate, but rather just anger at President Bush primarily from his left of center critics that spilled over into his democracy promotion policies.

By 2000 or shortly thereafter, democracy promotion had evolved to the point where it was broadly assumed by much of the foreign policy elite that America could and should seek to make almost every nondemocratic country in the world democratic. Of course, it was never quite that simple. Even in the days before the Iraq War, democracy promotion was always, either deliberately or indirectly, an assertion of American power and a demonstration of the power dynamic between the United States and the countries in which democracy promotion was practiced.

On a very basic level this meant that democracy promotion was not pursued in all nondemocratic countries, but only in those the United States perceived as weak or unfriendly, or both. Of course, at any particular moment this constitutes a majority of the world's countries. Thus, while countries like Armenia or Bangladesh have received U.S. democracy promotion funds for years, democracy promotion efforts in powerful but clearly nondemocratic countries such as China or Saudi Arabia have been either much more modest or do not exist at all.

Pursuing democracy promotion in powerful and consolidated authoritarian regimes like those of Saudi Arabia and China is extremely difficult. These countries, unlike most transitional countries, have distinctly nondemocratic ideologies to which their leaders are unequivocally committed. Moreover, they are not dependent on foreign assistance and, despite not being democratic, have a relatively strong and functioning state. Therefore, a strong external democracy promotion effort would necessarily mean seeking to change the governing regime. Obviously this would create problems in the bilateral relationships between the United States and each of these two countries. From a big-picture policy angle, jeopardizing relations with important trading partners on the off chance that a modestly funded set of programs can bring about democratic change seems like an unwise bet.

During the Cold War, on the other hand, democracy was only pursued in a few countries at a time, usually driven by a bigger geopolitical imperative. Although America sought to present itself as the defender of freedom, seeking to bring democracy was done only rarely and for specific political reasons. In addition, during most of the Cold War, the United States viewed democracy as the alternative to communism—and to a great extent only to communism—and rarely devoted substantial resources to changing or liberalizing noncommunist authoritarian regimes. This also meant that America was willing to support nondemocratic alternatives to communism and frequently welcomed the emergence of nondemocratic regimes or movements that could effectively combat or restrain communism.

That attitude changed in the post–Cold War era, as authoritarianism replaced communism as the opposite of democracy in the eyes of Washington policymakers. This reflected the changing political realities after the collapse of communism but also raised the issue of how democracy could be pursued in countries that, although authoritarian, were our allies. Unlike during the Cold War period, the strategic value of democracy promotion was sometimes unclear during the post–Cold War period. In the early years of this period, democracy was understood as a bulwark against the possible return of communism in eastern Europe, which at the time was a genuine concern. Helping countries such as Poland or Hungary rapidly evolve into democracies with functioning economies was one way to make communism seem less appealing to populations confronting political and social upheaval and uncertainty. In other parts of the world, however, the strategic benefits of democracy were less clear. One complex paradox of this period therefore was that democracy promotion was presented by Washington as at least partly altruistic and as not directly linked to U.S. interests, but also as having strategic import.

Larry Diamond offered an early description of the synergy between U.S. interests and U.S. altruism:

> With the value of the dollar diminishing and their economic future in doubt, it is not surprising that Americans are less inclined to support a foreign policy based on generous aims and grand ideals. Too often missing from the public debate, however, is an appreciation for how "hard" security and economic interests are inextricably, if often subtly, linked to the pursuit of liberal internationalist ideals. Throughout this century, and in some respects since its founding, American democracy has seen the promotion of democracy and freedom in other countries as part of its unique identity and purpose, but also as crucial to its national security and ultimately to the protection of its own liberty.[19]

Diamond is one of the leading scholars working on democracy promotion and a longtime advocate for U.S. democracy promotion. For these reasons, his words on the subject are significant and reflect the consensus view of most American supporters of democracy promotion. Diamond argues that "liberal internationalist ideals," in other words, the promotion of democracy, are essential parts of American security interests. Diamond makes this link as explicitly as possible.

It is not possible, however, for both conditions to be satisfied in every case. Certainly, some countries could have strong democratic institutions and be opposed to U.S. hegemony or influence. As proof, consider the various times in history that the United States has sought to overthrow democratic regimes that opposed American interests. In the post–Arab Spring era, this issue returned for the United States most prominently in Egypt. America was slow to condemn the ouster of Mohammed Morsi's Muslim Brotherhood government because it was replaced by a less democratic but more pro-U.S. military regime. Before that, the 2006 election victory of Hamas in the Palestinian Authority saw a party take power that was much more negatively predisposed to both America and Israel. The American response was to cut assistance to the Palestinian Authority following the election. Clearly, the connection between democracy and U.S. interests in some countries is not always evident.

Despite empirical evidence suggesting that democracy and U.S. interests do not always dovetail, maintaining the view that they do was important for positioning the United States in the post–Cold War order. This view contributed to conflating abstract good with U.S. interests and helped place the United States on the side of universal good rather than just on the side of its own national interests. Clearly this benefits a country that, like the United States, is an active global hegemon.

In the immediate aftermath of the Cold War, the strategic and indeed altruistic imperative for helping the countries in the former communist bloc, particularly the western half of that bloc, move toward democracy was clear. Countries like Poland, Hungary, and the Baltic states had strong historical ties to the West including, in many cases, large diasporas in the United States. They also fit into a narrative of being the victims of Soviet occupation that made it easy to see those countries as deserving of democracy and Western assistance. More substantive, because these and a few other countries were so clearly part of Europe, the strategic value of incorporating those countries into the peaceful European sphere was evident.

The expansion of this goal to include not just a handful of countries but most of the world was relatively quick. It also reflected America's changing role in the world. By the mid-1990s, the United States was a superpower with no political rivals, which provided a rationale for, or at least removed obstacles to, being engaged in almost every corner of the world. Initially this reflected U.S. power in the post-Soviet world but over time became a problem for the United States, as the ability to be involved anywhere in the world transformed into the need to be involved everywhere in the world. In the post–Cold War world, the absence of democracy in a poor, strategically insignificant country evolved from being something unfortunate but not terribly relevant to Washington to becoming a problem that America needed to solve.

The attacks on America on September 11, 2001, and the wars in Iraq and Afghanistan that followed also bolstered the perceived import of democracy promotion and placed it in a new, more visible, and more controversial context. The global war on terror was an unconventional war, wherein victory was measured not by the defeat of a hostile government but, at least in part, by winning the support of civilian populations around the world. Democracy seemed like a reasonable way to achieve that goal.

The more than twenty-year span since the Cold War has seen tremendous changes in the contexts in which democracy promotion has been pursued, but the changes in the programs themselves have been much more modest. This has led to a disconnect, wherein the structures and programs of democracy assistance have grown but not in a way consistent with the context in which they are performed. The result, not surprising, is that democracy promotion is generally not as successful now as it was a decade or more ago.

While this is partially because the external changes have created an environment that is more difficult and less welcoming for democracy work, it is also because the programs themselves have not evolved. Programs designed to guide or influence democratic transition or to facilitate or accelerate democratic consolidation—the major challenges in much of the postcommunist world fifteen to twenty years ago—are very different than programs that can initiate change or liberalization in consolidated nondemocratic regimes, which is the challenge facing democracy work in much of the nondemocratic world today.

Successful democracy programs in consolidated nondemocratic regimes require approaches that seek to change the political system; to the governments of those countries, therefore, they are much more troubling. Pursuing these types of programs would endanger U.S. relationships with a large number of nondemocratic but friendly regimes around the world in a way that governance or other less change-oriented programs would not. This explains why policymakers at USAID and elsewhere continue to invoke the transition paradigm: a transitioning country is ripe for less controversial and easier-to-implement programs that won't create problems between the United States and the country in question. The reality that the country is usually no longer in transition is a minor obstacle by contrast. Transitional countries, in short, are more likely to be influenced by technical programs, while consolidated nondemocratic regimes require more politicized approaches. The democracy promotion community's preference for technical programs creates a strong incentive to view all but the worst authoritarian regimes as transitional.

An unsuccessful democracy promotion project, while not ideal, is much better for the donor and the country than either a democracy promotion agenda that jeopardizes the bilateral relation or no democracy promotion at all. Not surprising, therefore, bureaucratic logic supports safe and uncontroversial democracy programs that are too often ineffective.

BUREAUCRATIC LOGIC OF DEMOCRACY PROMOTION

The bureaucratization of democracy promotion has brought with it a bureaucratic logic that has become increasingly important to the democracy promotion framework. Over the years institutions have developed incentives that are naturally more focused on surviving and growing as institutions than about the mission of democracy promotion. Because of this, discussions about democracy work often emphasize the kinds of programs that can be most successfully executed rather than whether or not there is any real value to pursuing democracy promotion in a given country. As a consultant for both democracy promotion organizations and USAID contractors doing evaluations, I have frequently been charged with making recommendations for future programming. It has always been made clear to me that recommending no future programming, because the problems cannot be solved with the tactics USAID has at its disposal, was not one of my options.

Government bureaucrats at USAID or elsewhere do not get promoted, or even have particularly interesting professional lives, if they do not manage increasingly large and expensive programs. People employed at NGOs working in democracy promotion also have a clear incentive for more programs in the countries in which they work. In addition, in many countries, the government can strengthen its relationship with the United States by allowing democracy promotion programs to be implemented. These governments may have to strike a balance between allowing enough programs, to send the right signal to the United States, and not endangering the continuation of their nondemocratic regime—and many governments do. Therefore, all the stakeholders have a stake in democracy promotion, even those that don't actually want democracy.

Pursuing substantially different tactics that might lead to greater democracy would, on the other hand, create potential problems for all the relevant bureaucratic actors. Undemocratic regimes would lose power if their countries became more democratic. Donor agencies would be forced to propose highly innovative projects and accept a fair degree of risk. And local NGOs that benefit from the existing system might not be chosen to receive funding if a genuinely different strategy is pursued.

CONCLUSION

Democracy promotion has for the most part fit well into the post–Cold War consensus foreign policy of the United States and is consistent with a foreign policy that engages with most of the world and seeks not only to further U.S. interests, but also to continue to position the United States as the leader, adjudicator, and enforcer on matters of human rights, democracy, and international law. Democracy promotion also fits more easily into a foreign policy outlook that, like the one that characterizes most of the post–Cold War period, accepts as almost axiomatic that America should not hesitate to intervene in the domestic political events of other countries.

The place of democracy promotion in broader U.S. foreign policy is not that simple, however. For close to twenty years, democracy promotion has been a pillar of American foreign policy, but it has never been the top priority and rarely even one of the primary goals of policymakers. Securing peace in various parts of the world, resolving long-standing conflicts, facilitating economic growth and trade that benefits America, and, since September 11, 2001, keeping America and its allies free of further terrorist attacks have all been more important to the United States than the promotion of democracy.

For the most part this has meant that democracy promotion has been quietly pursued in target countries while higher priority and higher profile goals have gotten more emphasis and attention. Occasionally, however, other goals have conflicted, at least in the short term, with the pursuit of democratic development. The most glaring example of this is in the area of national security where, particularly since September 11, it is not at all clear that keeping America and its allies safe from terrorism and promoting democracy are overlapping goals.

This has been most apparent in the Middle East, where elections in the Palestinian Authority, Egypt, and elsewhere have brought Islamist governments to power that are less likely to support U.S. efforts to combat terrorism. The election of Muhammed Morsi, a member of the Muslim Brotherhood, as president of Egypt in 2012 was clearly a step forward for democracy, but one probably not in the immediate interest of the United States. This partially explains the relative lack of outrage in Washington when Morsi was ousted by a military-led coup in 2013.

This dynamic has been an issue outside the Middle East as well. In Central Asia, for example, support for the U.S. war effort in Afghanistan from nondemocratic countries such as Uzbekistan or Kazakhstan has been essential to the United States. In those countries, maintaining a pro-U.S. government has been far more important than promoting democracy. A similar dynamic has occurred in Azerbaijan, given its strategic location and enormous oil reserves. None of this is new, but it demonstrates that democracy is generally a second-tier priority for the United States, and that the interests of the United States and the interests of democracy frequently diverge.

The viability of democracy promotion as a legitimate plank of U.S. foreign policy rests on a vision of America as uniquely positioned, because of its wealth and power but also because of its supposed moral stature, to support and advocate for democracy around the world. Much of the work of democracy promotion includes, either explicitly or implicitly, at least some element of modeling—of either telling other countries to do things the way America does, or evaluating other countries to determine the extent to which they do things like America. The viability of democracy promotion is therefore predicated to a degree on America's perception of itself and of the perception of America in the world. If either of those perceptions change, the domestic rationale for an ambitious agenda of democracy promotion will inevitably crumble as well. This is the dilemma America has begun to face as its own democratic shortcomings have become more visible to the world.

A broad and bipartisan consensus within the foreign policy establishment embraces the idea that America occupies, and should occupy, this unique high ground. This vision of American exceptionalism, as it is generally known, is for the most part limited to that foreign policy elite. Outside Washington, America is viewed very differently by the American people and also, frequently, by others even in countries and in groups that seek support and guidance. The effects of pursuing unilateralism and aggressive military interventions, flouting international law, and inconsistently applying standards of democracy and human rights has had a significant impact on the U.S. reputation globally. The United States has a long history of doing most of these things, but during the Bush years the hypocrisy of U.S. policy was most acutely perceived, possibly because it was also during this period that American rhetoric about democracy promotion was at its strongest.

It is critical to remember that the consensus on the unique role of America in global politics is bipartisan. While the presidency of George W. Bush is most associated with this view, it was Bill Clinton's secretary of state, Madeline Albright, who used the phrase "the indispensable nation" to describe the United States. The definite article in that phrase is significant, because it indicates that the United States is the only indispensable nation, thus implicitly making the assertion that all other countries are dispensable. It is unlikely Albright meant to imply that or that she or President Clinton believed that, but the words themselves are unambiguous. That this phrase is still recognized, even celebrated, in Democratic foreign policy circles demonstrates the depth of the bipartisan nature of support for this consensus.

Although the United States remains central to international efforts to expand democracy, and democracy promotion remains an important component of U.S. foreign policy, it is also noteworthy that part of the institutionalization of democracy promotion efforts has included an internationalization of democracy promotion. Although U.S. organizations like NDI and IRI remain the largest and most well-known implementers, and USAID the most significant donor organization, democracy promotion is far from an entirely, or even largely, American enterprise.

The most important election monitoring groups, for example, are multilateral organizations like the OSCE, EU, and other regional groups. Legislators are more likely to participate in study trips or receive expertise from countries in their immediate vicinity than from the United States. A group of MPs from Armenia or Kazakhstan participating in a U.S.-funded legislative strengthening program, for example, are more likely to go to Lithuania or Estonia, given their shared history in the Soviet Union, than to the United States to observe a functioning legislature. Civil society activists in Myanmar are more likely to have an exchange with activists in Thailand or Indonesia than with U.S. activists. Even American organizations like NDI and IRI are frequently

staffed by people from third countries. It is not at all unusual to see a
Serb working for an American organization in the former Soviet Union,
or a Bosnian doing the same in the Middle East.

In addition to the EU, OSCE, various arms of the UN, and other
multilateral organizations that provide funding for democracy promotion work, several governments besides America are bilateral supporters
of democracy promotion. Canada, the United Kingdom, the Netherlands, and others fund democracy programs in many countries. However, none do so on a scale comparable to the United States.

In the more than twenty years since the end of the Cold War, U.S.
democracy promotion has contributed to the spread of democracy to
much of eastern Europe and elsewhere and has demonstrated American
goodwill and competence. Most of this occurred in the first years following the collapse of the Soviet Union. The twenty-first century, however, tells a different story of American democracy promotion. That story
is one of a policy that has become institutionalized, in Washington and
overseas, and integrated to a great extent into American foreign policy.

Democracy promotion during the last fifteen years has had fewer successes and has not been able to smoothly adapt to the new political environment, characterized by competing powers, skepticism toward the
United States, consolidated nondemocratic regimes overseas, and reduced
resources and confidence domestically. Democracy promotion at the turn
of the century was associated with democratic consolidation in eastern
Europe. Today it is too frequently viewed as a poor post facto explanation for the adventurism of the Bush era or as a handmaiden of Islamist
governments in the Middle East.

Neither of these perceptions is entirely fair. Democracy promotion
has always been a project deeply tied to American foreign policy and
power and selectively applied to further U.S. interests. The wars in
Iraq and Afghanistan and the decline of U.S. power over the last decade
or two can be attributed to poor U.S. leadership, global trends, and
economic development, all much bigger than democracy promotion.
Nonetheless, twenty-plus years after the collapse of the Soviet Union, it
is clear that democracy promotion has stagnated and a new direction
is needed.

CHAPTER FOUR
PARADOXES OF IMPLEMENTATION

A GOOD DEAL OF THE debate around democracy promotion focuses on bigger-picture issues of U.S. foreign policy, the wisdom of seeking to influence domestic politics in other countries, the role of the military in these endeavors, and the like. However, understanding the programmatic side and probing the paradoxes that characterize the implementation of democracy promotion are both essential to a fuller grasp of democracy promotion and its challenges.

DEMOCRACY PROMOTION PROGRAMS

U.S. democracy promotion today takes the form of programs that, while addressing a wide range of issues involving democracy, still share similar characteristics. These programs are funded from one of two places: American taxpayers or private foundations. American democracy promotion is funded heavily by USAID, but the NED and several other agencies (for example, the Department of Justice) also support programs that seek to develop democracy overseas. These programs, unlike many foreign assistance programs, rarely involve direct transfers of funding to foreign governments or distribution of tangible goods like infrastructure, food, or medicine. Instead, they usually involve some combination of training, guidance, advice, and written materials, and efforts to transfer expertise from the United States to the recipient country. This protocol is now deeply embedded in all democracy assistance programs, so the assumption that the essential problem these programs need to solve is a lack of knowledge or expertise is almost never questioned.

Recent USAID documents, notably the 2013 "USAID Strategy on Democracy, Human Rights, and Governance," reflect a more nuanced understanding of the limits of technical support and capacity building: "Yet in the second decade of the 21st century, with its visible examples of successful political reform in developing countries, it is no longer credible to attribute this gap solely to a lack of capacity or knowledge. Rather, in many places, political and economic elites, vested in the status quo, block reform."[1]

Strategic insight of this kind in Washington, however, has not yet translated into a concretely different approach to crafting democracy promotion programs, where a program today, for example, "provide[s] technical assistance and works with committees and staff in the Armenian Parliament," "provide[s] technical assistance to the Cambodian government in its efforts to reform the justice system," or "cautiously engag[es] with civil society and Uzbek government counterparts, to promote an increase in civil society engagement, openness in government operations, and parliamentary oversight."[2] This is because there is no viable alternative to the capacity- or knowledge-building paradigm that underlies democracy work. If the transfer of information were removed from the core of democracy work, it is not at all apparent what programs or assumptions would replace it.

Programs themselves do not represent the totality of democracy promotion work, but for people in countries where America seeks, or has sought, to strengthen democracy, these programs are usually the public face of democracy promotion. It is striking that, for example, in many countries the NDI or IRI representative is a major political figure, often despite efforts by that person to remain in the background. Although the more effective work of democracy promotion might occur in a conversation between an American official and the country's president or in ongoing conversations between the ambassador and the government, the programs themselves are what the people in country, particularly the political, media, and civic elite, see and identify as democracy promotion. Political elites are usually very aware of what programs are being funded or discussed, who runs these programs, and what their goals are.

The high level of awareness in target countries about democracy promotion programs contrasts with domestic American understanding of democracy promotion, which sees democracy promotion primarily as constituting diplomatic and even military approaches. Given the areas in which much of democracy promotion functions, and the complex and multi-vectored nature of democracy promotion generally, this is probably inevitable. For example, a comparatively low-cost program building the capacity of the national legislature will come to the attention of MPs because they have direct interaction with the program. A much bigger and more expensive USAID-funded health program providing vaccines in a more remote part of the country may never come to the attention of MPs, except for those who have a particular interest in health care.

The political salience of these programs may surprise American audiences, who often characterize democracy promotion through the bigger lens of U.S. foreign policy and in the contexts of war, public statements by Americans, and elections. Those working on the ground, however, characterize the situation very differently. It is useful therefore to explore the implementation of democracy work in some depth.

Three major paradoxes characterize the implementation, or programmatic side, of democracy promotion. The first is deploying modest programs to accomplish ambitious goals. The second is introducing programs that intend significant change but that rely, either implicitly or explicitly, on cooperation from the governments they seek to change. The third is using nongovernmental agencies to implement programs that are overseen by the U.S. government and reflect U.S. government goals and priorities. Together these paradoxes create a complex programmatic arena wherein even effective programs might not have a significant impact, contributing to hampering the effectiveness of democracy work. The paradoxes also contribute to a structural environment that makes it difficult for even the most thoughtfully conceived and effectively implemented programs to have a large impact.

MODEST PROGRAMS, AMBITIOUS GOALS

Democracy promotion's core goal is to help countries move from being nondemocratic to democratic—or at least more democratic. This transition often represents an enormous change, as expanding democracy almost always means that wealth, privilege, status, and power are reallocated. Moreover, leaders of previous regimes may face criminal prosecution or other forms of transitional justice. In addition, new ideologies and fundamental beliefs about government, the state, and citizenship are adopted when democracy triumphs over older, less democratic systems. Supporters of democracy and human rights may applaud these changes, but should also recognize the major transformations they represent for most countries. Promoting democracy may be a worthy goal, but it also necessitates controversy and creates tension within existing government structures. Multilayered relationships and stress between the United States and target countries exacerbate these tensions.

The programs the United States employs to try to reach its ambitious goals are extremely modest. In most cases U.S. democracy work seeks to enact political change through capacity building, sharing information, and training. This disconnect is genuine and cannot simply be explained away by claiming that these modest approaches will lead to major outcomes. Modest programmatic approaches are not an obvious way to achieve such significant and transformative goals, nor, in recent years, have they been effective.

The modest programs are reinforced by the tone the democracy promotion community generally employs when discussing their work. It is almost an article of faith within that community that democracy promoters play a limited role, nurturing or assisting political change, not making or leading that change. This attitude grows out of good intentions and respect for the people and political actors in other countries and is evident in the descriptions NDI and IRI offer of their work—but it is also problematic. NDI states,

> NDI and its local partners work to promote openness and accountability in government by building political and civic organizations, safeguarding elections, and promoting citizen participation. The Institute brings together individuals and groups to share ideas,

knowledge, experiences and expertise that can be adapted to the needs of individual countries.[3]

IRI's mission statement describes the institute as

advanc[ing] freedom and democracy worldwide by helping political parties to become more issue-based and responsive, assisting citizens to participate in government planning, and working to increase the role of marginalized groups in the political process—including women and youth.[4]

The language employed by both of these organizations is important, as they are both sophisticated institutes that choose words carefully. The verbs and gerunds in particular stand out: "promote" (twice), "building," "safeguarding," "share," "help," "assist," and "work." These soft verbs suggest cooperation, support, and care, unlike hard verbs such as change, revolt, oust, or disrupt. Neither organization can be faulted for this, as the claims they make are all more or less true.[5] Nonetheless, it is significant that this is the way both organizations seek to present themselves—opting for an image that suggests caution and harmlessness rather than strength and risk acceptance—particularly as both organizations are often staffed and led by people who are bold, dedicated, and unafraid to take on injustice. This tone may accurately describe the understanding these NGOs have (or seek to present to the public) of their own work—that it is modest and uncontroversial—but in many ways the story is more complex. This is part of the paradox of urgency in democracy promotion work.

The tone used by democracy promoters is often contradicted by the urgency with which the democracy promotion community calls for democracy assistance and related programs in target countries. If programs are modest, aimed at nurturing and facilitating rather than creating or building, it would follow that they are not needed with the utmost urgency—but this is not the sense one gets from the NGOs and other organizations implementing democracy promotion around the world. Following almost every major global event, including invasion, conflict, war, and revolution, the democracy promotion community can be found seeking funds for democracy work in the affected country. Simple bureaucratic logic drives much of this activity, but the tone of these requests frequently suggests that democracy promotion is essential for the future success and stability of that country. Efforts to link democracy promotion to broader U.S. foreign policy goals suggest that this work is integral to U.S. success on a range of international issues. It is also not altogether surprising that programs that help, enable, and facilitate have encountered limited success against hardened authoritarian regimes.

It is tempting to attribute this approach entirely to bureaucratic behavior and the desire of these organizations to grow and get more funding, but this would be a substantial misstatement. These organizations are also caught in this paradox. If they speak of their work in less humble terms, they risk political backlash at home, and also in the countries where they work. Organizations like NDI or IRI cannot be seen, in most countries, as leading the charge for democracy. It is easy to envision the trouble that democracy promotion organizations would encounter if they discussed their work using language like "subvert," "overthrow," or "revolution." Of course, in many cases this is not the agenda of democracy promotion organizations; they are not using gentler words simply to disguise more aggressive programs. Their descriptions are accurate, as much, but not all, of their work is limited and plays a primarily supporting role. At times, however, democracy promotion focuses directly on making political change, albeit infrequently. Examples include involvement in events such as the Color Revolutions, supporting one side in an important election, or helping an opposition leader strategize at key junctures in a country's development.

This rhetorical and programmatic approach is one reason democracy promotion has stalled in recent years. The notion that democracy promotion needs to play a supportive and modest role rather than a more aggressive one is a political necessity, but it is also a product of a previous era, one when the goal of democracy promotion more generally was to facilitate transition. Today, on the other hand, expanding democracy inherently means creating real political change. The government of a newly democratic postcommunist country could have been—and, in many cases, was—encouraged to reform and could have benefited from the supporting and secondary roles played by foreign NGOs, but the government of a consolidated semi-authoritarian regime is significantly less likely to be influenced by these kinds of limited programs. To be successful, democracy promotion requires more vision and willingness to take risks than ever before, but the political environment is hostile to this notion.

This leads to a serious and persistent quandary in democracy promotion. The United States can either revamp and strengthen its programs and approach, or recognize that this work, in its current form, is unlikely to have a big impact. Neither of these options are good ones for policymakers. The former would create tensions with friendly nondemocratic governments that accept democracy promotion work in their countries precisely because it is unlikely to have an impact. The latter would call into question the whole purpose and project of democracy promotion, reducing it to a set of benign feel-good programs with little or no impact.

Moreover, it is not clear what a revamped and more powerful democracy promotion approach would look like. Simply expanding existing programs to, for example, support more civil society organizations, help more political parties, increase election monitoring, or redouble efforts to strengthen legislatures would likely have little overall effect on democratic development in most places. Revamping democracy promotion would require a degree of experimentation, innovation, risk taking, and expense for which there is almost no appetite in Washington. Even if these changes were to occur, there are no guarantees that they would be successful, as the tasks would remain dauntingly difficult.

Many in the democracy promotion field try to innovate and improve programs, but this is not easy given the narrow policy bandwidth in which most democracy work is stuck. Finding a better way to build capacity, or even a better place to focus capacity building work, is not likely to lead to dramatic change in most countries. In addition, democracy activists are acutely aware of one of the difficult lessons of recent decades: in many cases, getting rid of an authoritarian regime is the easy part, relatively speaking—building genuine and enduring democracy is much more difficult.

For every Czech Republic, Latvia, or Chile, where authoritarian regimes gave way to democracies, there are several Egypts, Russias, or Kazakhstans where one nondemocratic regime collapsed only to usher in another nondemocratic regime. In some countries, this cycle has repeated itself several times. Thus democracy policies aimed at changing regimes or bringing down authoritarian leaders are not only difficult to implement and politically dangerous but are also not at all guaranteed to lead to democracy. Overall, for democracy promotion to be success-ful in the current environment, it is imperative to determine new ways to pursue these policies, recognizing that simply finding ways to get rid of authoritarian or semi-authoritarian regimes, itself a formidable ac-complishment and effort, is not enough. The political and bureaucratic environment makes this very difficult.

Democracy promotion policy addresses these dilemmas by suggest-ing that modest, program-based interventions will make an impact—in other words, by failing to confront the magnitude of the challenge fac-ing democratic development in most of the world's remaining nondemo-cratic countries. By doing this, policymakers can continue to support a democracy promotion policy that relies on mobilizing modest programs to address enormous challenges. This is a clever and convenient way to sidestep the paradox, but it also undermines the likelihood that democ-racy assistance programs will make a meaningful impact.

DEMOCRATIC REFORM AND UNDEMOCRATIC GOVERNMENTS

USAID, like most of the rest of the rest of the U.S. government, links democracy promotion programs to governance programs. In most coun-tries, for example, USAID democracy programs are overseen by their program for democracy, human rights, and governance, which links these three distinct but overlapping concepts, implying that strengthening one of these three will have a positive effect on the other two. Democracy and governance do share significant overlap, but the two—or three, if human rights are included—are not the same. This is particularly true in countries with consolidated nondemocratic regimes. In a semi-democratic country, or an unconsolidated democracy, better gover-nance could lead to more democracy, but in a nondemocratic country this is not a likely outcome.

"Democracy" has many definitions, but in this context, USAID uses the term to refer to institutions that contribute to greater accountabil-ity, participation, and contestation in political life:

> Democracy refers to a civilian political system in which the legisla-tive and chief executive offices are filled through regular, competi-tive elections with universal suffrage. Democracy is characterized

by civil liberties, including the rights to speech, association, and universal suffrage, as well as the rule of law and respect for pluralism and minority rights. Democracy means "rule by the people" wherein the authority of the state is rooted in the explicit consent of its citizens.[6]

Stronger democracy, according to this definition, means greater representation for individuals and interests, more debates about policies, and a government more accountable through elections and other means. Democracy promotion therefore seeks to help make elections more free, fair, and competitive; nurture civil society organizations that can act as watchdogs toward the government; and help mobilize and organize citizens to advocate for their interests. Democracy also means working with government institutions, notably legislatures, to increase their representative capacity and bring them closer to the people they represent.

It should also be noted that USAID uses a definition of democracy that is almost entirely procedural, focusing on institutions and other related structures. USAID's definition of democracy is not very concerned with issues such as equality of outcome, economic fairness, or other substantive visions of democracy. This, of course, reflects the U.S. experience with democracy, but results in a limited and often politically biased approach to democracy and democracy promotion.

Governance, on the other hand, has a narrower definition. Programs aimed at improving governance seek to make state institutions run more effectively and efficiently. The areas of unambiguous overlap are apparent but not very numerous. Fighting corruption, for example, is a way to make government less corrupt while also strengthening accountability. However, other governance programs are less clearly likely to have an impact on democracy. Helping a government agency communicate more effectively might help the state of democracy, but only if the agency uses those skills to seek input from citizens rather than just have a better website or write better speeches. Some programs, such as those that help government agencies deliver services more cheaply or efficiently, are not related to democracy at all. The impact of these types of programs on democracy depends on the regime type of the government in question. Helping a nondemocratic government be more effective in its communication or reduce its bureaucracy leads to a less bureaucratic nondemocratic regime that is better at communicating, but it has no necessary impact on democracy, and could, in fact, be strengthening the regime in question.

In general, USAID does not sufficiently differentiate between democracy and governance. The 2013 strategy, for example, frequently refers to "democratic governance" and similarly links governance and accountability. Although democratic governance is important for democracy and human rights, good governance can be distinct from democracy. The numerous examples of well-governed but undemocratic polities include Singapore, some of the Gulf States, and even parts of China. By linking these two concepts, USAID programs too frequently imply that programs seeking to help governance are always good for democracy.

For example, the Turkmenistan Governance Strengthening Project that was implemented beginning in 2011 by a Washington-based contractor, the QED Group, and funded by USAID, "provides technical expertise, training and material assistance to the Government of Turkmenistan."[7] Examples of this technical expertise include

> help[ing] USAID train more than 60 government officials on effectively using email, online information sharing, Skype, and other programs. The GSP [Governance Strengthening Project] team is also organizing trainings for government officials from the Ministry of Finance of Turkmenistan, particularly on financial management and reporting, covering important aspects of governance such as transparent budget oversight and accountability.[8]

This program focused on governance, not democratic governance. It may have succeeded in helping the government of Turkmenistan function more effectively, but how training representatives of one of the world's most repressive governments how to use Skype or e-mail better strengthens democracy is a question for which there is no apparent answer. The possibility that making this repressive regime more adept with these tools strengthened authoritarianism in Turkmenistan should not be overlooked either. The question of how anybody at USAID thought this kind of program would contribute to greater democracy in Turkmenistan is also worth pondering.

The relationship between democracy and governance is implicit in U.S. democracy promotion strategy, but this relationship is relatively complicated. While it may be possible that the best governed countries are democratic, it is equally true that numerous nondemocratic polities are better governed than other more democratic ones. Singapore or Belarus, for example, are less democratic but better governed than Pakistan or Kyrgyzstan, despite the latter two countries being more democratic.

Strengthening governance, even in nondemocratic regimes, may in fact serve a national security interest for the United States, as strong regimes with functioning states are, in most cases, less hospitable to terrorist organizations. Terrorism generally is a bigger threat from failed or weak states than from authoritarian ones. In this regard, improving governance is a legitimate goal of U.S. foreign policy, but not one that always has bearing on democracy. It also demonstrates the inaccuracy of the belief that strengthening democracy is always the best way to meet other U.S. foreign policy goals, such as combating terrorism. Governance programs that support or strengthen governments that are not democratic but are solidly committed to combating jihadist terrorism are probably good from the U.S. national security perspective, but are not going to advance democracy.

Governance programs have additional appeal to donors because they are, appropriately, heavily technical. Unlike democracy programs that, because they seek to make political change, require a political component with which donors are not always comfortable, governance programs focus on capacity building and skill development. They are therefore easier to craft, implement, and evaluate.

The policy-related challenge is to craft programs and approaches that reflect the relative priority of democracy and governance in a given country. In some countries, this has been done well. U.S. democracy and governance support in Belarus, for example, has favored democracy much more than governance, which is appropriate given the authoritarian nature of that regime. Governance programs are also often helpful when a new democratic government is seeking to solidify support for the new regime. In the parlance of democracy promotion, this is known as making sure new democracies deliver. The importance of helping new democracies deliver is well summarized in a report by the Center for International Private Enterprise (CIPE), a major grantee of the NED, working on issues of markets and democracy.

In many countries where democracy has made inroads and elections have been held, the majority of the population has yet to

experience tangible improvements in their lives. In these countries, many may question the practicality of democracy or acquire
a distorted understanding of what democracy really entails. They
may become susceptible to populist or authoritarian appeals that
are camouflaged as democracy. The best way to improve the lot of
these people is to achieve greater reform and more complete democracy, not to compromise political or economic freedoms. The
paramount need is for better governance. While elections create
a basis for popular representation, a working, responsive government is the sine qua non for improving people's lives.[9]

New democracies that do not deliver are vulnerable to collapse or to
backsliding into less democratic regimes. Ordinary citizens generally
care about freedoms, but also about material concerns and government
services. Regimes that can provide both are among the most stable
and democratic. Democratic regimes that cannot provide for material
needs and basic services are not only fragile, but can lead people to
negative views of democracy, viewing it as a regime that focuses on
ideals rather than practical needs. In these newer democratic regimes,
governance programs are critical and very much part of effective
democracy promotion.

In Ukraine, for example, the democratic gains of the Orange Revolution in 2004 were largely rolled back by President Viktor Yanukovych,
elected in 2010. Yanukovych, who had tried to steal the 2004 election,
won in 2010 not because the voters of Ukraine no longer wanted
freedom of media and assembly, but because the leaders of the Orange Revolution government, including President Viktor Yushchenko
and sometime prime minister and 2010 presidential candidate Yulia
Tymoshenko, were perceived as governing poorly and of being bad
stewards of the economy. The global recession of 2008, which hit
Ukraine hard, contributed to this perception. Had the years following
the Orange Revolution been better economically, the history of modern
Ukraine would be very different.

This same urgency and relevance, however, does not apply to all
regimes. Helping nondemocratic regimes deliver better has a very different effect on political life. Too often, not enough attention is paid to this
important distinction, as governance and democracy are conflated, and
it is assumed by program designers that reinforcing one will strengthen

the other. In other cases democracy and governance needs are assumed to overlap entirely, as the two concepts are considered essentially the same thing.

Belarus is an authoritarian country where U.S. policy reflects the right balance between democracy and governance. Belarus is also one of the few countries where the United States has been relatively overt in its goal of regime change.[10] There, the United States offers no assistance to the authoritarian government, choosing instead to work with civil society organizations frequently based outside the country. Belarus is also an easy case for the United States because its strong ties to Putin's Russia make Belarus a nondemocratic country that is also rarely supportive of the broader U.S. policy agenda.

However, in many other countries that are only somewhat more liberalized than Belarus, such as Azerbaijan, the balance is noticeably different, emphasizing governance programs as much as democracy programs. The significance is that for governance programs to help democratic development, the goodwill of the government and a genuine commitment on the government's part to moving toward democracy are essential. Without this government support for democracy and governance programs, individual programs become either simply about governance or essentially a waste of time and money. For example, a legislative support program that seeks to make committees stronger, improve the research ability of parliament, provide training on crafting legislation for members of parliament and staff, or any of the other things that parliamentary programs generally do—and that USAID's Parliamentary Program of Azerbaijan from 2007 to 2011 sought to do[11]— can help make parliament more open and accountable, or make it move more quickly to implement the policies of the authoritarian president.

If the program helps provide more information to citizens by opening up committee hearings to public testimony, using social media as a way to inform people of how their representatives voted, or linking legislative research offices with civil society organizations, it will help democracy develop. However, if the legislature uses these skills to manipulate the media more effectively, keep input from civil society out of the process through creating complicated regulations and policies, and otherwise does not seek input from citizens, the governance program will have made the nondemocratic government stronger. This is the precise opposite of what the goals of a democracy program should be.

Democracy programs can be divided into those that work directly in partnership with the government, and therefore have a strong governance component, and those that work primarily with institutions outside of government, including CSOs and political parties. The former are much less contentious but, if the government is not genuinely committed to democratic reform, are destined to have little impact. The latter make it possible to skirt the challenge of working with nondemocratic governments to help strengthen democracy but, because they are outside government, also have limits. NGOs, political parties, and the like do not make laws and implement policies the way parliaments and governments, even in imperfect and undemocratic countries, do. For this reason, working with these institutions is important for democracy work, despite the obvious difficulties associated with doing this in many countries.

Programs that do not directly engage the government often rest on a very different set of assumptions. These programs come closer to recognizing that in many cases the government is the primary obstacle and that only by changing either its behavior or its makeup can democracy move forward. In rare cases, this is explicit, such as Belarus for most of the twenty-first century, or Serbia on the eve of Milosevic's defeat. In other cases, ambiguity surrounds this recognition. It is not unusual to see situations where donors believe that the government is still a possible collaborator in democratic reform, while the organizations they fund no longer hold that view. In many or perhaps most cases donors pursue both approaches simultaneously, working with legislatures or governments while at the same time supporting efforts to strengthen civil society and hold those government bodies more accountable.

Occasionally, that leads to a productive synergy, as CSOs funded by the U.S. government can play useful roles as watchdogs or in mobilizing citizens, while the U.S. government provides cover for them with the government of the target country. In other cases it leads to tension between the donor and the implementer, as CSOs push for change in a way that raises problems for a U.S. donor that wants to preserve the relationship with the nondemocratic government.

This dynamic also occasionally leads to tension between the United States and democracy activists, even those who receive U.S. funding. Democracy activists often make the mistake of taking American words on democracy at face value. U.S. rhetoric regarding democracy, particularly in countries where democracy promotion is occurring, is often very strong. Civic activists and others who receive funds or otherwise participate in these programs often do not fully understand the range of priorities facing the United States and its need to balance democracy with competing concerns. This frequently leads to dismay among democracy activists when U.S. democracy projects are not aggressive enough or too often give the benefit of the doubt to the government in office, which is much more likely to occur in the former Soviet Union than in, for example, Central or South America.

A few weeks before the November 2003 election in Georgia, which ultimately led to the Rose Revolution, I had a conversation with one of the smartest and most sophisticated leaders of what was then the Georgian opposition. He had sought me out in my NDI capacity to ask why the United States was not doing more to ensure fair elections in Georgia. We discussed it for several minutes as I tried to explain to him that in reality democracy was not the top priority for the United States in Georgia or indeed in most countries. Finally, exasperated, I told him that we would not be having the conversation in South America or the Middle East because there is greater awareness, and suspicion, of U.S. motives in those regions.

For people like that leader of the Georgian opposition in 2003, U.S. geopolitical considerations are naturally of less concern than the absence of democracy in their countries. Thus they consistently pressure, and in some cases expect, the United States to speak out against human rights or other abuses, push harder for fair elections, and the like, but do not always recognize that at times the United States cannot act without risking damaging its relationship with the government. In these cases, U.S. democracy promotion policies have put America in the position of making promises it cannot keep. Strong rhetoric regarding democracy, coupled with technical and financial support for CSOs working for democracy, suggests a U.S. commitment to democracy that often folds in the face of other priorities. Over time, even those receiving assistance from the United States become aware of this dynamic and wary of U.S. motives. Ultimately there is a cost associated with the discrepancy between U.S. words and actions on democracy, as activists grow wary of U.S. promises over time.

Tension is exacerbated because democracy promotion is only part of U.S. assistance in every country. In countries where the United States supports democracy, assistance often also includes money that in one form or another directly supports the government and helps keep it in place. Money that helps economic development, for example, often has the indirect effect of making the incumbent government stronger and more popular, whether democratic or not. Other types of assistance, like that which goes to security forces or the military, or occasionally direct budget transfers, strengthen nondemocratic regimes even if the security forces or military never are used against the people. Well-equipped forces help preclude the possibility of, for example, peaceful demonstrations and uprisings. If security forces are not well funded and equipped, they are much less likely to be loyal to nondemocratic regimes and thus less likely to side with the regime against the people. By helping arm and equip security forces, the United States, perhaps inadvertently, contributes to this dynamic.

In general, U.S. foreign assistance that focuses on improving governance often helps nondemocratic leaders remain in power. Democracy promotion policies and programs often have to be implemented in this framework that links democracy and governance. The United States can hardly be expected to seek to change a government it is either giving assistance to directly or working closely with to deliver assistance. This paradox often creates a seemingly insurmountable barrier for democracy work.

NONGOVERNMENTAL GOVERNMENTAL ORGANIZATIONS

During the last months of the Shevardnadze presidency in pre–Rose Revolution Georgia, I found myself in a conversation with yet another Georgian politician frustrated by his perception of American support for the aging Shevardnadze's kleptocratic and corrupt regime. At that time I was working for NDI in Georgia, so this politician told me he considered me part of that problem. When I protested that I was working hard for fair elections and worked for an NGO, not the U.S. government, he offered a Georgian saying. My translator got halfway through explaining it when I interrupted: "He means 'He who pays the fiddler, calls the tune.'" At that point, both Georgians nodded in agreement. For them, it was axiomatic that, regardless of what I called myself, I was paid by the U.S. government and therefore I worked for them. This perception underlies much of how U.S. democracy promotion work and the organizations that do this work are seen around the world.

Nongovernmental organizations (NGOs) are central to international development, not just to democracy promotion. NGOs comprise a variety of organizations ranging from one person sitting in an apartment in a medium-sized city in a developing country hoping to get a grant, to large organizations based in Washington with hundreds or thousands of staff, dozens of offices, and an annual budget in the tens, and occasionally hundreds, of millions of dollars. It is not surprising, then, that there are many different kinds of NGOs, with a taxonomy that reflects that variety.

In addition to their diversity of size, foreign NGOs that enjoy U.S. government support also represent a broad range of goals. Some are advocacy organizations seeking to pressure their governments to become more democratic. Others are watchdog organizations monitoring their governments and documenting various abuses and violations. The most visible of these watchdog organizations are often election monitors, but others seek to hold the legislature accountable, identify corruption in the government, or advocate for greater transparency for government bodies. Some NGOs are primarily focused on service delivery, working in areas ranging from health care to child welfare. Other NGOs function on a small business model, seeking and implementing grants to do research, provide services, or implement programs, usually with foreign grant money. These NGOs are similar to contractors, but retain their NGO status so they remain eligible to receive Western grant money.

"NGO" is a general term, but in many countries NGOs include INGOs and GONGOs and, occasionally, RINGOs and ENGOs, as well as the less-interestingly named local NGOs, which are also called CSOs. "INGO" stands for International NGO. In the democracy field this usually refers to large organizations, often American and occasionally European, usually based in Washington or a European capital, with field offices in many countries. Examples of INGOs are NDI, IRI, and IFES.

"GONGO" stands for government organized NGO.[12] This phrase is employed to describe organizations created, usually by a nondemocratic government, to look like an NGO but to pursue an agenda that supports that of the government. Examples of this include election monitoring groups funded by a government preparing to steal an election, or youth groups that organize young people to demonstrate their support for an authoritarian government. Among authoritarian coun-tries, Russia has been the most active in this area, creating organizations like "Nashi" (Russian for "ours"), a youth group loyal to President Putin. Nashi organizes patriotic youth camps for Russian youth, orga-nizes pro-Putin rallies, and otherwise mobilizes young Russians to sup-port the regime. "RINGO" and "ENGO," used less frequently, stand for religious international NGO and environmental NGO, respectively. Domestic NGOs are referred to as local NGOs and CSOs, to distin-guish them from international organizations.

These names help explain some differences, but they obscure some important similarities. The phrase NGO, particularly for those not di-rectly connected to development work, suggests that the organization in question is not part of the government, but the reality is significantly more complicated. Within a country where development money is being spent, the term "NGO" helpfully demonstrates distance between the organization in question and the state, but NGOs are often financially dependent on a government, or in some cases a few governments—just not the one of the country where they are working. Local NGOs that get their money, directly or indirectly, from foreign governments can-not therefore be so easily considered nongovernmental. While in many cases they have real autonomy, their existence, raison d'être, and pro-grams are also driven, at least to some extent, by decisions made by foreign governments. Also significant, some local NGOs are funded by foreign and local philanthropists, but in most countries those are the minority.

Some funding for local NGOs is indirect. It usually comes from USAID, but sometimes through a conduit such as an INGO or USAID contractor. Other funds come from the NED, which appears less a part of the U.S. government, but the NED, like USAID, gets its money from the U.S. Congress. Also significant, although the NED is called an "en-dowment," it does not have an endowment, in the usual way the word is used in philanthropy, and instead relies on regular funding from Con-gress. Similar institutions and structures exist for European support of local NGOs. These structures and conduits should not obscure the real-ity that this money is all ultimately drawn from the coffers of foreign governments. It is frequently used honestly in pursuit of good and impor-tant goals, but this structure makes it inaccurate to view local NGOs as fully independent of governments.

The relationship between government and INGOs is more direct. Most INGOs receive almost all their money from foreign governments. In the U.S. case, NDI, IRI, IFES, and others are funded almost entirely, but sometimes indirectly, by the U.S. government. Much of that money is then sent to the field, where it is used either directly for programming or allotted to local NGOs. The distinction between NGO and government in this context is significant but not simple. In the view of much of the world, including much of the United States, a large bureaucracy based in Washington, D.C., and reliant on the U.S. budget for its resources is part of the government, regardless of what it is called.

Organizations like NDI and IRI, however, cannot be dismissed so easily. They have independent boards, design their own programs, have substantial experience, pursue policies that are not always entirely consistent with those of the U.S. government, and, in fact, frequently argue with government representatives about programs and goals. This independence is real, but it is not complete. Despite these separations, NDI and IRI generally respond to program descriptions written by USAID, so the government clearly lays out the framework in which they operate. In the field, people working for these organizations meet and report regularly with USAID and when told what to do by, for example, the U.S. ambassador, they do it.

NGOs such as NDI and IRI that work as partners with USAID rather than as contractors are empowered to argue with USAID or the embassy, but it is understood that the embassy always has the last word. On the eve of the same 2003 election in Georgia where the United States, in the eyes of many in the opposition, was not doing enough to ensure fair elections, I was working very closely with a number of opposition parties on plans and strategies relating to fair elections. Shortly before the election, an American colleague and I were summoned to meet with a senior official from the U.S. embassy, where we were reprimanded for being "way too close to Saakashvili," and urged to cool our enthusiasm for what we were doing.[13] We were upset about this but had no choice but to do as the embassy had told us.[14] Although this incident occurred at a somewhat tense time in Georgia, the substance was not unusual. It is it not rare for embassies to become involved in the work of American NGOs in this way, but quite rare for those NGOs to successfully push back.

A related issue is that nondemocratic leaders occasionally accuse NGOs of spying for the donor governments. One example is a 2012 law in Russia that required NGOs receiving foreign money to register as foreign agents. This law applied only to Russian NGOs, but Russian suspicion of American NGOs had been in place for years. And not only Russia, or similar post-soviet authoritarian regimes, has expressed this view. Bolivian president Evo Morales made a similar statement in 2012: "Some NGOs and Foundations come here with the pretext of helping the poor, but really as a 5th round of capitalist espionage and empire."[15]

These accusations are usually met with statements of outrage from the democracy promotion community and occasionally the relevant embassies as well. However, the question is largely a matter of perspective. For NGOs who see their work as about helping develop capacity in a country, have often been invited into the country by the government, see themselves as independent from the donors, and genuinely believe in the causes of freedom and democracy, these accusations sting and seem unfair.

From the perspective of the host government the question looks very different. Both domestic and foreign NGOs that receive money from the United States or other foreign donors have a complex relationship with those donors. Although they do not work for the donors, there is a fair amount of gray area. Regular reporting, both formal and informal, means a great deal of information does make its way from the NGOs to the governments funding those NGOs. Moreover, it is rare that an NGO will withhold information if the donor requests it.

American NGOs would be more accurately characterized as SGOs, or semi-governmental organizations. A less charitable term might be PGOs, for pseudo-governmental organizations. The nomenclature is not as important as the extent to which democracy promotion can or cannot be separated out, not just from U.S. policy but from U.S. government programs and bureaucracy. Presenting democracy work as distinct from the U.S. government is somewhat disingenuous, but it also reflects a failure on the part of the United States to understand that most of the rest of the world views these NGOs as simply part of the U.S. government. Thus, democracy work itself is seen as being, to a substantial extent, in service of the U.S. government and of U.S. interests.

Again, in most countries America is not the only foreign donor, although it is frequently the single biggest. Democracy work is usually supported by European countries and occasionally by local powers as well. Nonetheless, democracy work can still be seen by many to consist of efforts by the Western countries to pursue their own interests.

In many cases this does not create a problem, as democracy activists, despite their frequent frustration with America and its allies, also recognize that these Western countries are the only ones willing to support their struggle for greater freedom and democracy. For the activists, including the American ones, this issue is nonetheless significant. Implementing U.S. government policy and working for democratic development are frequently and unavoidably going to be at odds with each other. The NGO structure, on the surface, addresses this issue by placing institutional boundaries between the U.S. government and democracy work. Issues of funding and policy approaches, however, abrogate these boundaries and make democracy work more vulnerable to charges, heard more frequently from the left, that it is just another iteration of the U.S. pursuing its own interests.

The structure of NGOs is significant, particularly when seen from the perspective of Washington. Legal constructs, advisory boards, and independence from the government despite receiving substantial resources from the government are all part of the conceit of democracy promotion, and indeed of the policy, research, and think tank culture in general. These institutions and structures have genuine independence from the U.S. government in many cases and on some issues, but that idea is only taken seriously in advanced democratic countries. In other types of regimes, the notion that these organizations have any genuine independence is seen as implausible.

Americans who work in democracy promotion, particularly for NGOs, are different from people who work in government. Many people implementing rule-of-law programs for organizations such as the American Bar Association (ABA) have practiced law, taught law school, or worked with the court system in their state. People working with political parties, legislatures, or civil society for American democracy promotion organizations also often have years, even decades, of valuable campaign, legislative, and civil society experience in America, Europe, or elsewhere. Thus, the NGO structure brings a more diverse group of people into democracy promotion work. The best NGO workers in democracy promotion are comfortable taking risks and innovating in a way that would make it hard for them to succeed in government. In addition, many of them have backgrounds that enable them to do their work very effectively, backgrounds found much less frequently among government workers.

These differences in skills, backgrounds, and work styles often exacerbate tensions between NGOs and their funders in various branches of the U.S. government. An NGO worker who has, for example, spent much of her professional life running partisan campaigns or advocating for U.S. interest groups may not immediately cotton to the rules and structures that permeate diplomatic work, making for difficult communication at times between NGOs and the donor organizations that support them.

These nuances are considerably more difficult for people in other countries, less familiar with the mores of professional life in the United States, to understand. For them, the unmistakable fact that all these organizations—as well as, for that matter, the military, if it is present—are supported by the U.S. government is likely to be much more salient. Most people who have worked for NDI or IRI in the field, for example, know this because they are frequently asked by the media to speak as a representative of the U.S. government. When this happens the NDI or IRI worker usually dutifully replies that she or he does not work for the government, so will just offer a personal opinion. In many cases, reporters acknowledge that politely but go back to assuming the NDI or IRI employee speaks for the U.S. government.

In many countries, some political actors assume that NDI and IRI, in particular, are simply the CIA in new and better packaging and attribute powers and impact to NDI and IRI that do not exist. In Kyrgyzstan, during the tumultuous early days of the Tulip Revolution, I encountered this phenomenon acutely. At one meeting in the home of a presidential candidate, I spent most of my time explaining that I was not CIA and that neither the CIA nor I was going to simply pick the country's next president. This conversation was conducted through a translator. As the meeting ended and we began to leave, I looked for my shoes, which I had removed when entering the house, but they were not there. I asked in Russian, "Where are my shoes?" My Russian is not good, but that is not a complicated sentence. My hosts were shocked to learn that I could speak Russian and hurriedly got my shoes for me. As we left, my translator turned to me and said "Now they're sure you're CIA." This demonstrates the level of suspicion directed toward NGO activists. The Kyrgyz leader with whom I was meeting was sufficiently convinced that I was CIA that he interpreted my one simple Russian sentence not as reflecting that I was only just learning the language, but that I was concealing my fluency from him to get an advantage in the meeting.

The relationship between NGOs and the U.S. government is complicated, as issues of NGO independence are rarely far from the surface, but NGOs do not implement all, or in some countries even most, democracy promotion work. Contractors are also key actors in democracy promotion and are too frequently overlooked or not given sufficient attention from scholars, journalists, and others studying democracy promotion.

Contractors differ from NGOs in a number of obvious ways, as well as in some ways that may be less obvious. Contractors are for-profit companies that bid to perform democracy promotion–related tasks that include evaluations and assessments of democracy work but also implementing programs in areas such as legislative development, civil society work, media, and even election observation.

Most of these contracting firms have limited internal expertise and instead recruit consultants and experts for projects on which they are bidding. They are usually able to attract skilled and experienced consultants because of the size and type of their projects and because they frequently pay more than NGOs. Many people who work for contractors have previous experience working for NGOs.

The major difference between NGOs and contractors is that NGOs work in collaboration with USAID to create and implement programs while contractors implement programs that have largely been designed by USAID. Contractors report much more frequently to USAID, are less able to challenge USAID on program-related questions, and have less flexibility in their programs. NGOs have more autonomy from USAID and are able to challenge programmatic ideas with which they disagree to a significantly greater extent than contractors can. In the terminology of USAID, NGOs are partners and contractors are implementers. That terminology captures the difference, but also overstates the autonomy of NGO partners, particularly in recent years. Of course, these kinds of distinctions and the different kinds of financial relationships have little effect on the view of people in these countries, who tend to see U.S. democracy organizations as all having more or less the same relationship with the U.S. government.

This partnership is being tested as USAID, according to numerous NGO workers, is asserting itself more with each passing year, thus undermining the spirit of partnership. The dynamic between USAID and its NGO partners occasionally brings to mind what John McMullen, a one-time minority owner of the New York Yankees and later owner of the Houston Astros, said about legendary and controversial Yankee owner George Steinbrenner: "There is nothing quite so limited as being a limited partner of George Steinbrenner's."[16] USAID's relationship with the NGO partners is not yet in Steinbrenner territory, but it may be moving in that direction.

As contractors take on more work, NGOs have begun to lose leverage with USAID, because of the fear that their projects will be given to contractors to ensure that USAID has more control. The issue here is not that NGOs are better at democracy promotion work than contractors. There is no unequivocal evidence of this, but it is indisputable that NGOs are more independent than contractors. As more work moves to contractors, the line between democracy promotion and U.S. foreign policy interests becomes even more difficult to identify.

It may be that democracy promotion is implemented better when it can be monitored more closely by USAID and when the implementers are less able to innovate and make judgment calls, but if that is the case democracy work should be more clearly viewed and presented as government work. NGOs often fight to maintain their independent status for reasons of institutional loyalty as well as principle and the belief they are right in their views of substantive issues. For contractors, even those who share those incentives, the position is much less tenable. A cynical interpretation would be that NGOs exist to give a veneer of independence to democracy promotion work, but with contractors even that veneer has been removed.

CONCLUSION

The United States pursues democracy promotion in a complex policy setting. The often ambitious-seeming goals of making nondemocratic countries more democratic, or at least more liberal, are pursued through policies that frequently appear modest or even incidental. Democracy promotion seeks to make states more democratic, frequently by working with undemocratic governments, through organizations described as NGOs but broadly understood, particularly in the countries where they are working as, at the very least, indirectly part of the U.S. government. Each of these paradoxes has roots in earlier conceptions of democracy promotion and democracy work, but each has a major impact on the work of democracy promotion today.

As democracy promotion has matured, or at least endured, these paradoxes have gotten stronger, and institutions and approaches have become more firmly entrenched as the years have gone by. But the challenges have changed. The questions of how democracy can be brought to entrenched nondemocratic regimes in Central Asia or the Middle East, not to mention China or Russia, through modest training programs and capacity building alone are ones that must be taken seriously. The bigger-picture political environment makes it difficult to ask these questions because the answers could lead the United States to policies it cannot embrace.

U.S. interests are real, and a policy of confronting every powerful authoritarian regime with radical programs aimed at overthrowing their governments would be disastrous. Given that, there is great incentive to avoid questioning the relevance of democracy programs designed for another era. Thus, the overarching principle behind the direction and structure of U.S. democracy promotion work is the broader geopolitical environment in which these programs occur. In other words, maintaining the U.S. relationship with nondemocratic regimes, crafting programs that do not overtly seek to change foreign governments, and framing these challenges in many cases as technical are central to U.S. democracy work. Balancing this with the goals of democracy promotion is difficult.

An America that sought to radically change every authoritarian government would find itself, and perhaps the whole world, in an even more unsafe and brutal place than it is in today. The current democracy promotion structure may have lost much of its likely impact, but it allows the United States to continue programs that on balance often do more good than harm without creating bigger problems for the United States. This is not a bad thing, but it also raises the question of why these programs even exist. Democracy promotion is caught between two unviable positions. Either commit to seeking to bring down some authoritarian regimes and to the decades of work it would take to ensure democracy in its place, or all but give up on the core mission of democracy work. A third option—to focus efforts on liberalizing nondemocratic countries, ensuring some democratic space and helping prevent nondemocratic regimes from getting worse—is an admirable agenda, but it is not truly democracy promotion.

The goal of democracy promotion is not, or at least should not simply be, to make a modest impact while allowing a complex bureaucracy to continue without unnecessarily angering nondemocratic governments. Ultimately, this cannot be justified, particularly to an American electorate increasingly concerned about government spending and perceived waste. And so the paradox persists, because to address it could create problems for U.S. foreign policy and bureaucracy; it means rethinking assumptions with which many have grown very comfortable. That explanation does not however fully address why democracy promotion still exists. If the point of democracy promotion is not to help democracy develop, as indicated by recent track records and programmatic approaches, then it might make more political and financial sense to get rid of it altogether. This view is not hard to reach when the logic underlying the paradox is taken to its natural conclusion, but of course this conclusion is neither wise nor acceptable to the numerous stakeholders involved in democracy promotion.

CHAPTER FIVE
DEMOCRACY AND DEMOCRACY PROMOTION

EARLY IN MY CAREER WORKING in democracy promotion I was having an informal chat over the phone with a senior USAID official in the country in which we were both working. My colleague was charged with working closely with all of USAID's democracy and governance portfolio. The call was friendly and informal as we kibitzed about the country's political situation and possible future political developments. At one point, as we discussed the possible makeup of the next parliament and the various competing interests in that parliament, I commented that it would be "like Fed 10." My colleague asked, "What is Fed 10?" Realizing I was speaking in political science shorthand, I said "You know, *Federalist Paper* No. 10." The relative silence on the other end of the phone suggested my colleague did not know what I was talking about. *Federalist Paper* No. 10, in which James Madison famously argued that the American constitutional model is uniquely crafted to "break and control the violence of factions,"[1] is one of the documents most central to American democracy. I then invoked Madison's name, but although my colleague vaguely knew of Madison, Fed 10 remained unfamiliar.[2]

This person was busy managing grants and staff, working with dozens of INGOs and local NGOs as well as a difficult bureaucracy back in Washington, and trying to stay informed about a complicated political situation in the country where we were working. Clearly a busy person like that can be forgiven for not reading Madison on the side. It is nonetheless striking that somebody in that position could be unfamiliar with the intellectual foundations of pluralism, competing interests, and the notion that the cure for factions is facilitating more factions and freedom. These ideas are, of course, central to American democracy as well as to the kind of liberal democracy the United States seeks to promote overseas.

A few years later, during the height of the Bush-era Freedom Agenda, a major African country was on the cusp of a historic election. I was working there briefly as a consultant for an American organization and had a conversation with a senior U.S. diplomat whose portfolio included democracy and elections. She confided in me over lunch that she was worried that a large number of different groups representing different people would end up in parliament after the election. I was dumbstruck by her comment, but managed to mumble that the term for what she was describing was "democracy." I had a lot less patience for this diplomat, so clearly contemptuous of the democracy she was charged with promoting, than for the hardworking and somewhat harried USAID officer who had simply not been sufficiently well trained or prepared for work in democracy. Although this woman's remarks struck me as extreme, efforts to equate democracy and unity throughout the democracy promotion community are not unusual.

UNDERSTANDING DEMOCRACY

Both these anecdotes, as well as many similar experiences I have had during the years I worked in democracy promotion, demonstrate another critical set of paradoxes around democracy promotion. Democracy is important to the United States as a policy and ideology, but it is also part of the American identity. Democracy promotion is, among other things, the foreign policy extension of this identity. There are many reasons America promotes democracy. Some of these are strategic, as we believe that democratic countries are less likely to make war and more likely to be sympathetic to our interests. There are also human rights–related reasons, as people living in undemocratic systems suffer more human rights violations and have little freedom. And many in the United States believe that democracy is the best system and something that should be shared with the rest of the world. However, these varied reasons over-shadow that the United States seeks to promote democracy because we cannot help ourselves. American policymakers almost without exception believe deeply not only that our political system is the best, but also that we are uniquely positioned and perhaps even obligated to spread this sys-tem. Vice President Joseph Biden, speaking in a moment of candor in October 2014, captured this notion well: "We Americans think in every country in transition there's a Thomas Jefferson hiding behind some rock, or a James Madison beyond one sand dune."[3]

Almost all Americans consider themselves knowledgeable about de-mocracy by virtue of being Americans, but too few have wrestled with or thought through some of the tougher issues surrounding democracy and its promotion. The experience of living in a democracy is, of course, valuable for the promotion of democracy, particularly with regard to understanding the feel of democracy, but a scholarly and analytical con-text for understanding democracy is also extremely valuable, and often missing at the level of democracy practitioners.

Even Americans who have had political experience, as is the case with many practitioners of democracy promotion, are disadvantaged without a broader understanding of democracy as a context for understanding their work. Many Americans working in democracy promotion have ample experience with the technical side of democracy—things like running political campaigns, doing constituency service or drafting bills for a legislator, or working for advocacy organizations in the United States—but have not had the opportunity, or need, to think about the meaning of democracy more generally. Without this broader experi-ence, American democracy becomes the too powerful exemplar, despite protestations in the democracy promotion field to the contrary. Some-times this is not even conscious. Leaders of both NDI and IRI have taken great care to demonstrate the genuinely multinational nature of their organizations and the work they do. Ken Wollack, the longtime presi-dent of NDI, has stated,

NDI is an international organization in that its staff members and volunteer political practitioners come from more than 100 coun-tries. In addition to the funding it receives from the U.S. govern-ment, the Institute receives support from, and works cooperatively with 35 countries and many intergovernmental institutions and nongovernmental organizations from every region of the world. Everything NDI does takes a multinational approach to sharing experiences and expertise from and with a variety of countries— new democracies, traditional democracies and countries in transition. Our role is to share diverse experiences and expertise and not to promote one type of system.[4]

On that same online forum, Lorne Craner, then president of IRI, echoed Wollack's remarks:

IRI also has a multinational staff, and our international roster of trainers ensures that we are able to bring diverse examples of new and old democratic development from Asia, Africa, Europe and Latin America. We also work closely with the burgeoning number of democracy development organizations from other new and old democracies.[5]

Craner and Wollack's comments reflect the efforts their organizations have made to promote a range of models of democracy rather than simply pushing for American-style democracy. On the ground, however, American practitioners often draw too heavily on the U.S. model, sometimes inadvertently. For example, people working on developing advocacy in democratizing countries may ground their efforts in a membership and money driven U.S. model that is unusual and difficult to replicate in other countries. People with backgrounds in U.S. electoral politics may also assume that a strong two-party system is the only workable party system and encourage smaller parties to merge with larger parties.

This enthusiasm for democracy is powerful and occasionally borders on being evangelical. Nobody articulated this evangelical enthusiasm for democracy better than President George W. Bush:

The advance of freedom is the calling of our time; it is the calling of our country. From the Fourteen Points to the Four Freedoms, to the Speech at Westminster, America has put our power at the service of principle. We believe that liberty is the design of nature; we believe that liberty is the direction of history. We believe that human fulfillment and excellence come in the responsible exercise of liberty. And we believe that freedom—the freedom we prize—is not for us alone, it is the right and the capacity of all mankind.[6]

At times this enthusiasm has created problems, but it has also led to extraordinary outcomes. The success of spreading democracy to former U.S. enemies such as Japan and Germany and efforts to spread democracy to the former communist bloc following the Cold War have also grown out of this sentiment. This enthusiasm has contributed to a situation where belief in the importance and value of democracy often outweighs understanding of democracy. Biden's remark about Americans looking for another Madison and Jefferson in the deserts and mountains of Iraq and Afghanistan can be seen as evidence of American naiveté, but it also reflects the optimism that underlies much of democracy promotion and indeed American foreign policy more broadly. Both are important fundamental dynamics of much U.S. democracy promotion.

Democracy is a complicated and contested concept that has meant different things at different times. Even today there is no agreed-upon definition; legal and structural aspects of democracy, as well as issues like equality and related economic questions, make agreeing on a definition difficult. Political scientist David Campbell has noted that "the spreading (expansion) of democracy feeds conceptually and empirically a certain need for differentiating between low-quality, medium-quality and high-quality democracy."[7] This differentiation raises the question of what kind of democracy America seeks to promote. Clearly, low- or mid-level democracies are freer and more democratic than authoritarian regimes, but they often feature limited party competition, legislatures that do not function well, and other flaws.

Understanding the distinction between procedural democracy (emphasizing laws and process) and substantive democracy (emphasizing outcomes and equality) is also central to understanding democracy and democracy promotion. Promoting procedural democracy is much easier, as it requires a focus on structures, laws, and constitutions, whereas substantive democracy requires trying to change political outcomes and potentially dramatically remaking political life in the target country.

More vexing is the issue of the gestalt of democracy, or as attorney Dennis Denuto (Tiriel Mora) says in the brilliant 1997 Australian film *The Castle*, while seeking to defend his client from eviction while holding up a copy of the Constitution of Australia, "The vibe of the thing." E. B. White identified the gestalt of democracy beautifully in a 1943 piece from the *New Yorker*:

It is the line that forms on the right. It is the don't in don't shove. It is the hole in the stuffed shirt through which the sawdust slowly trickles; it is the dent in the high hat. Democracy is the recurrent suspicion that more than half the people are right more than half the time. It is the feeling of privacy in the voting booths, the feeling of communion in the libraries, the feeling of vitality everywhere. Democracy is a letter to the editor. Democracy is the score at the beginning of the ninth. It is an idea which hasn't been disproved yet, a song the words of which have not gone bad. It's the mustard on the hot dog and the cream in the rationed coffee.[8]

The vibe or gestalt of democracy is absolutely central to the concept of democracy, but it is a difficult thing for America and its allies in democracy promotion to facilitate or encourage. The vibe of democracy is found in individual understandings of rights and responsibilities as well as in a complex balance of respect and irreverence toward political authority. In a democracy, those who govern work for the citizens, a concept that is hard to develop in a country that has had decades or in many cases centuries during which people have been subjects, not citizens, and have toiled for the good of the government and its corrupt, or at the very least extremely affluent, leadership. This distinction between citizens and subjects is one of the defining characteristics of democracy, but it is something that must be experienced to be fully understood.

It is difficult to imagine what a program aimed at promoting the vibe of democracy would be. Would USAID fund programs seeking to have citizens learn to demand more from their leaders or shout at them in public forums? Would USAID be able to implement programs aimed at deconstructing the trappings of pomp and ceremony around too many even minor officeholders around the world? The answer to both these questions is almost certainly no, because these kinds of goals do not easily lend themselves to programs and activities that USAID funds and that are compatible with USAID bureaucracy, and would be difficult to achieve even if programs could get funded. Nonetheless, if the gestalt or vibe of democracy is going to grow in transitional countries, these are the types of issues that need to be addressed.

Democracy promotion has been occasionally mischaracterized as simply an attempt to export American-style democracy to different parts of the world. A 1999 piece on democracy promotion during the Clinton administration illustrates this tendency, describing U.S. civil society support as "narrowly construed as building societies that embrace U.S. values and U.S.-style democracy."[9] At times this mischaracterization has been found in relatively high places. Hillary Mann Leverett, who served as director for Iran and the Persian Gulf at the NSC from 2001 to 2003, has said, "There was a strong push for policy toward U.S.-style democracy from the White House and the N.S.C. the entire time I was in the administration."[10]

This view, while still somewhat common, underestimates both the sophistication and international character of most democracy work. Americans and others working in democracy promotion usually recognize that our democracy is unique and not without its flaws, so models from Europe and elsewhere are also used a lot. At the higher levels of USAID, the NED, and other democracy promoting organizations, almost nobody continues to believe the U.S. two-party system is a good fit everywhere or that the uniquely constitutional relationships between various branches of government can be replicated. Viewing U.S. democracy promotion as simply an effort to export American-style democracy is something of a straw man argument, but it effectively underscores the problem of democracy being not well understood, or understood only through the prism of the American experience, by some in the field.

The problem of not sufficiently understanding democracy, however, goes deeper than that. It is not possible that everybody working in democracy promotion, even in a particular country, would have the same definition of democracy, but without a basic shared understanding, democracy work would be difficult. Most people would agree on a few basic components of democracy, such as freedoms of speech and assembly; free, fair, and competitive elections; and the need for a vibrant civil society, but after that things are less clear. Separation of powers, for example, is a value that Americans hold dear but that is less relevant to ideas of democracy in strong parliamentary systems. Rights for women strike many in the West as a basic tenet of democracy, but in some countries it is a subject debated within democracy. Some people look at a raucous parliament whose members are yelling at each other and see it as a sign of chaos and weakness of the legislature. Others look at the same body and see debate and disagreement of the kind needed in a democracy. Some democracies have a state religion while others are avowedly secular and try to treat all religions equally. In the former, aspects of life such as marriage and divorce are overseen by religious institutions, whereas this would be unthinkable in the latter. Some look at the power of wealthy individuals to use their money to influence politics and elections and call that freedom of speech; others see it as corruption. Even when it is well understood, democracy is a debated concept subject to significant disagreement.

WHAT DEMOCRACY IS AND ISN'T

Because of the way democracy programming works, democracy according to the U.S. government often takes on a relatively process-oriented and formal definition. USAID defines democracy as "a civilian political system in which the legislative and chief executive offices are filled through regular, competitive elections with universal suffrage. Democracy is characterized by civil liberties, including the rights to speech, association, and universal suffrage, as well as the rule of law and respect for pluralism and minority rights."[11] This is not surprising given the highly technical approach of democracy work. Competent legislatures, laws similar to those in the West, and free and fair elections are central to this U.S. government definition of democracy. These are all important components of democracy, but they also represent a limited understanding of democracy, one that does not devote any attention to issues such as equality and opportunity, or a gamut of economic concerns.

Democracy is a political system and an ideology, but in foreign policy it is too frequently conflated with three peripherally related concepts: support for the U.S. foreign policy agenda, a market economy, and a vague affinity for the West generally. First, in many cases democracy is assumed to be linked to support for U.S. foreign policy; a measure of a country's democratic evolution is therefore its orientation toward the West. The evidence of this can be seen in how nondemocratic regimes are judged differently in Washington based on their relationships with the West.

For example, former Georgian president Mikheil Saakashvili was often described as a democrat despite evidence that, as his tenure went on, Georgia was becoming less democratic.[12] The reason for this was that he wanted to orient his country toward Washington, not Moscow. This may have been a good policy for both Tbilisi and Washington, but had no direct bearing on democracy. A similar situation occurred in Kyrgyzstan where, by 2009, Kurmanbek Bakiev presided over what was, by almost any measure, a repressive regime, but because he continued to allow the United States access to the Manas Air Force Base, which was of great importance for the U.S. war effort in Afghanistan, the depth of the authoritarianism to which his regime had sunk was not fully recognized in Washington until after he had been ousted.[13]

Democratic regimes that do not support U.S. foreign policy, by contrast, are subject to much greater scrutiny and, occasionally, even U.S.-backed coup attempts. Examples of this can be found throughout the postwar history of America, including Chile in 1973 and Iran in 1953, but more recently in the American perspective on elections in Venezuela and left-of-center regimes in Latin America.

In a similar way, democracy from the American policy perspective is frequently linked to a market economy. The 1998 national security strategy document refers to the need "to secure and strengthen the gains of democracy and free markets while turning back their enemies," suggesting democracy and free markets are two sides of the same coin.[14] The 2006 national security strategy uses stronger language, arguing that governments that cannot deliver the "benefits of effective democracy and prosperity to their citizens," will become "susceptible to or taken over by demagogues peddling an anti-free market authoritarianism." Note the juxtaposition between democracy and "anti-free market authoritarianism," again linking these two different concepts.[15]

While it is hard to imagine a totally centrally planned economy existing in a democratic state, one of the major tasks of democracy is to determine the state's relationship with the economy. Issues such as the rate of taxation, whether or not major industries are owned by the government, and the rights of workers are the central subjects of democratic debate. The basic purpose of democracy is to establish agreed-upon lawmaking structures for working out these and other related issues. If democracy is linked too strongly and inextricably to private industry, low taxes, or the free market, then a core function of democracy—determining economic policy—is removed before democracy has occurred. Questions such as, for example, whether or not major industries should be owned by the state are central to democracy. If democracy is associated with only one answer to that question, then it is being restricted.

Last, democracy has become for many a shorthand way of saying "things we like." The "we" in that sentence refers broadly to the West. Robert Dahl likens "the term democracy" to "an ancient kitchen midden packed with assorted leftovers from nearly twenty-five hundred years of continuous usage."[16] That analogy, offered by Dahl in a book about democratic theory, should resonate throughout much of the democracy assistance community as well.

"Democracy," "liberalism," "equality," "unity," "peace," and "economic development" are related terms; they are all desirable qualities for a country, but they are not the same thing. More significant, the existence of democracy does not guarantee any of those qualities, with the possible exception of liberalism. Democracies go to war and occasionally get attacked by foreign powers. Many have episodes of domestic unrest and even violence. Almost all have intense polarization and angry, divisive politics. Although it does not usually make democracies stronger, many have substantial economic inequality and sometimes inequality based on race, religion, or ethnicity. Nor are democracies immune from economic downturns and stagnation. Liberalism is different, as a modicum of liberalism is essential for democracy, but the range and extent of civil liberties and freedoms fluctuate in even the oldest and strongest democracies. Democracy is best understood as a political system that is effective at avoiding or precluding authoritarianism or other bad outcomes, but unlike many other political regime types, it makes no claim to achieving perfection or alleviating all problems.

Additional problems associated with using democracy as a stand-in for all good things are that it makes it harder to focus on real issues of democracy and that it leads people in the countries in question to have unrealistically high expectations for democracy. Building democracy, and assisting in that process, is not the same as helping the economy develop or ensuring national security. Once, in a meeting in a rural area of a country in the former Soviet Union, during a discussion about democracy in that country, I was asked "How can this be democracy, if we still don't have jobs?" I am confident that my academic explanation of what democracy is and is not was not the answer the man was looking for, but the question itself demonstrates how easily these ideas are confused by people in transitional countries, as well as, unfortunately, policymakers in donor countries.

Programs that seek to achieve these other goals may or may not have any bearing on democratic development. Moreover, democracies often make mistakes in these areas. If a newly elected legislature votes for an economic policy that contributes to an economic downturn, that is a political or economic problem, but it is not a problem of democracy. It seems apparent that allowing people and countries to make their own mistakes is central to the promotion of democracy, but this is not always reflected in the work of democracy promotion. Further, it is also important that people inside these countries understand that democracies are prone to policy missteps and cannot guarantee policy outcomes.

Democracy may, in fact, be more likely than other political systems to lead to economic growth, peace, and other good things. If citizens believe democracy is a guarantee of all these public goods, disappointment with democracy itself will be difficult to avoid if these goals are not quickly achieved. Joblessness, foreign threats, and even terrorism are problems that plague many countries regardless of their political systems. Democracy may, and probably does, equip a country to better fight these problems, but it offers no guarantees.

DEMOCRACY, UNITY, AND CONFLICT

A related and absolutely central point is the often misunderstood relationship between democracy, unity, and conflict. Democracy is necessary, as Madison argued in *Federalist Paper* No. 10, because conflict is an inevitable result of freedom. "As long as the reason of man continues fallible; and he is at liberty to exercise it, different opinions will be formed. As long as the connection exists between his reason and his self-love, his opinions and his passions will have a reciprocal influence on each other."

Democracy is not about creating unity. It is about accepting conflict and managing it legally and without violence. Institutions—like legislatures, fair elections, CSOs, and even laws—grow out of conflict and disagreement. These institutions, when they function well, help prevent conflict and disagreement from turning to violence and oppression. Democratic institutions lead to compromise with which both sides can live and the belief, on the losing side, that they will be able to fight another day and possibly be on the winning side in the future. Managing conflict and ameliorating its most violent possibilities is the fundamental purpose and value of democracy.

Some unity is needed, of course, for a democracy to function. People living in a polity should be able to agree for the most part on being part of that state, and also need to share some basic values—most significantly, that democracy is the appropriate form of government. Beyond that, however, unity is not necessary for, and can even undermine, democracy. The problem is that unity is an appealing concept for development workers and even promoters of democracy.

Authoritarian regimes also prioritize unity because, ironically, it is much easier to govern an unfree society if there is widespread agreement. In its most extreme form, regimes such as the Soviet Union sought to wipe away older identities and create a new kind of person, known as *homo sovieticus*, that would reflect the communist monolith. Other authoritarian regimes aggressively seek to limit religious pluralism and differences of opinion on economic or political issues and to restrict the rights of those who are not members of the ethnic majority. All this is done in the name of, among other things, unity. Real democracies take a different approach to these issues.

The heart of the dilemma is that unity is often essential for bringing democracy about. When an entrenched authoritarian government is in power, an opposition divided on partisan ideological or ethnic lines helps that regime remain in power. Only when the opposition comes together in a united front, agreeing on the basic need for change and often little else, can the authoritarian regime be overthrown. Authoritarian governments are frequently dominated by omnibus ruling parties that draw from many different ideological streams. This is particularly true in the former Soviet Union but also in many secular authoritarian regimes throughout the world. These regimes cannot be defeated by a narrow ideological appeal in most cases, so a broad opposition coalition is needed. Therefore these opposition movements often seek to create a broad appeal based around very general ideas, such as freedom or economic growth. This political necessity dovetails with a democracy promotion policy community that has an endless capacity for dialogue and coalition building exercises.

These are the kinds of technical programs— multiparty retreats and study trips, ongoing dialogues between parties, and large civil society coalitions—that democracy promoters do well and that provide opportunities for important political work. Bringing politicians together to work on unity or coalition building affords good practitioners opportunities for the informal discussions that might not show up in grant proposals and quarterly reports but are often the most important programmatic work undertaken by democracy promoters. These programs and exercises are also important at specific moments during the democratization process. Once those moments have passed, however, bureaucratic incentives continue to fuel the programs even though they are no longer what is needed to make the next steps toward democracy.

The unity that makes a national liberation movement powerful or successful is less valuable in a country trying to consolidate or deepen democracy. Once democratic institutions are established, conflict and competition is absolutely essential for their survival and for the overall consolidation of democracy. Many newer democracies stumble not because of an absence of opposition but because of an absence of pluralism.

Pluralism is an American iteration of democracy, building on the work of Madison in *Federalist* No. 10 as well as twentieth-century political scientists such as Arthur Bentley, Theodore Lowi, and David Truman. Robert Dahl argues in *Who Governs* that the interactions between interest groups in urban America are evidence of functioning pluralism and indeed democracy. In his later works, notably *Dilemmas of Pluralist Democracy*, Dahl argues that independent organizations, essential for pluralism and democracy, contribute to problems because "they may help to stabilize injustices, deform civic consciousness, distort the public agenda, and alienate final control over the agenda."[17]

Pluralism views democracy as dependent on groups competing with each other for public goods, usually in the form of economic benefits, laws, or regulations. An idealized version of pluralism implies that the magic of the political marketplace leads to an equitable distribution of these political goods. A more grounded understanding of pluralism recognizes that some groups have more access to the resources necessary to get what they want in a democracy. Nonetheless, the notion of pluralism is central to any modern democracy where policies are contested.

Without conflict and competition (what Madison refers to as "factions") and their political expression as groups, organizations, and representative political parties, politics quickly becomes driven by patronage, personal relationships, and charismatic leadership rather than by interests or competing visions and policies. The unified political opposition that so skillfully brings in an authoritarian regime can, if it remains unified, quickly turn into a political elite that gives rise to one dominant party where policy differences are worked out internally with little input and accountability from the people.

Conflict is, of course, present to varying degrees and in different ways in all societies. In many Western countries economic divisions, debates over religiosity, and racial tension define the most acute conflicts, but in smaller countries the conflicts may have different roots. Urban-rural divisions, sharp ethnic tension that may not always be apparent from the outside, divisions based on historical differences, and the like are among the many conflicts that lead to pluralism in various countries.

Elections that do not reflect these conflicts quickly become "Seinfeld elections," because they are about nothing.[18] Elections without competing visions or debates over issues and interests lead to patronage, corruption, and personality-driven parties rapidly rushing to fill the vacuum created by the absence of pluralism. Absent conflict, legislatures do not attract people seeking to further their interests or represent people, and instead draw people interested in cronyism and using their position to make money. These legislatures further erode democratic institutions because of the kinds of people seeking to serve in them.

In many nondemocratic countries, poorly functioning legislatures are both a major characteristic and a cause of the absence or weakness of democracy. In almost every country where the United States is actively supporting democracy promotion, there is a legislative support program aimed at solving this problem. Understanding the roots of these weak legislatures and the political conditions that give rise to them is therefore important.

In a semi-democratic system, a polarized electorate may be a sign of the vibrancy of democracy. In a country that has some democratic elements, it is no longer appropriate or even helpful to expect a unified opposition, especially if elections are becoming better. In addition, different electoral systems require different degrees of unity. Low-threshold party list systems lead to little structural incentive for unity, as small parties can make it into parliament on their own. Obviously, elections systems with single-mandate seats require unity, or at least cooperation, between like-minded parties.

This preference for unity, particularly from Americans, also draws on the American party system, dominated by two large parties, both of which are based on relatively diverse coalitions. In the U.S. system, the possibility of groups splitting off from parties is almost always considered a negative, raising fears of spoilers or other disruptive elements. In multiparty systems or countries with different electoral rules than those in America, these considerations do not apply.

All societies have conflicts and competing interests. When these interests are not represented in political party systems, legislatures, or other institutions, they do not simply disappear. They continue to exist, potentially leading to instability or violence. A loud legislature where people yell at each other and occasionally threaten each other or come to fisticuffs does not necessarily reflect a strong democracy, but is better than the alternatives of working out those differences on the streets, or with weaponry, or—less dramatic but equally undemocratic—for the governing party that controls the legislature to discuss and resolve differences internally without input from the people.

Highly polarized elections often reflect the strength, or potential strength, of a democracy, but they are frequently portrayed as problems. Preelection reports often cite increased polarization as a cause of concern, but polarization around an election is often a sign that citizens take the election seriously and are channeling their political energies in a healthy and democratic direction. It is sufficiently obvious that it barely needs mentioning, but many elections in consolidated democracies are highly polarized. America in recent years is no exception. However, few believe that the intensity of feelings and differences of opinions between Democrats and Republicans are prima facie a meaningful threat to American democracy. The difference is that in consolidated democracies institutions are strong enough that high degrees of political polarization can be managed. This is less frequently true in nondemocratic or democratizing countries.

In Georgia in 2012, preelection reports decried the degree of polarization, linking it with and presenting it as a symptom of real problems in the preelection environment. ODIHR's election report a few weeks before voting noted that "the polarization of the campaign has increased.

The tone of campaign messages of both UNM (United National Movement) and GD (Georgian Dream) senior leadership and majoritarian candidates is confrontational and rough."[19] An NDI report in June of that year raised concerns about "growing political polarization in the country and a dearth of civil discourse among political leaders."[20] In both these cases polarization was not explicitly defined as a problem, but it was associated with a "confrontational and rough" tone and a "dearth of civil discourse." These issues may have reflected problems of Georgian democracy at the time, but linking them to polarization suggests that polarization itself was the cause of the problem.

The polarization that NDI and ODIHR identified in Georgia in 2012 was a sign of the resurgence of democracy in Georgia. The 2012 election there was the first in years that was sufficiently competitive to give rise to strong passions. Previous elections in 2008, 2009, and 2010 had been dominated by the ruling UNM party to a degree that precluded polarization. The polarization that outside observers saw in the months leading up to that election was real, but it was also a sign that the semi-authoritarian regime was weakening and that pluralism was reemerging in Georgia.

The NDI and ODIHR reports also suggest that if polarization did not exist, these problems would not exist either. That may or may not be true, but it also raises the problem identified by Madison in *Federalist Paper* No. 10, "Liberty is to faction what air is to fire, an aliment without which it instantly expires. But it could not be less folly to abolish liberty." In this case polarization is to democracy what air is to fire. Getting rid of polarization in places like Georgia in 2012, and many other elections in nondemocratic systems where incumbent governments are widely disliked, might make for a more gentle campaign, but it would ultimately undermine democracy.

As countries move closer to becoming democratic, it is essential for the opposition to transform from a broad national liberation movement to a group of political parties competing against each other. This also has bearing on the importance and perception of unity. Democracy assistance programs aimed at fostering dialogue between opposition groups, building coalitions between political parties, and the like are valuable in environments where ridding a country of an authoritarian regime is the most pressing issue. These programs, however, often continue because dialogue, unity, and coalitions are ideas that have a strong appeal to implementers and funders of democracy promotion, despite frequently not being what is needed anymore in that particular country. After the authoritarian regime is gone, the role of democracy promotion should change accordingly, but old habits are often hard to break, particularly when they have been effective in the past and lead to easily funded programs.

This distinction is also a reminder that overthrowing authoritarian regimes and building democracy are related, but often very different, tasks. The belief that the unity needed to overthrow an authoritarian regime is also essential for democracy reflects the same poor understanding of these two different phenomena that led many to be too optimistic about events like the Arab Spring and, before that, the end of communism.

Failure to make this transformation can result in the gains made from the democratic breakthrough giving way not to democracy but to another one-party-dominant system, wherein the new party in power controls much of the government and gradually limits the democratic space.[21] In the middle of the last decade, when Color Revolutions were considered the path to democracy throughout the former Soviet Union, I participated in a workshop with a coalition of political parties from one of the more authoritarian countries in the region. The workshop was being held in a democratic country in eastern Europe so that we could speak and strategize more openly. At the end of the several days we spent together, as I was saying my good-byes, one of the politicians said, "I hope next time you come to our country, we are in charge." I responded, "I hope next time I come to your country, you are running against each other." Everybody in the room looked at me quizzically, reflecting the extent to which the belief in unity is deeply ingrained in our sense of politics, even when it is no longer helpful. This also demonstrated how difficult and unintuitive many of the basic ideas underlying democracy are, even for people with a good deal of political sophistication and interest in democracy.

WHAT DEMOCRACY SHOULD BE ABOUT

Another reason conflict and disagreement is necessary for democracy is that democracy needs to be about something. This seems obvious, but a democracy promotion policy that focuses intensely on procedural understandings of democracy can lose sight of this. The most familiar subjects of democracy are questions of the government role in the economy. This is the left-right axis that still frames how many people think about democracy and politics generally. This framework remains important in many consolidated democracies, but is only part of the story in those countries. Other issues and axes are also significant. For decades in the United States, for example, religiosity has been at the core of democratic debate, as some believe in a more socially conservative view and of structuring society based on their interpretation of the Bible, while others take the opposite view. This, of course, drives the debate in the United States on issues like marriage equality or abortion rights and is evidence that the left-right axis may no longer be the best way to understand political cleavages in any country.

It is not always easy, however, to differentiate between issues that should be debated and fought out through democratic institutions (issues *within* democracy) and those that have bearing on the political system itself (issues *of* democracy). Some are obvious: a debate about how much pensioners should receive is clearly within democracy, while efforts to make elections fair or enforce constitutional limitations on the executive are issues of democracy. Another way to envision this is that there are some reasons a party or individual should not be allowed to participate in democratic politics. It is easy, however, to confuse those reasons for voting against a party. For example, a party with an armed wing or one that commits acts of terrorism may reasonably be asked to renounce those things before running for office. A party with bigoted views toward women or gays and lesbians, however repugnant to many, should probably still be allowed to contest elections.[22] The former is an issue of democracy. The latter is an issue within democracy.

Drawing these lines is often difficult, particularly because in many semi-democratic and semi-authoritarian countries, the central issue within civil society, the media, and certainly elections is democracy itself. This is also the prism through which many domestic and international actors view politics and elections in nondemocratic countries. Parties in these countries frequently run a platform calling vaguely for democracy, and election debates center on the democratic failings or successes of the incumbent regime rather than on issue differences of the kind seen in consolidated democracies.

Furthermore, incumbent governments in many of these countries have a record that, if looked at critically, could disqualify them from participating in elections because of criminal behavior, violent repression of freedoms, and the like. However, disqualifying incumbent governments from participating in elections is rarely a viable approach. Many religiously oriented parties have views on women, gays, and others that also seem fundamentally undemocratic to some. In addition, excluding organizations and viewpoints from political participation rarely accomplishes anything. These views do not go away simply because they are pushed out of the electoral process. Instead they may seek more violent and less democratic means to express their views.

The core of the paradox of defining and understanding democracy is that many in the U.S. government, including those working in the field of democracy, have a lingering misunderstanding, even fear, of the thing they are trying to promote. This fear may not always win out, but it rarely goes away entirely. Anybody even casually familiar with the history of American foreign policy knows that from the Middle East to Central America and from Asia to the Caribbean, America has a policy of undermining and disrupting democracy that is at least as long and well pedigreed as its democracy promotion policies. Most of these cases have occurred because of a perceived U.S. need to protect its interests, but a desire for stability can be an equally strong disincentive for democracy. The preference for stability over democracy is still present in much of official Washington. Supporters of democracy can argue that democracy is a guarantor of stability, but to the extent that is true, it is mostly true in the longer run.

In many countries greater democracy does not, and will not, lead inextricably to policies that are better for the United States, particularly in the shorter term. In recent years, this has been most apparent in the Middle East and North Africa, where elections in places like Egypt, at least initially, and the Palestinian Authority have brought parties to power that are opponents of the United States and its regional ally, Israel. Examples in other parts of the world include the 2013 election in Venezuela won by Nicolas Maduro, a strong critic of the U.S. role in South America. The election itself was controversial, with disputes about the voting machines and other irregularities, but probably less so than many elections that are won by pro-U.S. candidates.[23] However, U.S. efforts to declare the election undemocratic and to hold back recognition of Maduro as the winner were much greater than what is usually seen in worse elections when the United States approves of the winning candidate.[24]

Given this, the concern many policymakers have about promoting democracy is understandable, but it nonetheless creates problems. These problems are exacerbated by implicitly redefining democracy to mean a regime that does not violate human rights on a widespread scale and has a pro-U.S. outlook, and by an approach that does not recognize that promoting unity, peace, and economic development is often constructive but is not necessarily the same as democracy. The United States frequently tries to soften its support for pro-U.S. candidates by linking them, sometimes wrongly, to democracy. Unfortunately, when these two different concepts are too frequently conflated, the meanings blur together and democracy gets lost.

Many events and issues that suggest chaos and instability are also signs of democratic development. Increased polarization in the national legislature, for example, can be a sign of instability, but it can also be a sign that groups that have been excluded from political participation for years are now able to express their views through legitimate political means. Legislative stalemate and the failure to address meaningful problems can be a sign of incompetent authoritarian leadership, but it can also be evidence of a polity where democracy is getting stronger, making it hard for an executive to simply push legislation through.

A related point is that while, on balance, there is reason to think democracies make better policy decisions, democratic countries often make poor policy decisions through democratic methods. A country that implements a tax code or monetary policy that is likely to stifle economic growth may therefore be making an economic mistake, but that must not be taken for evidence of an absence of democracy. Moreover, democracy promotion should not be involved in policymaking at that level, but when democracy is defined too broadly, that can occur.

One of the specific ways this manifests itself in many democratizing countries is that USAID tends to endorse civil society organizations that support progressive and liberal causes such as environmental movements, women's rights, and religious pluralism. In many countries, support for these causes, particularly on issues such as the environment, is not part of the democracy and governance portfolio, but part of broader USAID efforts. Nonetheless, the links between these efforts and democracy work can be strong.

For democracy to work, however, groups opposing these views, despite how unappealing their positions might be, also need the skills necessary to function in a democratic system: the people who want to pollute the river or limit LGBT rights need to use the same political tools as those trying to save the river or win equality for LGBT people. The tools and resources of democracy have to be available even to those whose views are unappealing, otherwise those people will not see the process as legitimate and will pursue other measures. It is no surprise that groups espousing these views do not usually get support from USAID or other Western donors. Interest groups and civic organizations that oppose the United States are even less likely to have access to the technical and other support offered by democracy promotion organizations. It is also true that these groups are less likely to trust these American-backed organizations, often for good reason, and therefore less likely to seek their support. Democracy promotion that helps only one group gain access to these tools and leaves the other side unequipped to compete in the democratic arena is not only unlikely to succeed, but is also undemocratic. The goals of democracy promotion, perhaps counterintuitive, should include giving legitimate and legal voice to the narrow-minded, backward-looking, environmentally insensitive, anti-American, and economically confused, as well as to the good Western-leaning liberals.

I encountered a stark example of this incomplete understanding while doing a civil society assessment for a USAID contractor in Kosovo. The assessment required me to conduct interviews with numerous Kosovar NGOs. However, I was told not to speak with, or include any analysis, of an NGO called Vetevendosje (self-determination). Vetevendosje was a large membership-based organization that was influential in Kosovar politics. It also had been relatively critical of the United States and took positions considered radical by American diplomats. Thus Vetevendosje did not appear to USAID as a relevant piece of the NGO environment in Kosovo. Leaving this group out of the analysis guaranteed an incomplete understanding of the civil society context in Kosovo. Groups like Vetevendosje, despite having views that may be counter to those of the U.S. government or counter to liberal values, are often precisely the groups that are most important to bring into democratic and pluralist processes. Excluding them inevitably limits the reach of democracy work.

These types of dilemmas are unavoidable because democracy promotion almost always exists alongside other U.S. goals. The United States wants democracy in most countries, but it also wants support on key foreign policy issues and various domestic political outcomes for the country in question. In some cases, the interests of the United States have been buoyed by greater democracy, for example, in eastern Europe in the years immediately following the fall of communism, but this is often not the case. However, if democracy is perceived by the United States as being in conflict with American economic or security interests, democracy will lose out. This paradox is rarely confronted and is more frequently avoided by adopting a less accurate definition of democracy. This is perhaps inevitable, but it makes democracy work challenging.

The strongest argument for democracy in this context is that democracy almost always ends up being good for the United States. This argument is powerful and appealing, if unprovable. The idea that political systems that keep those most hostile to the United States inside the political process rather than outside with an incentive to disrupt that process are better for the United States, in the long run, is intuitively resonant. Policymakers, however, have little incentive to think or plan in that type of time frame.

CONCLUSION

The paradox surrounding understanding democracy imperfectly while seeking to promote it is contentious. Few Americans working in democracy promotion, and for that matter few Americans in general, would concede that they do not have a strong understanding of democracy. As Americans we are exposed to democracy daily and in many different ways, but perhaps because it is around us all the time we do not always fully think it through. Moreover, despite the internationalization of democracy promotion work, many Americans have an understanding of democracy that is specific to our country. It is therefore not surprising that many in the field are unfamiliar with ideas like those of Madison's in *Federalist* No. 10, Condorcet winners in elections,[25] or various models of pluralism and democratic theory.

This lack of understanding is overlaid by a Washington foreign policy culture that is still driven by an overly macho notion that much of politics is about "getting the measure of the man." This leads to macroblunders like President George W. Bush's nattering about Russian president Vladimir Putin's soul,[26] but it also leads to crafting policies flawed in less flagrant ways. The stubborn persistence of the big man theory of history leads too many in Washington to see democracy as linked to the presence of dynamic democratizing figures. In some cases—for example, Mikheil Saakashvili in Georgia—many Americans see the energy and charisma and assume the democracy, even though it isn't there. Even when the leader who is considered a democrat in Washington has indeed been a democrat, this belief has caused problems because it has contributed to overlooking the deeper institutional challenges to crafting lasting democracy. The failures of Viktor Yushchenko in Ukraine and of Ang San Su Kyi in Myanmar to always act in the best interest of democracy and human rights are examples of this.

In the United States, primary and secondary school education, which still focuses on civics, is the lens through which young people learn about democracy. This education is reinforced by a media and punditry that tend to talk about American institutions specifically rather than about democracy as an abstract. Obviously, almost all Americans working in the field of democracy promotion have ample postsecondary education. Many even have graduate degrees, but the areas of expertise most commonly found in the field are law, international relations, and area studies. While these fields offer a great deal of valuable skill and knowledge, they rarely include emphases on the study of democracy per se. Not everybody who works in democracy promotion needs a PhD in political science, but a deeper understanding of the nuances and debates that have surrounded democracy for centuries would help those doing democracy promotion think about their programs differently and provide some perspective.

At the very least, some agreement on what the relevant terms mean and a basic understanding of the key concepts would be helpful. However, even a relatively in-depth definition of democracy would not sufficiently address the poor understanding of democracy in the field at U.S. embassies, USAID, and even the offices of various USAID partners. In these settings, democracy is frequently defined informally by people on the ground. Most of these definitions are reasonable, but their variety does not contribute to a consistent approach. Moreover, many in the field have specific approaches to democracy. Some ambassadors and senior USAID officers are known, for example, for caring largely about the media, while more than a few are known to distrust political parties. Also, many democracy promotion organizations draw heavily on their own experiences. Americans working on legislative development almost always, and quite naturally, place a great emphasis on constituency service. Europeans from party-list systems place a similarly substantial emphasis on things like platform development, which may be less relevant in other types of democratic systems.

The lack of a strong understanding of democracy influences program decisions; for example, there is a strong bias toward programs that either encourage unity or support good policy outcomes that have little direct impact on democracy. Parties are by their nature in a competitive relationship with each other. Some form of dialogue is good, but more important is recognizing that the differences between parties—and their ability to work out those differences within democratic institutions—are the crux of democracy and more important than unity.

Determining the appropriate balance of unity and disagreement, particularly in a nondemocratic country, is a daunting challenge and lies at the heart of democracy promotion. Parties should agree on the political system, but not much else. Turning that notion from a platitude into a reality is of course difficult. Multiparty systems based around several leaders with similar views but clashing egos would benefit from coalition and unity-oriented projects, whereas party systems based on parties with strong demographic, geographic, or economic differences would not.

There is also something unmistakably patronizing about a view of democracy that emphasizes unity over conflict and debate. It seems to suggest that some people can handle only a watered-down version of democracy, without the vibrancy, risk taking, and conflict taken for granted in most Western countries. In these cases, democracy is more accurately defined as simply a relatively liberal regime, or any regime that is not particularly repressive.

A vibrant democracy is one where foreign and domestic policy are hotly debated and are often nonlinear and unclear. This means that for most countries, as democracy strengthens, the relationship with the West, particularly the United States, should become a topic of debate.

Slow and consistent movement toward the West or NATO may be a sign of stability and is probably good for Western interests, but on its own, it is not a sign of democracy. In nondemocratic but pro-West countries, a more clear sign of democracy is when the anti-American protesters are allowed to peacefully demonstrate in the capital or are able to elect people to office that represent their views. But this is viewed differently when seen through the myopia of too many USAID offices and embassies.

A strong understanding of what democracy is would force the United States to ask some essential questions—beginning with, is democracy what we really want to promote in every country—but it would also make democracy promotion more internally consistent, facilitate the crafting of more effective and relevant programs, and perhaps even lead to more democracy in the countries where the United States seeks to promote democracy.

CHAPTER SIX
THE POLITICS OF DEMOCRACY PROMOTION

DEMOCRACY PROMOTION, LIKE MUCH OF U.S. foreign policy, can no longer be completely disaggregated from domestic policy. Democracy promotion was brought into the domestic politics discussion largely because of the rhetoric of the administration of George W. Bush. One example of the rhetorical flourishes President Bush used in support of his administration's democracy work occurred on May 1, 2003, in a speech made from the deck of the USS *Abraham Lincoln*. This speech became known, to the eventual chagrin of the Bush White House, as the "Mission Accomplished" speech: "In the images of celebrating Iraqis, we have also seen the ageless appeal of human freedom. . . . And we will stand with the new leaders of Iraq as they establish a government of, by, and for the Iraqi people. The transition from dictatorship to democracy will take time, but it is worth every effort."[1]

President Bush's words reveal much about how his administration viewed democracy promotion. By referring to the "ageless appeal of human freedom," the president alluded to his belief in the universality of freedom and democracy. This belief underlay much of Bush's Freedom Agenda. Mentioning it in reference to a Muslim country like Iraq was not insignificant in mid-2003, at a time when anti-Muslim sentiment in America was quite strong. The rest of Bush's statement captures the duality of viewing Iraq as a democracy work in progress—"democracy will take time"—with the certainty that Iraq was headed in the right direction, therefore making it easy to "stand with the new leaders of Iraq," who Bush seemed to believe were on the cusp of creating a democratic government the likes of which would make Abraham Lincoln proud.

During the Bush presidency, democracy promotion experienced a transition, from a policy that few outside foreign policy elites and those working in the field were aware of to one presented as central to Bush's foreign policy. In turn, it became central to much of the criticism of that policy. Despite Bush's absence from the White House now for almost two full terms, democracy promotion still remains at least somewhat polarized by his presidency.

The domestic discussion of democracy positions is deeply ridden with some of the major paradoxes framing democracy promotion, as it brings out the contradictory positions on both the ideological left and right. The domestic context for democracy promotion also includes a fiscal component, as the changing fiscal climate in the United States has an effect on support for democracy work. In addition, democracy promotion is deeply and unavoidably tied to America's view of itself. As that has changed in recent years, domestic views toward democracy work have changed correspondingly.

It is significant that the domestic discussion on democracy promotion is relatively new. For many Americans, democracy promotion started when they became aware of it, during the Bush presidency, and has evolved as a reaction to the actions and rhetoric of that presidency. This has naturally influenced perspectives of the policy because many know much less about the more successful and uncontroversial democracy work the United States pursued in the 1990s.

Although it is inaccurate to consider democracy promotion as the only thing the United States was doing in Iraq and Afghanistan in 2003–07, it is also wrong to dismiss that work from the democracy promotion portfolio of that time. While much democracy work occurs in less controversial places like Armenia or Tanzania, often taking the form of relatively benign capacity building programs, the democracy work in Afghanistan and Iraq cannot be ignored altogether. A proportion of democracy work—small in terms of number of countries but large in terms of budget or emphasis—is strongly tied to American military action and the political agendas of the White House.

DEMOCRACY PROMOTION LEFT AND RIGHT

Although democracy promotion is still not central to most foreign policy debates in America, it is on the periphery of many, and has become an issue that is frequently seen through a left-right lens. This lens distorts more than it clarifies, however, as it is often a reaction to the Bush administration and the use of U.S. power rather than a well-thought-out critique of democracy work.

Democracy promotion draws on many policies and attitudes central to American foreign policy. It rests on a deep commitment to an internationalist foreign policy as well as a belief in the superiority of the American system. When these assumptions, which also underlie many other U.S. policies, including military interventions in Iraq and elsewhere, come under scrutiny, democracy promotion naturally becomes a subject of that scrutiny as well.

The progressive critique of democracy assistance is to great extent a reaction to the foreign policy excesses of the Bush administration. The conflicts in Iraq and Afghanistan, the use of democracy promotion as a post facto explanation for those conflicts, and the frequent and premature declarations of victory, both on the battlefield and in the field of democracy, discredited the Freedom Agenda, as the Bush administration called it, in the eyes of many. The chosen wording is important. George H. W. Bush, Bill Clinton, and now Barack Obama have supported democracy promotion; George W. Bush had a Freedom Agenda. With rhetorical flourishes like that, it cannot be surprising to anyone that democracy promotion became laden with ideological baggage during the Bush presidency.

The rhetorical transition, albeit temporary, from democracy promotion to Freedom Agenda, was evidence that George W. Bush was approaching democracy work somewhat differently than had his recent predecessors. It also clearly linked democracy work to foreign policy goals and projects that were distinct to the Bush presidency rather than to U.S. foreign policy more generally. "Freedom," of course, was a word that President Bush used a lot and that became more or less his signature foreign policy meme.

As the activist left began to oppose democracy promotion, largely because of its association with the militaristic foreign policy of President Bush, the neoconservative right began to embrace it even more actively for the same reason. The Bush presidency is an important explanatory variable, but it does not fully elucidate the appeal of these respective positions to these two ideological poles.

During the Bush presidency democracy promotion became associated with the right wing of American politics not because of anything intrinsic to the policy itself, but because of its advocates and detractors. The most prominent supporters of democracy promotion during these years were neoconservatives like Paul Wolfowitz, Richard Pearl, and others in the Bush administration. Visible critics of these policies included people on the left, such as Noam Chomsky, as well as Libertarians such as Ron Paul and the Cato Institute.

Since the Bush administration ended, a similar cleavage regarding democracy promotion has emerged in relation to countries like Ukraine, where the strong support by many conservatives for those seeking to rid the country of the corrupt leadership of Viktor Yanukovych in late 2013 and early 2014 was clearly tied to those same conservatives' views of Russian president Vladimir Putin. If Putin had not been meddling in Ukraine during and after the Yanukovych presidency, it is unlikely that conservative support would have been quite so significant.

During the Bush years, the positions of many on democracy promotion in both Iraq and Afghanistan were never distinct from positions regarding the wars. Thus, people who opposed the war in Iraq tended to belittle or criticize democracy assistance there, rather than see it as separate from the war. As Rosa Brooks summarizes, "During the Bush Administration, the idea of democracy promotion became tightly and inexorably bound up with regime change and the carnage of the Iraq War. Because it came to us in a package that included bloodshed, occupation, torture, and indefinite detentions, Bush's 'Freedom Agenda' left a bitter taste in the mouth."[2] In addition, particularly in Iraq, many of the truisms used to defend democracy promotion—that it is not forced on countries by the West, that it is not related to military adventurism, that is multilateral and more about facilitating domestic actors than aggressively seeking regime change—simply did not apply.

To some extent, this was also probably unavoidable, as a position of opposing the war while supporting efforts to make Iraq more democratic after the initial mistake of the war would have been hard to maintain. Although there is no internal logical inconsistency to that position, it was nonetheless politically almost impossible, and made more difficult by the complete lack of confidence and trust felt toward the Bush administration by many on the left after the invasion of Iraq.

This put many on the left in the position of not only wanting to avoid a dishonest and unnecessary war, but of also arguing that after that war the Iraqi people did not have a right to determine their own future through democratic means. Moreover, by opposing democracy promotion in Iraq following the Western invasion, progressives found themselves continually arguing that the invasion was wrong, rather than proposing post-invasion policies. This left them out of most of the policy discussions during the early years of the war. This paradox may have been unavoidable, but it was also barely noticed on the left, both during the war and in its aftermath.

Many progressives have sought to reconcile this by supporting democracy but not democracy promotion of the kind practiced in the Bush years. Brooks expressed this as well:

> Can democracy promotion be saved, in the face of all our mistakes, all our inconsistencies, all our false starts, hypocrisies, and hesitations[?] . . . Democracy promotion should remain a vital part of our foreign policy—not *despite* our mistakes, inconsistencies, false starts, hypocrisies, and hesitations, but *because* of them. We should embrace and promote democracy not because *it* is perfect or because *we* are perfect, but because democracy remains the only political system yet devised that builds in a capacity for self-correction. . . . The basic contours of the idea remain both clear and sound. If everyone counts, then everyone must be allowed to speak and organize and assemble with others; everyone must have a shot at arguing with and persuading others. This is how ideas emerge, struggle for life, gain prominence, and are tested. Some survive; some vanish; some fade for a time and re-emerge again later on.[3]

From this perspective, the right of people to choose their own governments, determine the direction of their country, and rid themselves of unwanted and undemocratic leaders is recognized, but the U.S. role in this process is not. This is a difficult balance to strike because if the belief in the right to democracy is sincerely held, it is difficult to maintain that the United States should do nothing in support of these rights.

One way to resolve this conflict, which became more important as the failures of Bush's foreign policy mounted, is to ask not what the United States *should* be doing in places like post-invasion Iraq, but what it can *effectively* do in those places. The U.S. record on democracy promotion is characterized by numerous successes and failures, but over time the balance has tipped more toward the latter. Looking at Iraq after a U.S. invasion in terms of what the United States is obligated to do therefore leads to one set of recommendations, but focusing instead on what is or is not likely to be effective may lead to a different, and more modest, policy prescription.

But in the eyes of many progressives, the years of the Bush administration had separated democracy promotion from its stated goals. In short, democracy promotion was no longer about democracy but was simply another expression of American power, in service of American imperial goals. One analysis of that era describes how

President George W. Bush's invasion of Iraq signaled the unambiguous return of "democratic imperialism" in American foreign policy. Entailing what is tantamount to the imposition of democracy upon a foreign country, this can be seen as the ultimate manifestation of America's traditional obsession with its role as a global moral crusader.[4]

This perspective is consistent with the opposition to American wars, going back at least to Vietnam, that have helped define progressive politics in the United States for the last half century or so. Presenting Bush's Iraq policy this way made it easy for many on the left to oppose democracy promotion or, more accurately, made it difficult for progressives to craft a defense of democracy promotion, regardless of their views on democracy itself.

The heart of the left critique, which had long existed but became much stronger in the Bush era, was that while democracy was a good and even desired outcome in most if not all countries, the intention and ability of the United States to help those countries achieve that goal was severely wanting. The political appeal of this is clear, as it dovetails neatly with an antiwar and anti-interventionist approach to foreign policy.

The contrast between democracy promotion during the Bush and Clinton presidencies is striking, but so are the similarities. Both administrations pursued internationalist foreign policies, but of course President Clinton never instigated a war of the scope of the U.S. invasion of Iraq. Nonetheless, the 1990s were a time when U.S. power went around the globe to resolve problems and strengthen political institutions. President Bush pursued a Freedom Agenda, while President Clinton cloaked some similar policies, not least in the Balkans, in the language of "humanitarian intervention."

Shashi Tharoor and Sam Daws point out the contentiousness of the notion of humanitarian intervention:

> But we must begin by acknowledging that the term "humanitarian intervention" is itself contentious. To its proponents, it marks the coming of age of the imperative of action in the face of human rights abuses, over the citadels of state sovereignty. To its detractors, it is an oxymoron, a pretext for military intervention often devoid of legal sanction, selectively deployed and achieving only ambiguous ends. As some put it, there can be nothing humanitarian about a bomb.[5]

Nonetheless, humanitarian intervention was a less divisive policy, and a less divisive-sounding phrase, than Freedom Agenda.

The evidence supporting claims that the United States was in most cases either unwilling or unable to cultivate democracy is mixed and was even more mixed in the early years of the twenty-first century, when Bush was most vocal in his belief in the Freedom Agenda. The 1990s had been a period of historic democratic expansion in the formerly communist countries of eastern Europe and the former Soviet Union, as well as South America, East Asia, and elsewhere. Democratic gains in those countries all included a usually modest but also clear role for Western democracy assistance. Earlier precedents of America contributing to democratic development, for example after World War II, were even more apparent. Thus, by 2003 or 2004 a reasonably compelling argument could have been made that the United States indeed could and probably should play a role in helping countries achieve the democratic aspirations of their people.

This sentiment, however, was completely overshadowed by the scope of the conflict in Iraq and the extraordinary disconnect between the rhetoric about democracy from the Bush administration and what was really happening and what the United States was really doing in Iraq. Every time the Bush administration, in what might generously be described as a radically and surreally premature manner, referred to Iraq as a democracy, it provided more fodder for the narrative that U.S. democracy promotion could not, and should not, be taken at face value. This rhetoric also made many question the value of democracy. By constantly describing a war-torn, violent, and destroyed country like Iraq as democratic, the Bush administration made democracy much seem less appealing.

President Bush's optimism regarding democracy in Iraq was extraordinary. In a speech in London in November 2003, he commented, "Iraq has a new currency, the first battalion of a new army, representative local governments, and a governing council with an aggressive timetable for national sovereignty."[6] A few weeks before that, at a speech at the NED, Bush referred to Iraq as being part of the "global democratic revolution."[7] A few years after that, this time in Philadelphia, Bush sounded another optimistic note about Iraq: "The Iraqi people have assumed sovereignty over their country, held free elections, drafted a democratic constitution, and approved that constitution in a nationwide referendum. Three days from now, they go to the polls for the third time this year, and choose a new government under the new constitution."[8] President Bush's ability to speak this way despite a seemingly endless stream of bad news from Iraq is, on some level, impressive. However, by the last years of his presidency, Bush's early optimism on Iraq was proven a sad reminder of what might have been rather than a harbinger of what actually happened.

This intense rhetorical emphasis on democracy and relentless optimism about democracy in Iraq ended up reinforcing both progressive criticisms of democracy promotion and the assertion that democracy promotion was not about democracy, but about U.S. interests. This criticism was not always valid during the Bush administration, or that of any other recent president, but it was valid enough that it made the progressive critique of democracy promotion resonant.

The progressive disdain for democracy promotion ceded the energy, ideas, and enthusiasm surrounding democracy promotion to the neoconservatives who dominated American foreign policy, and the Republican Party, from 2001 to 2006. This, not surprisingly, contributed to an approach to democracy promotion and a definition of democracy serving the interests of that ideological faction rather than forwarding principles of democracy, at the same time minimizing potential progressive contributions to democracy and democracy promotion.

During the Bush administration the right wing embraced democracy assistance, seeing democracy not only as a basic human right or superior form of government, but also as a way of furthering American interests. This contributed to a working definition of democracy that conflated democracy with pro-American positions. Support for the Orange and Rose Revolutions, whose leaders sought to move Ukraine and Georgia, respectively, further into the American and European orbit, for example, was motivated by geopolitics and American interests more than concern for democracy. This is normal behavior from a global power, but the Bush administration's view of the role of democracy also helped policymakers overlook the severe problems in Georgian democracy and the overall weakness of Ukrainian democracy.

This policy ultimately weakened the regimes of staunch Western allies in both Georgia and Ukraine during the second Bush term. By overlooking problems of democracy, the Bush administration did not help their friends; in fact they weakened them. By the end of 2012, both Mikheil Saakashvili and Viktor Yushchenko, the respective leaders of the Rose and Orange Revolutions, had been replaced, albeit through elections, by leaders who were less enthusiastically pro-West.

Democracy as an expression of American values clearly is and should be resonant across the political spectrum. The idea of democracy has a deep appeal on both the left and the right, but less so the notion that the United States should commit itself to aggressively promoting this value. During the Bush years, however, right-wing ideology led to a new kind of democracy promotion and, predictably, a tendency to conflate democracy with things like the Western orientation of a leader or rhetorical support for the free market. Even the language of individual freedom, so much part of the dialogue about democracy in places like the former Soviet Union and the Middle East, was gleefully recognized by conservatives.

Democracy itself, however, is much more complex and often considerably more ambiguous with regard to conservative interests. Real democracies do not seek an alliance with the United States because of a foreign assistance package and a visit to Washington, but they debate the question of what kind of relationships they want with the United States in the legislatures, media, and occasionally the streets. Likewise, free markets and low tax rates are not axiomatic in democratic systems. Indeed, questions of the role of the state and how much should be paid in taxes are at the very core of what politics is about in most democratic countries.

To some extent conservative interest in democracy promotion was genuine, but also at times seemingly disconnected from any true belief in democracy. In some ways it was a mirror image of the left, which used the language of anti-imperialism and even democracy to distance itself from a policy that had become way too closely associated with an unpopular and militaristic administration.

DEMOCRACY PROMOTION AFTER THE CRASH

From roughly 2005 to 2008, progressive criticisms of democracy promotion, originating in a strong dislike for anything to do with George W. Bush, were the biggest obstacle preventing democracy promotion from receiving broad support from the American public. By late 2008 and early 2009, during the final days of Bush's presidency and the first few months of Barack Obama's presidency, this had changed. Following the sharp economic downturn of 2008 and Obama's election, spending and the deficit became once again important issues in American politics. A Republican Party that had been comfortable borrowing money at a healthy clip during the Bush administration began to consider deficits a problem as soon as a Democrat moved into the White House. Accordingly, beginning in 2009, Republican views about the need to cut spending began to again dominate governing discourse with regard to both domestic and foreign policy.

Support among the American people for democracy promotion had declined from 24 percent believing it should be a top priority in October 2005, a time that was more or less the height of Bush's Freedom Agenda, to 21 percent feeling that way in November 2009, and only 18 percent expressing that sentiment in November 2013. When Bush took office in 2001, fully 29 percent of respondents believed democracy promotion should be a top priority for the United States.[9] Thus it is likely that democracy promotion became less popular over the course of the Bush administration, due at least in part to responses to both Bush foreign policy and rhetoric regarding democracy.

This new political reality was reinforced by an economic climate very different from the heady 1990s and even from the middle years of the Bush administration, when the country had begun to recover from the downturn at the beginning of the century. Widespread joblessness, declining worth of stock portfolios, the bursting of the real estate bubble, and rising numbers of home foreclosures all contributed to a widespread understanding that things had changed in the United States and that economic strength and future prosperity could no longer be taken for granted.

In the early years of the Obama administration, this outlook began to frame popular perceptions of democracy promotion, even though democracy promotion, in the context of the overall U.S. budget or even of the overall foreign assistance budget, remained very small or even miniscule. Many Americans find something particularly galling about democracy promotion spending. When done effectively, democracy promotion is a nuanced, even delicate, exercise of soft power, best done discreetly and in collaboration with other democratic allies. This makes it uniquely vulnerable to American public opinion, particularly in times of economic decline. Foreign policy expenses for the military, assistance in responding to natural disasters, combating human rights crises and the like are reasonably straightforward and easy to explain. Not everybody agrees with these expenses, but everybody understands them.

The question of whether to spend money on democracy assistance is both a real and a symbolic issue for many Americans. While these policies are not expensive, they are not free; and every penny spent on democracy assistance is either a penny borrowed from China or a penny not spent at home. The issue is also symbolic because at times of economic difficulty, many Americans naturally begin to question the rationale behind an expansive and occasionally ill-defined foreign policy. Moreover, democracy promotion is implicitly an exercise of power and confidence, so when the American people are not feeling confident, it is not surprising that they begin to question the value of democracy work.

Democracy promotion is a policy expression of soft power. Moreover, it is often targeted toward countries where anti-American sentiment is strong. The question of why the United States should be spending money seeking to strengthen democracy in countries where popular governance would be characterized by strong anti-American views and perhaps policies is a legitimate one, and one that supporters of democracy have yet to answer to the satisfaction of many Americans.[10] Additionally, the actual expenses are difficult to characterize and often not exactly compelling. Helping NGOs in other countries run more efficiently or helping foreign legislatures hold executives more accountable are difficult concepts to explain to Americans who are increasingly concerned with the ample economic problems facing their own country.

USAID programs such as the collaborative governance program (CGP) in Kyrgyzstan, which "works with government institutions and civil society organizations (CSOs) to improve the regulatory framework for social procurement, philanthropy, and charity; to enhance the capacity of the government to engage CSOs in delivering social services and technical assistance; and to establish a strategy for cooperation among the government, CSOs, and the private sector,"[11] may have a real impact in the field but are unlikely to be seen as a top priority by Americans in times of shrinking economies and stressed budgets. It is also difficult for many Americans to understand the activities or purposes of these types of programs.

This lack of understanding should not be overstated, however. Democracy promotion remains a policy about which, in the bigger picture, there is little awareness at all. Even when democracy promotion was at its most popular, in 2001, it was still, according to Pew, the seventh-highest foreign policy priority among the public.[12] Nonetheless, even at the elite level, the economic rationale for democracy promotion is weaker during poor economic times. Should a true fiscal conservative (or just somebody who does not believe in democracy promotion, particularly if that person is not a creature of the interventionist foreign policy consensus) ever become president or chair a powerful congressional committee, it is not difficult to see how democracy promotion could quickly be cut or how popular support could be built for those cuts.

This is not just a political issue. The economic downturn of 2008 has had a strong and enduring impact on politics in the United States. Responsible government in the United States needs to ask the question, not whether or not democracy promotion is a good idea, but whether in difficult economic times it should remain a budget priority for the United States. The reality that there is not much money involved is relevant, but is not exactly an answer to the question.[13] This standard, of course, is not applied to any other government programs. Almost nobody defends any small social welfare programs or tax subsidies for corporations by making the argument that not a whole lot of money is really involved. If voters believe the idea that democracy promotion is not a great use of resources, then the fact that there is very little of it in the first place is cold comfort.

The changing American economic climate is exacerbated by the presence of more outside powers competing with the United States and the West. Fifteen years ago, most countries seeking foreign assistance looked largely to the West. Today, Russia and China as well as regional powers like Saudi Arabia can compete with the United States. A foreign leader accepting money from China or Russia may be asked to accede to the Russian or Chinese view on various foreign policy questions, but is left to do as he pleases with regard to human rights and democracy. U.S. soft power may be substantial, but in the eyes of a nondemocratic leader, it cannot compete with Russian or Chinese money unencumbered by meddling in domestic politics.

In addition, many countries where America does democracy work also receive a great deal of other assistance from the United States. The governments of these countries generally see democracy assistance as something in which they must participate in order to get the other foreign assistance money they genuinely need. If there are other sources for that money, as is increasingly the case, the argument for allowing democracy assistance will quickly erode. This is most striking in parts of Asia—for example Cambodia—where Chinese involvement and investment dwarfs that of the United States. The United States is unable to respond to this situation by spending more money on other assistance-related programs because of financial realities at home.

Thomas Carothers and Saskia Brechenmacher describe this new world of democracy promotion for the United States:

This growing hostility was startling for a democracy and rights community that had felt the wind of history at its back ever since the fall of the Berlin Wall and had become accustomed to doors opening to its work rather than closing. When the pushback trend first made itself felt, it appeared to be a reaction to a particular juncture in international politics. President George W. Bush's use of democracy promotion as a frame for the U.S.-led military intervention in Iraq and the U.S. war on terror more generally (with its emphasis on Bush's "Freedom Agenda") changed many people's views of the democracy promotion enterprise. Western democracy assistance was no longer seen as a post–Cold War effort to foster a globalizing set of political values, but instead as the hard political edge of a newly militaristic, interventionist U.S. geostrategy.[14]

The emergence of other potential patrons for the governments of developing countries may also begin to drive up the costs of political influence and exercise of soft power. Smart nondemocratic leaders in Central Asia, South Asia, and elsewhere have become skilled at playing powers like China, Russia, and America against each other. For the United States, this has meant that to have its democracy promotion considered seriously, it has to offer bigger packages of support than those being provided by China and Russia, which has proven both difficult and costly.

LOOKING INWARD–DEMOCRACY PROMOTION AND SELF-PERCEPTION

American democracy promotion, in its current form, is to a significant extent an outgrowth of the post–Cold War period of triumphalism in the United States. At that time, the United States had just won a decades-long struggle against the Soviet Union and communism. U.S. self-confidence was very high and was buoyed by an expanding economy at home. In that context democracy promotion, an idea that at heart rests on the notion that the U.S. system is more or less the best and should be shared with the rest of the world, was a natural policy development.

One of the most surreal things about U.S. democracy promotion is the absolute certainty with which employees (often mid-level) of U.S. NGOs or American donor organizations speak of the U.S. system as the best and do not question the notion that all countries would want to emulate it. In the democracy promotion community, it is understood without question that democracy is the best system, and that democratic countries are "normal" countries. Many democracy promotion organizations are staffed by local people who are particularly pro-U.S. in their political orientation, thus creating a reinforcing loop for this notion. While democracy promotion does not seek to promote a specifically

American form of democracy, this perspective is still almost omnipresent, if not always consciously recognized.

When asked, many who work in democracy promotion will deny this perspective, but it permeates many aspects of the work implicitly rather than explicitly. This helps explain why young Americans with a few years of campaign experience often hold important jobs in the field; why former and current elected officials who have not distinguished themselves in any real way and are often not burdened by any great expertise or intellect are asked to share their expertise with legislators in democratizing countries; and why so many who work in the democracy promotion field are so certain they are pursuing the right goals, and doing it in the right way. The paradox is that despite this deep belief being problematic, it is absolutely essential for democracy promotion. Without a high degree of confidence, the capacity building and similar types of programs on which the democracy assistance endeavor rests would be much more difficult.

Even Americans in the field who are often critical of U.S. politics still hold on to this conceit, which is a product of the extraordinary cultural and political hegemony that the United States still enjoys. For many Americans, the idea that the United States, as the most powerful and wealthy country in the world, has the best system seems almost too obvious to need to be said out loud. Nonetheless, the almost incessant repetition of that idea from American politicians and other opinion leaders makes it even easier to believe. However, from the outside looking in, U.S. democracy looks decidedly mixed in the twenty-first century. To some extent, this depends on from where one is looking, but the problems of American democracy and governance in recent years are hard to miss and harder to excuse away.

American soft power has been tarnished by events such as the 2000 election, the invasion of Iraq, the rise of ugly divisive politics, the disappointment many feel toward President Obama, and the recurrent threats of government shutdowns and fiscal cliffs in recent years. Much of this may have initially grown out of the Bush administration, which was unpopular internationally, but it has not changed a lot during the Obama presidency. The Obama presidency initially signaled to the rest of the world that the United States was changing, but the legacies of President Obama, including widespread surveillance, drone attacks on innocent civilians, and the institutionalization of permanent war for permanent peace have betrayed much of this initial hope. More recently, Donald Trump's nativist presidential campaign, the inability of U.S. political elites to even discuss growing income inequality, and widely publicized incidents of racially motivated police brutality have further reduced U.S. soft power.

These changes have had a mixed effect on democracy promotion. For critics of the United States, it has become easier to identify the flaws in the American system and question its relevance as a model for the rest of the world. These developments have also given pause to many Americans working in the field. More frequently, however, they have morphed into things that can be explained away or pointed at as evidence of the strength of the American system. So, for example, the revelation of widespread torture by the U.S. government is presented as an example of the U.S. capacity for honesty and accountability.[15]

In recent years, however, doubts about this fundamental foundation for democracy promotion have begun to emerge both inside and outside the United States. The changing media climate has contributed to this as well. The rise in Internet technology, widespread access to video-recording equipment, and social media sites like Twitter and YouTube have made American foibles, missteps, and misgovernance much more visible to the whole world than they were a generation ago. The same tools that can be used to expose the brutality of an authoritarian regime can also be used to show the absurdity of American political life. Stories of NSA surveillance, WikiLeaks, and the treatment of people like Bradley Manning and Edward Snowden are now discussed globally and have further reduced the ability of the United States to be a model for an open society.

Additionally, non-American powers have also learned how to exercise soft power. Glossy, well-produced programs on television networks such as RT, Al-Jazeera, and CCTV today bring different perspectives on events inside the United States and on the U.S. role in the broader world than those seen on American media. In the months following the Russian invasion of Crimea, RT (formerly Russia Today) drew a lot of attention; it was frequently described as a propaganda tool of the Kremlin, on balance an accurate characterization.[16] However, while RT's coverage of Russia and countries such as Ukraine or Georgia, which are of great interest to Moscow, is strong propaganda, with frequently only a tenuous relationship to reality, its coverage of the United States is different. It is RT's coverage of the United States, always critical and frequently insightful, that is the real source of its soft power within the United States.[17]

This more competitive soft power environment has made it more difficult for democracy promotion to succeed, but it has also undermined domestic support for democracy promotion. A population that is constantly bombarded, at both the elite and non-elite level, with stories about the worst Congress in history, the possibility that constitutional arrangements are outdated and need revision, angry partisanship from both the left and the right, antigovernment fervor, government shutdowns, and threats of default on debt is not likely to believe that their country can or should seek to help other countries develop their political systems. Elites may hold on to a position supportive of democracy promotion longer, as it is consistent with the internationalist consensus that characterizes the political establishment, but for many Americans, the policy will become increasingly difficult to defend.

In the 1990s, for example, it was clear that post-soviet regimes were emerging from decades of repression and needed Western help to survive and thrive. Twenty years later it is equally clear, at least according to much of the media, that the crisis facing America's political system is severe and requires immediate attention. In the decade or so following President Bush's reelection in 2004, books and articles with titles such as "Is the US Government Really Broken?"[18] "Why Our Government is Broken,"[19] "Admit It, Political Scientists: Politics Really Is More Broken Than Ever,"[20] *Broken Government: How Republican Rule Destroyed the Legislative, Executive, and Judicial Branches*,[21] or "The System Is Broken: How the Midterms Expose Our Dying Democracy,"[22] have become almost ubiquitous. In this context, it is hard to build support among the American people for observing elections in Cambodia or strengthening free media in Tanzania.

Yet these types of democracy promotion programs and activities continue with little change from the headier days of the middle years of the Bush administration and the 1990s. None of the changed perceptions about the U.S. role in the world or the ability of the United States to influence political outcomes in various parts of the world have led to changes on the programmatic side of democracy promotion, but they have indirectly reduced the effectiveness of these programs. Democracy promotion is most effective when it is able to adapt to both local conditions and macropolitical and economic factors. In recent years, the policy has proven relatively inflexible in this regard. This is largely because the bureaucratic logic of supporting free media, stronger civil society, or better functioning legislatures, as well as the potential value of these kinds of activities, remains constant despite the relative standing of the United States and its democracy.

The inability to adapt and recognize how the changing perceptions of the United States lead to a new environment for democracy promotion has made the work less effective. Members of parliament asked to participate in a training by an American expert are less likely to take that training seriously after reading news of the shutdown of the American government. Similarly, free media programs are a lot harder to persuasively implement when news of Edward Snowden is all over the Internet. Implementers and organizers of these programs know that participants are aware of what is going on in the rest of the world, particularly in America, and are rarely shy about confronting Americans about this.

Any American who has spent a significant amount of time working in democracy promotions has encountered this phenomenon. During the Iraq War, members of parliaments and governments with whom I was working on anticorruption issues raised the question of Halliburton's role in receiving contracts in postconflict Iraq; and the abuses at Abu Ghraib were brought to my attention with some frequency. People working in the field today undoubtedly encounter similar questions about CIA torture or NSA surveillance. These criticisms are not always based on accurate reporting, but in a context where there is some truth it is easy for opponents of the United States, and critical thinkers more generally, to expand on that dishonestly and portray the United States in a more negative light.

The heart of this issue is that despite all heartfelt and legitimate efforts to the contrary, there is something deeply patronizing about democracy assistance. This is the inconvenient and uncomfortable truth that cannot be ignored if democracy promotion, in all its strengths and weaknesses, is to be fully understood. This patronizing cast is almost unavoidable given the goals of democracy work, the underlying power and money dynamics, and, often, the way programs are implemented in the field. It is hard to imagine how this can be avoided given that, at its core, democracy promotion is based on the belief that the world would be better off if political systems everywhere looked like those of the wealthiest countries in North America and western Europe. Recognizing this should not preclude democracy work, but ignoring it is intellectually dishonest. The deeply held assumption that the West knows best and is showing the others the way permeates much of the work, even when it is undertaken by people who would blanch at this assertion if confronted with it. This assumption is perhaps an inevitable outgrowth of a project like democracy promotion that, even at its best, seems to walk a thin line between supporting a friend and showing an inferior what is best.

The patronizing aspect of democracy promotion has long been an obstacle to the work itself. People do not like feeling patronized or spoken down to; the best people in democracy promotion work very hard to avoid this perception. Ironically, however, if those doing the democracy promoting don't feel like they are the more knowledgeable party representing the superior political system, the project also falls apart. Thus, the logic of democracy promotion rests on a set of assumptions that cannot be fully revealed nor probably even fully accepted by the practitioners themselves. Successful implementation of democracy promotion programs rests on being able to present models of how to do things ranging from marking up a budget to conducting an election while not coming across as patronizing or pedantic. This is a difficult needle to thread in the best of circumstances.

CONCLUSION

Democracy promotion has strong ideological roots in both the left and the right and as such should be able to generate support across the political spectrum. In recent years, this has been turned on its head as opposition to democracy promotion has emerged, albeit for different reasons, from both the left and the right. It is a reflection of the complexities and the paradoxes that characterize democracy promotion that it is seen by some as an example of a waste of American tax dollars[23] and by others as an example of American imperialism.[24] These dueling perceptions contribute to the precariousness of the future for democracy promotion, as it is vulnerable from several different angles.

Carothers points out that in recent years, the U.S. commitment to democracy support has already begun to wane:

U.S. assistance to advance democracy worldwide is in decline. Such spending has shrunk by 28 percent during Barack Obama's presidency and is now less than $2 billion per year. The decline has been especially severe at the US Agency for International Development, which traditionally funds the bulk of U.S. democracy assistance and established itself in the 1990s as the largest source of such aid worldwide. According to data provided by the agency, USAID spending to foster democracy, human rights and accountable governance abroad has fallen by 38 percent since 2009. . . . [It is] not a product of a broader contraction of U.S. foreign aid spending, which remains robust overall. Rather, it is a policy choice, reflecting both skepticism about the relative importance of democracy work by senior U.S. aid officials and, more generally, the muted emphasis on democracy-building by the Obama foreign policy team.[25]

The changing domestic political environment has been one of several factors that have contributed to this change in policy by the Obama administration. In most countries, U.S. democracy promotion budgets are down slightly; in others, democracy is sufficiently strong that democracy promotion programs are no longer needed. But in general, programs today look similar to a decade ago in ambition and approach, just smaller.

This reduction is perhaps unavoidable so long as democracy work is seen through a programmatic prism. Once it is accepted that programs funded by USAID and implemented by NGOs or contractors is the preferred approach to democracy work, the range of possible programs that are fundable and can be implemented is not likely to be very big. Likewise the official U.S. attitudes surrounding democracy promotion, despite the budget changes described by Carothers, are also largely unchanged. The belief among much of the foreign policy leadership that the work is important and that most countries still look at the United States as a model of democracy and openness has also remained the same.

It is possible, perhaps even likely, that further reductions in democracy promotion support from the United States will occur in the next few years. Many domestic political issues—ranging from legitimate budget constraints to attacks, from the right, on spending grounds, or from the left, linking democracy promotion to excessive interventionism more generally—have the potential to weaken or reduce democracy promotion spending. Additionally, if these programs continue to be perceived as relatively ineffective, the rationale for continuing them will be further undermined.

Like much of American foreign policy, reducing U.S. democracy promotion creates its own set of challenges. First, a network of people, organizations, scholars, and others who work on democracy promotion has now been created and would resist seeing these programs significantly cut. Although numerically and financially these people and organizations are minute, they are still influential. Some of the organizations in question have powerful boards with numerous former senators, congress members, and others who would help efforts to oppose major cuts. For example, NDI and IRI are chaired by Madeline Albright and John McCain. Officers and board members of the NED include former members of Congress Norm Coleman, Martin Frost, and Vin Weber. The individuals in senior and sometimes not-so-senior positions in these organizations are often well connected, with strong relationships in Congress and throughout the foreign policy establishment. In addition, the network of scholars and others working in support of democracy promotion have access to opinion pages, influential websites, and other media that can help shape public opinion.

Carothers, for example, concludes his *Washington Post* piece on declining U.S. support for democracy promotion by arguing that

> supporting democracy, human rights and better governance more substantially and effectively will not produce instant solutions to these and other crises. But patiently and seriously pursued, such aid can be a crucial part of the longer-term solutions we seek. Troubled though our democracy can seem at home, our society still enjoys its unique stability and security thanks to its pluralistic, open political system rooted in democratic accountability and the rule of law. That formula remains the right one for our pursuit of stability and security abroad.[26]

Tom Bridle, a scholar-practitioner of democracy promotion, writing in *Foreign Policy*, argues for a broad and robust democracy promotion policy: "Democracy assistance is central to America's values, to our interests and to our security. But in a complex world, where progress toward democracy and better government are fragile and rare, we are more likely to accomplish our goals if we have more tools and strategies at our disposal, not fewer."[27] Carothers and Bridle are only two of the dozens of scholars, although two of the best, who write with some frequency in support of democracy promotion.

Second, even if defunding democracy promotion were possible domestically, it is not clear how the United States would be able to do it without creating bigger problems. In almost any country where the United States would consider simply ending its democracy promotion programs, except for in those few that have become democracies, such an action would be seen as a concession to a nondemocratic government and a sign of defeat for the United States. If, for example, after ten or twenty years of working to make a country like Pakistan, Kyrgyzstan, or Mali more democratic the United States ended its commitment, it would be perceived, regardless of the reasons, as the United States simply giving up. This would be damaging inside the country in question, as it would empower the authoritarian elements, but also outside the country, where it would be seen as a sign of American weakness. This would also send a message to democracy activists that the United States is not able to be a reliable ally in their struggle for democracy. The United States has backed itself into a difficult corner with regard to democracy work.

Moreover, in many of these countries U.S. money, despite all the contradictions and problems, supports good local NGOs. The NED and USAID support hundreds of NGOs in dozens of countries. Obviously not all these organizations are effective, but many are. Simply ceasing to support organizations that function as government watchdogs, anticorruption crusaders, or domestic election monitors would make it easier for nondemocratic regimes to consolidate their authoritarian hold on the country. If U.S. and European funding for these types of organizations simply ended, many of the organizations would not survive, and important voices that help make nondemocratic countries a little more free and nondemocratic governments a little more accountable would be silenced. The effect this would have on civil societies in many countries would be severe.

Withdrawing support for these organizations could also give rise to stronger anti-American sentiment from influential segments of society that, in some countries, are currently among the rare bastions of pro-U.S. sentiment. These activists would likely feel abandoned by the United States and would become even more vulnerable to persecution at the hands of their governments. NGOs that see their U.S. funding eliminated because of domestic political concerns in the United States would not see that as a reason to think better of America or the American people. In countries where alternate models of opposition exist, this could be particularly bad for the United States.

Democracy promotion has additional value to the United States that should not be overlooked. NGOs, both foreign and domestic, working on democracy-related issues in many countries develop access to information and key relationships that are not otherwise easily available to American diplomats. Similarly, American-democracy NGOs in particular make it possible for the United States to have deeper and stronger ties with political leaders in many countries. NGO workers, unlike diplomats, are more able to establish informal relationships with party members and other political figures. It is easier for them to have casual meetings, where the absence of the notebook and reporting entailed with official U.S. meetings generally makes everyone more comfortable. In addition, many democracy promotion activists have a battery of political skills and knowledge that allow them to understand domestic politics in a given country better than the diplomats do. Losing these relationships and this perspective would make U.S. diplomacy less nimble and make it harder for the United States to rapidly adapt to political changes in some countries.

Finally, perhaps the most difficult thing about changing democracy promotion policies is that it would force the U.S. foreign policy establishment to question some of its deeply held assumptions. Democracy promotion springs from beliefs that the United States has a unique, or at least special, role to play in the world; that our political system is the best, not just for us, but for the planet; and that most people if given a choice will want to be like us. Democracy promotion has allowed us to reframe our political system as a universal good. Obviously this paradigm is not accepted globally, but it is almost never questioned in Washington.

A frank discussion of democracy promotion as a discrete and bounded policy therefore cannot occur, because that discussion would challenge the core beliefs of the foreign policy establishment. For example, the question of whether or not the U.S. political model should be emulated or exported is clearly central to democracy promotion, but addressing that question requires a much broader exploration of U.S. foreign policy, an exploration that is not likely to be smooth or easy. Likewise, examining the question of whether democracy can be supported by a programmatic approach that assumes the major problem is a lack of skills, knowledge, and expertise is essential for a meaningful debate around democracy promotion, but that question also has broad implications for U.S. foreign policy, and for numerous organizations and individuals working in that field.

Crafting a policy that recognizes the possibility that democracy promotion, as currently constructed, is no longer effective or feasible in a changing political and economic context would be cognitively dissonant to a foreign policy establishment that holds their beliefs to be true. Accordingly, because the alternative is too difficult, the easiest course is to continue with democracy promotion as-is, despite growing misgivings from the American people and growing evidence that the policies are considerably less effective than they were a decade ago.

Despite how the changing political environment has affected perceptions of democracy promotion, and despite evidence that the policy has begun to run its course, it is not likely to go away. The political costs of dismantling democracy promotion, at least for now, seem to outweigh the problems associated with the policy. However, doing nothing and simply continuing the policies as they are today will exacerbate the problems of democracy promotion until they become more serious and irreparable. Failing to address the problems will make democracy promotion more vulnerable to critiques that the work is useless or a waste of money. Thus, in the short run, failing to rethink democracy promotion is an appealing strategy because it will lead only to manageable budget cuts, but those seemingly manageable budget cuts will lead to even less defendable projects, ultimately making it harder to build support for democracy promotion.

CHAPTER SEVEN
DEMOCRACY PROMOTION
AND AMERICAN POWER

DEMOCRACY PROMOTION IS AN INTERESTING policy topic for study, but not because the U.S. government spends a few million dollars in a few dozen countries around the world on programs that, on balance, may do more good than harm but are no longer of critical importance. Nor is democracy promotion a compelling policy to study just because of its interaction with the changing domestic political environment in the United States. Democracy promotion is of particular significance because the examination of democracy promotion provides powerful insight into the construction of American power in the late twentieth and early twenty-first centuries, as well as into the assumptions and stories that are the foundations of that power.

AN EXPRESSION OF AMERICAN POWER

Democracy promotion has always been an expression of American power. Although it has at times been a positive and benign expression of that power, democracy promotion cannot be disaggregated from this power dynamic. At its core, democracy promotion is a policy pursued by powerful countries in less powerful countries, a reality that frames the actions of some foreign leaders. For example, in recent years Russian leader Vladimir Putin has expressed frustration and anger with American democracy promotion efforts in his country, and in September 2012 closed down all USAID-supported democracy projects in Russia. Putin's remarks in 2014, that "in the modern world extremism is being used as a geopolitical instrument and for remaking spheres of influence. We see what tragic consequences the wave of so-called Color Revolutions led to. For us this is a lesson and a warning. We should do everything necessary so that nothing similar ever happens in Russia,"[1] demonstrate his concern that a Color Revolution could occur in Russia and topple his regime. The statement also captures the Russian leadership's suspicion of democracy promotion as well as their dissatisfaction with being treated like just another poor, weak, formerly communist country.

Russia views democracy promotion in this way not only because it views the programs as a threat to its regime structure, but also because it is a reminder that the United States sees Russia as a weak country, more like Armenia than like China. For Putin, U.S. democracy promotion is as much a question of power and sovereignty, even respect, as it is of democracy or human rights.

Matthew Rojansky, quoted in the *Washington Post*, explains Russia's feelings about U.S. democracy promotion:

> Russian authorities have made clear for the better part of a decade that they see Russia as a great power, and a provider of assistance, not a recipient. Add to that tension over the pre- and postelection protests, which the Kremlin alleges were orchestrated by U.S.-funded NGOs, plus the deep disagreement over U.S. democracy promotion activities in the Middle East, and you can see why this decision [to expel USAID] may have come now.[2]

Rojansky was speaking about a specific incident, but his words apply to Russia more generally.

Equally significant, certainly from Moscow's perspective, is that democracy promotion programs in China have generally been limited. USAID describes its most democracy-oriented comments, programs, and goals on its China webpage:

USAID . . . is working with China to improve environmental law and environmental governance. Activities also will strengthen environmental due diligence among national agencies and the private sector and reduce China's environmental footprint. USAID assists China's efforts to develop a legal system for fair, participatory, and transparent governance; as well as its efforts to introduce reforms within the justice system.[3]

U.S. support for democracy and human rights in China is much less than it is in Russia, and is an even lesser issue in their bilateral diplomatic relationship. In the three years before USAID was kicked out of Russia, during fiscal years 2010–12, USAID spent $68.6 million on democracy and governance in Russia. During that same time, the USAID democracy and governance budget in China was only $8.2 million.[4] The approach to democracy work in Russia and China differs not because there is an abundance of democracy in China, even relative to Russia, but because China is a powerful country.

A key component of the democracy promotion power dynamic is that almost all democracy promotion programs funded and implemented by outside sources would not be allowed in the United States. With a few exceptions, the U.S. government has never embraced foreign support for domestic civil society organizations engaged in politics. Organizations such as the Confucius Institute, funded by the Chinese government, are accepted at many American schools, but the focus of these institutes is Chinese language and culture. The Institute of Democracy and Cooperation (IDC) is a Russian-funded organization with offices in the United States that issues reports and makes statements about democracy in the United States and other Western countries, but it does not engage directly with American citizens and political activities. Moreover, statements, reports, and activities by the IDC get almost no attention from American politicians or media and are treated, appropriately, like Russian propaganda. In general, this kind of activity is tolerated in the United States, but these organizations are rarely involved in politics in the way that Western-supported NGOs involve themselves in politics in other countries.

A foreign organization, even one funded by strong American allies, would not be allowed to conduct workshops for Congress or congressional staff. Newly elected members to the U.S. Congress can participate in orientations sponsored by Harvard University's Institute of Politics or the Congressional Management Foundation, but these workshops and events are opportunities for new members of Congress to learn from experienced Americans only. If a delegation from the French or Lithuanian legislatures or the Netherlands Institute for Multiparty Democracy proposed a workshop for new members of Congress like those conducted by organizations such as NDI or IRI all over the world, they would be met with a cold shoulder.

America also expresses its power and its view of its role in relation to less powerful countries by persistently presenting itself as the arbiter of democracy, determining which countries need democracy support and in what way. However, if a less powerful country, one not considered a consolidated democracy, were to experience the hyper-partisanship, congressional inability to legislate, frequent threats of government shutdowns, and unwillingness to meet debt obligations that are now part of everyday political life in America, the United States and its European allies would set up working groups, seminars, and other means to address these issues. Likewise, any country in the former Soviet Union, Asia, or Africa where money played the same role it does in U.S. politics would see projects aimed at reducing such corruption.

Almost no foreign-funded programs like these exist in the United States, however. One can only imagine the bipartisan rancor that would greet, for example, an EU-led yearlong workshop in Washington aimed at getting money out of American politics; it would be considered an attack on American sovereignty almost across the political spectrum. It is therefore worth at least thinking about how political elites and ordinary citizens in other countries feel about similar but not hypothetical efforts made by the United States. There was a time when these efforts were welcomed, and often even requested, by foreign governments, but today that is rarely the case. Nobody in the democracy promotion field thinks American democracy is perfect; most working in the sector are quick to recognize American democracy's ample shortcomings. Nonetheless, the contrast between the scrutiny America places on other countries' political institutions and the unwillingness to have its own institutions similarly examined cannot be overlooked.

To the extent that America is on the receiving end of anything that vaguely resembles democracy promotion, it occurs around elections. International election organizations, notably OSCE/ODIHR, usually send observers to the United States, but these missions are limited. In addition, although the resulting reports are perhaps interesting to scholars and others, they have no policy relevance, are barely reported on in the United States, and do not lead to efforts to improve American elections.[5] More often, the United States brings foreign election officials to America to see how U.S. elections are run. In fairness, these projects often show foreign election officials a relatively realistic portrayal of American elections and do not seek to brush over the problems.

In the days leading up to the 2012 election, U.S. NGOs including the NAACP and the ACLU appealed to an OSCE election-monitoring delegation to raise their concerns about possible voter suppression. The response from the right was predictable and consistent with conservative views on international organizations becoming involved in American politics. Catherine Engelbrecht, a conservative activist working to oppose alleged election fraud in 2012, responded by saying, "These activist groups sought assistance not from American sources, but from the United Nations. The United Nations has no jurisdiction over American elections."[6] The Tennessee state legislature has also sought to ban UN election monitors.

These examples highlight conservative intolerance for international election monitors and other similar organizations because opposition to any international role in American elections, or American democratic development more generally, is stronger on the right, but the sentiment is also bipartisan. Progressives and Democrats very rarely advocate for a larger international role in American elections or meaningfully engage with international organizations working on U.S. democracy related questions.

This reluctance to engage international election monitors occurs in a context that includes several characteristics of American elections that would strike any experienced election observer as less than ideal. For example, in many American states, partisan elected officials are responsible for administering elections. Most international election-monitoring groups discourage this, preferring either nonpartisan appointed experts or a multiparty commission appointed by the courts or the legislature. However, in many U.S. states, the top election official is elected. Katherine Harris, the secretary of state in Florida in 2000 during the contested presidential election in that state, is the most well known of these officials. Harris was a Republican who was instrumental in helping Republican candidate George W. Bush carry Florida and thus become president.

Harris's role in that election naturally aroused suspicion and concern from progressives who believed she was unwilling to make decisions unhelpful to Bush. During the recount in Florida in 2000, when Harris refused to call for a recount of heavily Democratic West Palm Beach County, *Salon* reported, "Rep. Peter Deutsch, D-Florida, argued that Harris's decision to not extend the deadline to at least Friday, is 'bizarre,' while also pointing out that she's Bush's state campaign co-chair. 'I honestly think what's going on is a strategic decision by the Bush campaign to hurt the litigation efforts,' Deutsch said."[7]

The absence of nonpartisan domestic election monitors in the United States is also unusual by international standards. Election monitoring in America is done largely by partisan organizations, such as groups of lawyers associated with a major party or NGOs that are clearly aligned with one party or candidate. In many respects this approach works well, as Democrats are good at watching for Republican election abuses and Republicans are similarly able to keep an eye on the Democrats. However, nonpartisan domestic monitors are valuable because they have more credibility across party lines.

Moreover, the antiquated equipment used in some places in the United States—most visibly, until recently, in New York City—would raise concerns from international observers in most parts of the world. It may make me feel kind of cool, as a New Yorker, to know that I cast my vote for Barack Obama on the same kind of machine my grandparents used when they voted for Franklin Roosevelt, but those machines, which often broke and could be easily tampered with, may not have been the best thing for America democracy. In general, U.S. elections remain unobserved in any meaningful way by the rest of the world, not because American elections are any kind of model compared with other democratic countries, but because America is powerful.

MEDDLING AND THE MORAL HIGH GROUND

America and its European allies not only involve themselves through democracy promotion in the domestic workings of the politics of other countries to a degree that would almost certainly be seen as infringements on American sovereignty if the reverse were to occur, but U.S. organizations and governments often claim the moral high ground when foreign governments chafe at this involvement. For example, in 2013 when President Evo Morales expelled USAID from Bolivia, he used strong language to explain his decision: "[USAID] still has a mentality of domination and submission. . . . They surely still think they can manipulate here politically and economically. . . . That belongs to the past."[8] Morales's claims may not be precisely true, but they certainly would resonate with anyone familiar with the U.S. role in that part of the world over the last century or more.

The State Department's response, while perhaps not inaccurate, was self-righteous, indicating no empathy at all for the Bolivian view. A spokesman for State referred to "the baseless allegations made by the Bolivian government," and noted that "those who will be most hurt by the Bolivian government's decision are the Bolivian citizens, who have benefited from our collaborative work on education, health and the environment,"[9] reflecting the belief that America knows what is best for Bolivians better than their elected president does. U.S. secretary of state John Kerry defended U.S. involvement in Bolivia by describing it as "our backyard," a choice of words that could not have been well-received in La Paz. This response is a profound reflection not only of Washington's attitudes, even today, toward much of Latin America, but also of how the United States sees its democracy promotion mission as one of helping people and making countries better.

The disagreement between Morales and the State Department is about policy, as each sees the impact of American democracy work in the region very differently. It is also, however, about context. President Morales placed USAID and contemporary U.S. involvement in Bolivia in the context of several centuries of history during which American policies toward Bolivia and its neighbors were very destructive, while the United States sees its actions in no context other than that of America as a post–Cold War force for universal political good.

This issue is complex because, in most cases, it is not the friendly and mostly democratic governments seeking to become more democratic that take the most umbrage at U.S. democracy promotion efforts. It is usually undemocratic governments that see Western democracy promotion as both an affront and a threat and therefore pass laws limiting foreign money, harass Western democracy promotion workers, and occasionally kick democracy organizations out of their country. Leaders like Putin, Morales, and others often seek to leverage anti-American sentiment to push democracy promotion away. By doing this, they build nationalistic opposition to democracy promotion, thus strengthening their nondemocratic regimes.

The undemocratic cast of these regimes too frequently obscures legitimate concerns raised by their leaders. When, for example, Russia's government passes laws limiting how much foreign money an NGO deeply involved in politics can receive, they are not doing anything very different from what the United States would do in a similar situation. The 2006 NGO law passed in Russia, according to Human Rights Watch, has

> significantly expanded state officials' discretion to reject the registration of NGOs, to inspect NGOs, and to require reporting from NGOs. It is primarily this broad and vague discretion now accorded to state officials to interfere with the founding and operation of NGOs, open to discriminatory and arbitrary misuse, that is having a detrimental impact on human rights NGOs. . . . This discretion, combined with the abusive use of some potentially mundane, if onerous, administrative regulations, threaten both the freedom of association to establish and run NGOs and the freedom of expression of NGOs. . . . The 2006 law introduces restrictions on who can found an NGO, and expands the grounds on which the state may reject the registration of a non-commercial organization.[10]

Since then, Russia has passed other anti-NGO legislation, including a 2012 law that "requires all NCOs to register in the registry of NCOs, which is maintained by the Ministry of Justice, prior to receipt of funding from any foreign sources if they intend to conduct political activities."[11] Laws like this one clearly limit the growth of democracy in Russia, or in Central Asian countries that have passed similar laws in recent years, but they are also an assertion of Russia's sovereignty and its discomfort with America seeking, albeit indirectly, to play a larger role in its domestic politics.[12]

When Putin or others accuse democracy promotion workers of being spies, as these laws implicitly do, these accusations are met with righteous outrage from the West, but these accusations should not be dismissed outright. In 2005, Nikolai Patrushev, the director of Russia's FSB, stated, "Foreign secret services are ever more actively using non-traditional methods for their work and with the help of different NGOs' educational programmes are propagandising their interests, particularly in the former Soviet Union."[13] The *Moscow Times* reported that the response of the U.S. embassy to these charges was to have a spokesperson dismiss them as "utterly baseless" and to "deny them utterly."[14] This tone captures both the righteousness and confidence that characterizes the American view that NGO activity is not remotely related to spying.

In 2006, Putin addressed this topic directly:

> In his first comments on the discovery of alleged British spies in Moscow, Russian President Vladimir Putin on Wednesday linked the scandal to foreign financing of nongovernmental organizations in Russia, a connection that grass-roots activists say is tangential and being used to smear their work. "The situation is regrettable, as we have seen, when attempts are made to use secret services to work with nongovernmental organizations and when financing is carried out through secret services' channels."[15]

Although none working for NDI, IRI, or other similar organizations see themselves as spies, employees of those organizations seek and have valuable information about countries, their governments, and their opposition. Moreover, the information is gathered as part of a broader effort to transform the domestic workings of those countries. Most NGO workers usually cite their NGO credentials and stress that they are not part of the U.S. government in order to get this information. I certainly did when working on democracy promotion projects. However, when asked to share this information with an embassy or a visiting official from the State Department, they have little recourse other than to do so. This may not be the precise definition of spying, but it is a distinction sometimes without a difference.

Even NGO workers who are not comfortable sharing information often have a difficult time saying no when an embassy or government official requests that information. Once when working on a political party–related project for an NGO that involved gathering extensive information about the inner workings and political orientation of every party in the target country, I was asked by the U.S. ambassador if he could see my report before I submitted it. He seemed surprised when I told him I could not do that. Had he asked the NGO, as I suggested he do, they most likely would have given him the report, knowing he would have been able to get it some other way.

Democracy promotion is also unmistakably an expression of American power because it frequently occurs in places where the United States has won a military victory. Moreover, in recent decades it has at times been almost directly linked to military action: almost all significant American- or NATO-led military actions in the last two or three decades have been followed by democracy promotion. From World War II to the Cold War to the Bush-era wars in Afghanistan and Iraq to more recent military efforts in Libya, Western military intervention and victory, of one form or another, have been followed by democracy promotion. The U.S. military actions in the former Yugoslavia during the Clinton administration also occurred almost hand in hand with democracy promotion efforts.

Although there is no readily apparent reason why democracy promotion should be an essentially inseparable part of U.S. military action, that is what it has become. This affects democracy work, as it sharpens the real and perceived connection between democracy promotion and U.S. aggression. It also changes the nature of military intervention, as it not only all but guarantees a long American involvement in any country where America intervenes, but also makes it possible for supporters of U.S. military actions to frame those actions positively, as efforts to help people and bring democracy, even when those efforts begin with bombs and invasion.

In some cases this relationship has been positive; countries like postwar Germany and Japan or post–Cold War Lithuania and Poland have become consolidated democracies enjoying relative freedom and prosperity. Even in countries such as Afghanistan or Iraq, where the result has not been as positive, it is not the democracy promotion itself that has caused the problems. Democracy promotion has been helpful in some ways, as domestic and international organizations funded by the United States and other outside donors have pushed, with moderate success, for more liberal policies, stronger rule of law, and the like in both Afghanistan and Iraq. However, the ongoing presence of these organizations has also framed policy in Afghanistan and Iraq in such a way that a continued American role, despite numerous public assurances to the contrary, seems inevitable. In addition, it is clear that democracy promotion there is closely linked to American military power. Had the military not over-thrown the Taliban or Baathist governments, democracy promotion would never have come to Iraq or Afghanistan.

HARD AND SOFT POWER

Democracy promotion is an exercise of American soft power. John Ikenberry defines soft power, building on Joseph Nye's work, as "the ability of a country to persuade others to do what it wants without force or coercion."[16] Democracy promotion is, at least on the surface, an example of soft power, relying as it does on emulation, modeling, and technical support. Supporting and encouraging civil society organizations, facilitating exchanges and study tours with legislatures and other relevant organizations in democratic countries, or providing grants for media freedom–related projects are almost textbook definitions of soft power. Moreover, the notion that democracy promotion is bolstered through the examples of democratic institutions, media, and other freedoms and citizen engagement of Western countries is at the very core of the concept of soft power. Although it often goes unsaid, democracy promotion rests implicitly on a belief that people in nondemocratic countries want to be like us or, if not precisely like Americans, like our European friends and allies. This belief deeply reflects the soft power approach to foreign policy.

Soft power is an important part of the arsenal of most powerful countries in the twenty-first century. The United States probably has deeper reservoirs of soft power than any country in the world, drawing from the enormous influence U.S. culture, commercial brands, consumer behavior, and media have on most of the world—influence that surpasses that of any other country. Most of this soft power is unspecific and serves to help create a general positive image and affinity for the United States that exists often in spite of negative views of U.S. military and political decisions.

Democracy promotion, however, is not that kind of soft power. Democracy promotion is much more specific and done in service of direct American foreign policy goals. It is an assertion of soft power, but nonetheless an assertion of American power overall as well. Members of foreign parliaments do not listen to a twenty-five-year-old American tell them how to set up their national legislatures out of respect for that twenty-five-year-old, or because of their affinity for American culture, but because of American power, both hard and soft.

In addition, the instruments of democracy promotion are NGOs, USAID grants, seminars, workshops, and guidebooks; these instruments are a long way from bombs, bullets, and other instruments of hard power. Democracy promotion is an expression of soft power, but like much soft power, it relies on a foundation of hard power. It becomes a lot easier to urge citizens of another country to emulate you if you have already defeated them militarily or if they rely on you for security or foreign assistance. In places where efforts to strengthen democracy have followed military interventions this is most obvious, but these are not the only examples of the hard power element of democracy promotion. In much of the former communist world, the ability of the United States to exercise soft power draws very directly from the American victory in the Cold War.

The bilateral relationships from which most democracy promotion emerges rest unambiguously on an imbalance of hard power. It is not simply a coincidence that the world's most powerful country by any measure of hard power is most active in seeking to spread its form of government to the rest of the world. Poor countries, those without strong militaries or powerful allies on whom they depend for security, do not seek to do anything similar. Hard power is what gives America the entree to exercise soft power, including democracy promotion, in much of the world.

Some countries tolerate U.S. democracy promotion because they value military alliances, whether real or potential, with the United States. Others tolerate these types of democracy promotion activities because they help keep relations with the United States smooth, thus precluding any kind of U.S. military action or other efforts to more actively disrupt their political system. Some have no choice, as democracy promotion arrives shortly after a U.S. military action. Most countries where U.S. democracy promotion occurs, however, allow it as part of a broader U.S. assistance program on which the country in question depends or that it at least values a great deal. Economic assistance, of course, is in a gray area between hard and soft power, as it is not quite the same as military power but is not the softer power of influence, cultural capital, or international prestige.

To some extent there is nothing new about this dynamic. For decades and probably centuries, powerful states have sought to change the political systems of less powerful states to align more clearly with the goals of the powerful states. Not all powerful countries have tried to create governmental systems similar to theirs; most were satisfied to create political systems, or support political leadership, sympathetic to their worldview. During the Cold War, the United States was less interested in democracy than in ensuring that regimes, particularly in the Americas, were pro-U.S. In the centuries during which European powers colonized much of the world, many of these powers, notably Britain, frequently created the frameworks of political institutions. Most colonial powers supported political regimes that recognized colonial arrangements, facilitated trade, and did not challenge the worldview of the colonial power.

In this context, twenty-first-century democracy promotion is one of the more benign and less brutal expressions of this dynamic. Establishing NGOs, pushing for fair elections, and seeking to expand freedoms of media and expression clearly are qualitatively different than Soviet efforts, many of which were successful, to overturn governments and install compliant communist regimes in the years following World War II, or of various colonial powers to overthrow existing regimes and establish governments friendly to their interests.

U.S. democracy promotion is not the same as these historical precedents, but the similarities cannot be ignored. In all cases, more powerful and more global powers sought to remake the domestic political arrangements of weaker countries. In addition, and also significant, the more powerful country, or representatives of that country, believed in all cases that they were acting at least partially out of morality and altruism. The colonial British believed they were bringing civilization and good government to places like India or parts of Africa. Likewise, Soviet communists believed their system was better than the capitalist systems that they saw devastating the lives of millions all over the world. Obviously neither all communists nor all colonial British officers felt this way, but some did. That dynamic is certainly alive in contemporary American democracy promotion, and understanding democracy promotion in that context is, therefore, important.

COMPETING FOR INFLUENCE

The absence of competing models or patrons was a critical characteristic of democracy promotion in the early post–Cold War period, but the environment has begun to change with the emergence of China and to a lesser extent Russia as major global political powers in the twenty-first century. This has raised new challenges for U.S. democracy promoters, as the work now occurs in a competitive context. Sometimes this competition is ideological, but more frequently it is based on economic competition, as each side seeks to offer economic support in exchange for geopolitical alignment and a favored domestic political system.

The demonstrations and unrest in Ukraine that began late in 2013 reflected this dynamic, at least at first. In November 2013, Ukraine was poised to sign an association agreement that would have moved it further down the path to greater integration with Europe and potential membership in the EU. For many in Ukraine, particularly those who did not support its president, Viktor Yanukovych, this hard-won diplomatic victory was cause for celebration. Yanukovych and many of his supporters saw the situation differently, and Yanukovych's decision not to sign the EU association agreement led to major demonstrations that ultimately forced him from office.

Yanukovych, however, did not decide to decline the association agreement independently; rather he turned to his patron, Russia, for political and economic support in his decision. Russia, of course, did not want to see Ukraine move closer to Europe, so was happy to provide alternatives to Yanukovych. Putin's offer of $15 billion in assistance and loans, a good chunk of which was likely to make it into the pockets of Yanukovych and supporters, made it easy for the Ukrainian president to make his decision.[17]

Ultimately, Russia was unable to provide enough support for the teetering, corrupt, and criminal Yanukovych government, and Yanukovych resigned and fled the country in February. Subsequent Russian actions in Ukraine in 2014, including the barely disguised invasion of Crimea and the similarly Russian-sponsored effort to destabilize southern and eastern Ukraine, demonstrate that America and Western powers seeking to influence either domestic political structures or foreign policy directions in Ukraine cannot avoid Russian resistance.

Russia's strategic actions in Ukraine in 2014 veered toward the violent and military, but in other countries, such Armenia and Kyrgyzstan, Moscow has not had to rely on force to provide a counterweight to Western influence. In those countries, Russian economic support, organizations such as the Eurasian Economic Union (EEU), and policy advice has proven valuable to nondemocratic regimes seeking to stay in power. In the 1990s, when Russia's economy was much weaker, Moscow was unable to play this role, thus leaving the West alone in their efforts to influence politics in the post-soviet space. In the second decade of the twenty-first century, this is certainly no longer the case.

China presents a different kind of competition for America than does Russia. China rarely seeks to become as overtly and visibly involved in the internal workings of neighboring countries as Russia does, but still has a great deal of influence on many countries, primarily through trade and assistance. China offers trade deals and development opportunities, usually for resource-rich but otherwise poor countries, notably in Africa and Asia. For these countries, Chinese investment and assistance is distinct from Western assistance because there is no desire on the Chinese part to become involved in or change the politics of the country in question. Nor does China call for better human rights or greater freedoms in those countries. For nondemocratic leaders, this is appealing. Thus, while few countries want to, or can, emulate China's political institutions and structures, China is nonetheless a desirable partner for many countries.[18]

SOVEREIGNTY

Democracy promotion is also part of a broader redefinition of sovereignty in the post–Cold War world. Sovereignty is inevitably a complex notion, particularly given the high level of economic, environmental, and structural interdependence in the twenty-first century. It is also deeply related to relative strength and wealth. In a geopolitical context where dozens of states and multilateral organizations combine to give out billions of dollars in assistance in dozens of countries, sovereignty takes on a different meaning, as few states can genuinely function independent of foreign assistance. A large fraction of this money is, of course, used for assistance other than democracy work, but it is part of the context in which democracy work occurs.

Money spent on democracy promotion, however, cuts to the quick of the sovereignty question because democracy promotion engages some of the areas most essential to national sovereignty. Accepting democracy promotion money means accepting a relatively high level of foreign presences in elections, legislatures, and other sensitive political areas. Even for governments that value democracy promotion and would like to make their countries more democratic, this is a concern. For example, in many countries that receive democracy assistance from the United States, foreign powers, including the United States, help pay for elections. If an outside power pays for something as central to sovereignty and politically intimate as elections, this cannot help but raise questions, such as, to what extent does that country have real sovereignty? It also places the donor in a position to feel comfortable making demands about, and evaluating the quality of, those elections. In a global political environment with so much economic interdependence between countries, it is easy to overlook these kinds of questions, but in many places they remain important, if largely unstated.

Although assistance aimed at improving health, alleviating hunger, or responding to natural disasters may also in some respects undermine the sovereignty of the receiving country, most countries and most people are still happy to receive this assistance. Money used to promote democracy is different—one key difference is that it is not mutual—and cuts to the question of sovereignty in a different way.

When a major natural disaster hits a donor country, many countries offer support of various kinds to help respond to that crisis. We have seen this following earthquakes and hurricanes in the United States, earthquakes and tsunamis in Japan, and in other cases. Few see this support as anything other than what it is, a gesture of goodwill and assistance from one country to another. Thus disaster assistance is mutual, at least in theory, in that all donor countries could receive it at one time or another. America, for example, has accepted disaster relief from several countries including China, Australia, Japan, Israel, and France following Hurricanes Katrina in 2005 and Sandy in 2012.

Democracy promotion, however, is different. Democracy assistance is provided by the powerful, or those allied with the powerful, to the not powerful. Power and alliances are at least as important in determining where democracy assistance is funded as are democratic deficits and needs. An assessment of the state of democracy in America in the middle of the second decade of the twenty-first century, for example, would undoubtedly draw attention to antiquated political institutions that are ill-suited to the modern world, the lingering effects of racial prejudice, the rise of fundamentalist extremists, and the extent to which income inequality has undermined political and economic life. However, although USAID commissions democracy, rights, and governance (DRG) assessments for many countries to identify these types of needs and propose corresponding programs, no assessment of that kind for the United States will be undertaken by a foreign country and no follow-up programs will be established—not because they are not needed, but because the United States is rich and powerful. This may be obvious to the point that it is almost awkward to bring it up, but it is nonetheless true.

Despite its complicated relationship to American power both hard and soft, democracy promotion has, on balance, helped make many countries freer and more democratic while limiting the power of, and occasionally helping depose, authoritarian leaders across the globe. This is one of the most significant paradoxes of democracy promotion. Although it is an expression of American power that raises a number of important questions in key areas such as sovereignty and intervention between powerful and less powerful countries, democracy promotion has been far from an unambiguously negative force.

Nonetheless, the benign and often positive aspects of democracy promotion have been overshadowed in some countries by the broader negative effects of the U.S. role and in other countries by general ineffectiveness. In all countries these policies are only possible because of American power; but American power has changed since the halcyon days of democracy promotion in a postcommunist world eager to join the EU and NATO, and be part of the West.

AMERICAN POWER TODAY

Twenty years ago American power was defined by victory in the global struggle against communism. This victory was not only a significant accomplishment, highlighting the strength of the West and the United

States, but was also a moral victory, as the United States had, for the second time in half a century, played an instrumental role in defeating a brutal and murderous ideology. Today, however, the nature and extent of American power has changed substantially. In the twenty-first century, American power is still grounded in the size of the American economy, which—recession and debt notwithstanding—is still formidable. The enormous reach of American consumer and popular culture is also part of the foundation of American power, particularly soft power. In the area of geopolitics, however, American power is no longer defined by a victory over communism but by a war on terror that is best described as a stalemate. Moreover, in many but not all of the countries where the United States seeks to promote democracy, the moral position of the United States is now different. The victory over communism is for many a distant or irrelevant memory, while the lingering effect of the war in Iraq has colored the moral position of the United States in a very different hue.

The struggles against communism and, before that, fascism were ones in which the United States had many allies. These included countries that had fallen to fascist or communist forces and sought support from the United States in throwing off those authoritarian regimes, as well as countries that were threatened by fascism or communism. Today, no comparable dynamic exists. Jihadist terror is a real threat, of course, but it is targeted largely at America, Europe, and other Western allies; the best way for a country to avoid being targeted by those terrorists is to keep its distance from the United States. The war on terror is a global struggle therefore not comparable to the Cold War. This is a fundamental difference between the U.S. position in the world now compared with the period between 1941 and 1991.

The first decade or so following the collapse of communism saw U.S. democracy promotion bolstered by the perception that America was at the apex of its power. As that perception has changed, the effect and even relevance of U.S. democracy promotion has changed as well. Democracy promotion twenty years ago could be described as an outgrowth of U.S. power that contributed to the consolidation of democracy in several countries in different regions. Today it may still be, but it is also, in a significant way, an expression of U.S. power, encountering fewer successes in a world where authoritarianism has hardened in many countries.

For the United States, being able to support democracy in a given country serves many purposes. One may be a genuine commitment to making that country democratic. This is still part of what motivates much of democracy policy as well as many individuals, Americans and those in target countries, working on U.S.-supported democracy promotion projects. Another goal is to move that country toward a position that is more beneficial to the United States. These two purposes overlap, but only partially.

Last, and very significant, a major purpose of democracy work is to affirm the power dynamic between the United States and the target country. This intent may not be overt, but democracy promotion work is so steeped in this dynamic that it is unavoidable. In countries where America provides democracy support, the United States is almost constantly assessing the country, monitoring its progress through one rating or another, seeking to identify potential democratic leaders, and evaluating proposed laws and political development. These activities are the very essence, even the definition, of democracy assistance and are reflected in publications by U.S. democracy assistance donors and organizations. Titles such as "Best Practices in Democratic Governance: A Guide for Local Governments"[19] and "Tracking Democracy: Benchmark Surveys for Diagnostics, Program Design and Evaluation"[20] abound. A USAID-funded 2012 DRG assessment of the Democratic Republic of Congo (DRC), for example, notes in the executive summary that

> the core challenge to democratic governance in the DRC is that declines in checks and balances and in public accountability, and the failure to deliver public services have led to a breakdown in the social contract that was established with the 2006 transition. The practice of using government offices to serve private interests frustrates the population and starves the state of resources needed to provide public services. Limitations on political and civil rights and the concentration of executive power prevent both the public and other state institutions from ensuring the state acts in the general public interest. Failures in democratic governance lie at the root of the DRC's persistent economic stagnation and ongoing insecurity and conflict.[21]

This is a good assessment of the specifics of the challenges the DRC faced in 2012—but the problems are also massive in scale. The report follows up with several program recommendations, many of which are good but, taken together, are prima facie not sufficient to address the myriad problems facing the DRC. This type of assessment represents the power dynamic wherein the United States is the party identifying the problems—which are often very clear to many in the country—while implicitly, and often falsely, believing it is uniquely positioned to solve the problems. This approach may be part of any good-faith effort to strengthen democracy, but it is also a reminder and an expression of the power dynamic at every step.

Despite the U.S. vulnerability to critiques of its weakening democratic institutions, disturbing concentrations of wealth and power, or rising extremism, all these topics are viewed by Americans as domestic issues that are none of the business of the rest of the world. The consensus around this attitude spans party lines and is shared by both political elites and ordinary Americans.

Thus, the right of America to judge democracy in other countries is one of the rewards, and measures, of American power. Although democracy promotion is an expression of U.S. power, as America seeks to influence domestic politics and pass judgment on other countries, democracy promotion also becomes, ironically, a reflection of America's relative powerlessness. America has enough power and wealth to fund democracy programs in dozens of countries, but collectively these programs are bearing decreasing fruit in recent years. The power dynamic is close to becoming one of America using democracy programs simply as a way of asserting power for its own sake, rather than for any real chance of effecting change.

In some respects, therefore, it is less important whether or not U.S. democracy work is effective; most important to foreign policy elites is the fact of the work itself, as it reaffirms their view of the world and of the U.S. role in the world. Thinking about the best ways to remake the domestic politics of another country, determining what programs are best suited for that endeavor, and similar democracy promotion activities are in and of themselves expressions and reflections of American power.

This is a cynical interpretation of democracy work, but it resonates with the implementation of democracy promotion. Much of the internal

working of democracy assistance policy is focused not so much on outcomes but on identifying and securing ways for the United States to
become or remain involved in democracy work in each country. As mentioned, I have done various democracy-related assessments for donor
agencies like USAID and also for implementing partners like NDI, where
recommending that USAID discontinue its programs would not have
been accepted. Moreover, many of these assessments were program evaluations where I was asked specifically not to evaluate the impact of the
program but instead to focus on whether or not the contractor had implemented the program consistent with the requirements given by
USAID. It is obviously important that contractors receiving tax dollars
are honest and fulfill their obligations, but to simply ignore the effect
of their work on the broader development of democracy demonstrates
the bureaucratic and political imperatives underlying much of democracy work.

Becoming or remaining involved is obviously essential to democracy
work, but it often becomes a goal in itself; involvement in democracy
work increasingly becomes its own reward. In countries like Azerbaijan
or Cambodia, where millions of dollars for U.S. democracy work have
not led to marked improvements in democracy, the fact of the involvement itself is increasingly considered a meaningful and positive policy
outcome.

The question of U.S. involvement is too frequently framed as being
about whether or not the United States can find a way, a program, a
budget line, a local partner, or whatever else is needed to be involved in
country rather than about whether or not the work itself, in the terms
allowed by the undemocratic government, is what is needed to move democracy forward at that time. Bureaucratic logic is culpable, but that is
only part of the story. This direction for U.S. democracy promotion also
reflects America's internalized self-image as the global arbiter and eval-
uator of democracy and freedom and as a country uniquely able to solve
problems facing countries throughout the world. That self-image grows
in importance as it becomes increasingly difficult to effect democracy-
related outcomes around the world. Democracy promotion has become
a more important way to measure and express U.S. power, just as, para-
doxically, that power is waning in much of the world. The cost in money
and political capital of maintaining that vision of power is generally overlooked, but it is real.

This reflects paradoxes inherent in both U.S. power and democracy promotion. U.S. power is big enough that America is involved in every corner of the world, but sufficiently dispersed that it has limited influence in most parts of the world. Moreover, the United States is expected, by itself and by its allies, to be involved in every part of the world, so a failure to play a role in a country—regardless of its geographical remoteness or limited interest to the United States—is seen axiomatically as either an American moral failing or a reflection of declining U.S. power, or both. Therefore the reasons for America to not be involved in a country are almost always overlooked or downplayed. America is so powerful that it can no longer choose to stay out of a country without being seen as weak; this quandary also informs U.S. democracy promotion policy.

There are many countries where democracy work is unlikely to yield immediate results, largely because the problem—a consolidated authoritarian regime—is beyond the scope of the programs that constitute most democracy promotion work. However, to concede this and make an otherwise economically and politically prudent decision to stop doing democracy work in that country is an option that is rarely even entertained, because that decision would also be seen as a concession of weakness by the United States.

In this respect democracy promotion must be viewed in the context of the broader foreign policy and also the bipartisan foreign policy establishment that for the most part dominates thinking about U.S. foreign policy. For reasons including ideology, precedent, and its own self-preservation, this establishment is deeply committed to an approach to foreign policy that does not question the ability or appropriateness of the United States seeking to influence domestic and international political outcomes more or less everywhere. To discuss the practical side or efficacy of democracy promotion would inexorably lead to more general questioning of the U.S. role in the world and would threaten the consensus that leaders from both parties have worked so hard to build.

Obviously, this consensus frays from time to time, most notably when military intervention is being discussed. Although the wisdom of individual interventions is often vigorously debated, America's overall role in the world is still taken for granted. Democracy promotion is relevant to that dynamic, as it is one of the more benign-seeming forms of U.S. engagement and therefore can mobilize broad ideological and partisan support. This was not the case during the height of the Bush administration, but was true for decades preceding that and is again the case.

The core assumption undergirding most of U.S. foreign policy is that America can and should be deeply involved in the world's affairs. This is the primary cause of a foreign policy environment where everything that happens in the world is viewed not through the lens of trying to figure what is going on and why, but of what America should do about it. Promoting democracy fits into this framework well because it provides both a rationale and prescriptive guidance for how America can become involved in most countries and can be applied across the domestic American political spectrum. It is not difficult to make both progressive and conservative arguments supporting U.S. democracy promotion.

Democracy promotion is to some extent a goal of American power. The United States, according to this framework, seeks to project its power to help strengthen democracy globally. Democracy promotion, however, is more accurately understood as an expression of American power, as the United States, according to this frame, promotes democracy because it is powerful. This distinction is significant because it explains why America is likely to be committed to democracy promotion regardless of whether it is successful or not. Promoting democracy reinforces America's image of itself as powerful and able to influence outcomes throughout the world, regardless of the extent to which this perception is or is not true.

Democracy promotion has evolved as America's role in the world has changed. Modern democracy promotion was born out of a bipolar world where America needed allies and an ideological response to the Soviet Union, but the greatest successes of democracy promotion, and its institutionalization, occurred during a period when U.S. hegemony was at its highest. As America's influence has changed, democracy promotion's relationship to broader American foreign policy has changed as well.

CHAPTER EIGHT
THE FUTURE OF DEMOCRACY PROMOTION

DEMOCRACY PROMOTION IN ITS CURRENT form has been an integral part of U.S. foreign policy for more than a quarter of a century; in different but still significant forms it has been around considerably longer. In many respects it is inseparable from several of the central goals and activities of U.S. foreign policy, reflecting the policies and assumptions of the American state in the second decade of the twenty-first century and also those of the five or six decades preceding it. Democracy promotion is nonetheless a policy fraught with contradictions and paradoxes and grounded in assumptions about the United States and its position in the world that no longer apply the way they did even ten to fifteen years ago.

THE FUTURE OF DEMOCRACY PROMOTION

The future of U.S. democracy promotion will be framed by the changing role of the United States in the world, the evolving views of the American public concerning both U.S. involvement overseas and budget-related issues, and the consolidation of the world's nondemocratic regimes. During the 1990s, the formative years of modern U.S. democracy promotion, U.S. hegemony was strong, with few powers able to compete financially, politically, or ideologically with the United States. This made it possible for the United States to exert its influence regarding democracy and other issues throughout the globe in a way not seen before or since. In the last decade or so the world has become increasingly multipolar, thus limiting American influence in democracy and most other matters.

Powers like Russia can now oppose U.S. democracy promotion efforts through their own soft power, economic influence, energy resources, and military might. Likewise, China can exercise enormous economic power and provide substantial amounts of foreign assistance, a situation that simply did not exist twenty years ago. The field for U.S. democracy assistance is therefore not nearly as open as it was in the aftermath of the Cold War.

Domestic politics in the United States will also have an impact on the future of democracy promotion. Democracy promotion has never been, and is still not, a major concern of the American electorate, but the American people's changing view of the U.S. role in international affairs may well limit how democracy promotion can be pursued. As the economic downturn of 2008 hardens into a new and difficult reality for many middle-class and working poor Americans, the American appetite for an engaged interventionist foreign policy is also likely to continue to wane. Equally likely, it is only a matter of time before an ambitious politician or political party campaigns and wins on just that promise. Democracy promotion, as it is currently constructed, can exist only if the elite consensus on America's role in the world continues to set the tone for U.S. foreign policy generally.

The sharp change in the rhetorical emphasis on democracy promotion between the George W. Bush administration and the Obama administration demonstrates that even when the parts of the foreign policy consensus remain, democracy promotion can easily fade away from a central place. President Obama has not just shifted the rhetoric around democracy promotion, but has also reduced its role in U.S. foreign policy.[1]

Fiscal realities and perceptions will also likely reinforce this movement in public opinion against an active, engaged, and expensive U.S. foreign policy. For most of the Obama administration, the Republican

Party has focused its political attacks on government spending and the growing debt. Whether that is a real problem or a political talking point, there is a growing awareness among the American people that the state is spending too much. This will make it easier for those seeking to roll back U.S. involvement in international affairs, including democracy promotion efforts. Democracy promotion, while not expensive in the context of U.S. government spending, is vulnerable because the activities are seen alternately as either ineffective or insignificant.

The global environment for democracy promotion is also influenced by the evolution of nondemocratic regimes around the world. Although at any given time a handful of countries, such as Myanmar or Ukraine today, are either postconflict or genuinely transitioning, most of the world's nondemocratic countries are consolidated authoritarian or semi-authoritarian regimes. Azerbaijan, Vietnam, and Bahrain, for example, cannot be legitimately described as transitioning anymore. In these countries it is difficult to advance democracy through democracy promotion as it is currently structured, particularly because most democracy promotion programs continue to rely on the unstated assumption of at least some cooperation between the NGOs and the government. In consolidated nondemocratic regimes, this cooperation is not going to occur. This atmosphere is a striking contrast to the 1990s, when many countries emerging from communism or other forms of authoritarian governance were led by people anxious to consolidate democracy. Promoting democracy today in consolidated nondemocratic regimes forces the United States either to commit to ineffective and wasteful programs or to recognize the paradox inherent in trying to change the government in a country that is often a U.S. ally. This is a difficult quandary for the United States, but continuing to ignore it is unlikely to bolster democracy work.

This changing dynamic could raise important questions for democracy promotion and U.S. foreign policy. Azerbaijan is an example of this phenomenon. For reasons of resources and security—its access to Caspian Sea oil and its position as a moderate Shia Muslim country that borders Iran—Azerbaijan has been an important ally of the United States. It has also never been democratic and has been resistant to U.S. efforts to move it in that direction. In 2014 and 2015, as Azerbaijan became increasingly and more visibly repressive, cracking down on all opposition, arresting journalists, and the like, the alliance with the United States became strained. This led Azerbaijan to explore shifting its alliance to Russia, or at least ensuring less tension with Russia.

Russia's strong alliance with Armenia probably precludes a close Moscow-Baku relationship, but again Azerbaijan is operating in a context of competing powers, of which Russia is one. U.S. foreign policy analysts, most of whom are keenly aware of the authoritarian slant of Azerbaijan's ruling Aliyev family, must weigh the cost of putting more pressure on that regime in the context of competing interests.

Despite these problems facing democracy promotion, the policy is unlikely to go away. The default setting for the future of democracy promotion is for it to continue in more or less its current form. The policy will not disappear simply because it is no longer effective or because it is more suited for an international environment that no longer exists. This is not how the logic of bureaucracy and institutions function in Washington. Too many powerful interests support democracy promotion for it to be politically worthwhile for any policymaker to try to dismantle it without first building broad public support for the idea. In its current form there is only limited room for democracy promotion to adapt, for programs to be crafted differently, for cooperation with governments to be reduced, and for changes of a similar scale to be implemented.

While the structures used to implement democracy promotion and the assumptions underlying them may be out of date, those considerations are separate from the value of democracy promotion as a whole. The question of whether democracy promotion is effective in its current form is different from the questions of whether democracy promotion could work or whether it is wise for the United States to continue to pursue it. The goals of democracy promotion have at best always existed in the gray area where national interests and an altruistic belief in democracy and freedom overlap. If those are still goals the United States thinks are worth pursuing, and if America is disappointed in how progress in these areas has slowed down, then rethinking how democracy promotion is done is reasonably necessary.

Several possible scenarios present themselves for the future of democracy promotion. Determining which is best for the United States and how best to implement it is the heart of the challenge for those who believe the complex goals of democracy work are still worth pursuing.

CONTINUING TO STUMBLE THROUGH

The first and most likely scenario is that U.S. democracy promotion two, five, or even ten years from now will look a lot like it does today. In this scenario, democracy will continue to stumble through as a policy decreasingly relevant and effective but nonetheless benign and able to make a positive, albeit modest, impact. This path of least resistance does not involve bureaucratic shakeups, legislative innovation, or bold political leadership. Democracy promotion could also improve in this scenario, although probably only incrementally, as programs improve, new technologies and methodologies are incorporated into the work, program evaluation becomes more effective, and other innovations are implemented.

The infrastructure of democracy promotion in the United States, including donor organizations like USAID and the NED and semi-governmental organizations like NDI, IRI, and IFES, as well as numerous contractors and consultants, is relatively strong and can easily endure for several years. Infrastructure could change slightly: some NGOs could become less important, more funding might shift to contracting, the United States might increase its direct funding to local NGOs, or new American NGOs could assume major roles in democracy promotion. These or similar types of changes, however, would not alter the framework within which democracy programs are implemented and executed. Funding would probably also continue to decrease, but gradually.[2] This scenario is one in which bureaucratic logic and institutional entropy would play a growing role in the future of democracy promotion, as it would require more political resources and effort to change it than it would to keep it in its current form.

In this scenario, the paradoxes that have characterized democracy promotion and limited its effectiveness would continue unchallenged and unresolved for the foreseeable future. Democracy promotion strategies and approaches would not be changed to reflect the current state of democracy and authoritarianism in many countries. In other words, the transition paradigm would still frame much of American democracy work. Avoiding the difficult questions and paradoxes surrounding democracy work is no way to make the work more effective, but it may in fact be a good strategy for ensuring its continuation.

Inevitably in this scenario, democracy promotion would return to the periphery of foreign policy, as it would not be a valuable tool for policy-makers. Successes would be limited and would continue to be programmatic rather than outcome-oriented—a good program, well thought out and implemented efficiently, would be considered a discrete success regardless of its overall effectiveness. For example, a good domestic observation campaign or a successful workshop for MPs might be successful programs but may have limited impact. And, as has been the case since around 2009 in most democratic breakthroughs (or more accurately, collapses of authoritarian and semi-authoritarian regimes), U.S. democracy promotion has not been at the center of most significant political changes in nondemocratic countries. From 2009 to 2014, in countries in the former Soviet Union such as Kyrgyzstan, Georgia, and Ukraine, as well as the Arab Spring countries of North Africa, the democracy promotion community was largely on the sidelines seeking to catch up to events. This dynamic is unlikely to change.

This scenario is appealing, at least in the short run, as it demands little from any of the major players in democracy promotion. NGOs and contractors do not have to rethink their approach to the work they do, and policymakers do not have to question the assumptions with which they have become comfortable or resolve the paradoxes that hamstring their work. Those policymakers who want less U.S. involvement in the international arena or who are concerned about cutting spending would also be satisfied in this scenario, as they could point to stagnant or decreasing budgets and a democracy promotion policy that is becoming less significant over time. In the long run, however, it would likely lead to decreasing budgets and relevance: democracy assistance would have fewer successes, and organizations working in the field would find themselves more frequently at the periphery of politics in the countries where they work and at the periphery of foreign policy discussions in Washington.

If this scenario comes to pass, democracy promotion could begin to occupy a different position. Currently democracy assistance has elements of both political and development work. Some democracy work, particularly that which involves working closely with and advising political leaders and actors, is explicitly political; other elements of the work that emphasize capacity building and civil society are better understood as development work. If democracy promotion does not change, it will begin to move more clearly to the development side of the spectrum as the relationships and openings necessary to do political work will continue to fall away. This means that capacity building, leadership training, exchanges, and the like could become a bigger part of democracy assistance, while advising political parties, supporting democracy movements, and similar work would be minimized.

This scenario does not preclude innovation by those working in the field, as democracy promotion will still draw smart, hardworking, and dedicated people, but this innovation will occur in a circumscribed environment. Party programs will be more thoughtful, election monitoring will continue to become even more comprehensive, and new technologies will continue to provide legislatures the tools to be more responsive and accountable, but these will be technical improvements and thus have only limited impact. Democracy promotion has long been strongest and best positioned to address precisely these types of technical issues; in this scenario, it will soon be all that democracy work can do.

The stumbling through scenario is probably the most likely; it has been happening in the democracy promotion area for several years now. Democracy promotion policies, although not always the technical substance of programs, have remained largely unchanged over the last five to ten years despite their changed context, quite different from the one in which the programs were developed and thrived almost twenty years ago. The policy has continued because the cost of changing it, to both domestic politics and international perception, has been too high; but neither has it been fixed or substantially improved, because the steps necessary for that are too difficult.

This scenario works for most of the stakeholders in democracy promotion but is unlikely to meaningfully advance democracy anywhere in the world. It keeps the United States involved in many countries, but in a limited way, and allows the United States to postpone having to resolve the paradoxes in its policies on democracy. In this regard it is an outcome with which everybody can live and about which nobody will be excited.

REDUCING OR ELIMINATING DEMOCRACY PROMOTION

A second scenario that could occur in the next few years is that the scope of democracy promotion could be substantially reduced or almost eliminated. The latter is only possible if the anti-internationalist segment of the American electorate is able to win significant electoral power, probably including the presidency. While this appears unlikely at the moment, it certainly cannot be ruled out over the next ten to fifteen years. In 2011, more than a third of the members of the House of Representatives supported the abolishment of USAID. There is a lot of distance between that and actually abolishing or even substantially cutting USAID, but it demonstrates how popular those types of ideas already are and can become.

Democracy promotion is not likely to be radically cut in 2016 unless an ideological Libertarian such as Rand Paul or a far left Democrat such as Bernie Sanders were to get elected. Both of these candidates have extremely slim chances of winning in 2016. Most of the other major candidates, including Hillary Clinton, Marco Rubio, and Ted Cruz, are firmly in the mainstream of foreign policy thinking and would not seek to make such a drastic change to democracy policy should they become president. The foreign policy beliefs of entertainer candidates like Donald Trump and Ben Carson are less clear, but will probably be much more in the Republican mainstream on these issues if they become successful as the campaign goes on. However, the party that loses the election in 2016 may find a strong anti-interventionist caucus in their own party, particularly as that sentiment has its adherents on both sides of the ideological and partisan divide. Should the Democrats nominate Hillary Clinton and lose, there will be pressure to do things differently the next time. A similar fate could await the Republicans if they nominate someone other than Rand Paul—who is not likely to depart the national political scene anytime soon—and lose. In either case, a smart ambitious national politician, who could come from either party, will see that political opening and possibly try to exploit it.

This scenario, unlike the previous one, would require a proactive policy decision and would upset several powerful stakeholders, so it is less likely to happen. However, there is also political gain to be had for those who lead the implementation of this scenario. A member of Congress, riding a powerful isolationist and budget-conscious wave of public opinion, could devote herself to this effort and be rewarded with a visible national profile.

The political argument for this approach is straightforward and likely to appeal to an electorate that has lost much of its confidence in America's ability to accomplish things overseas and is increasingly wary about spending. It would not be at all hard to publicize the money spent on democracy work, the relative lack of success in recent years, and even to highlight a few programs that can be presented as costly and wasteful. Examples of study tours for people who ended up on the wrong side of democracy, trips overseas for unpopular American political figures to talk about democracy, workshops for parliaments that were soon disbanded, and the like would strike many Americans, particularly if presented strategically, as compelling reasons to defund democracy work.

Although democracy assistance still has many supporters, those supporters tend to be insiders, as there is little widespread popular support for—or even popular understanding of—democracy work. Many in Washington, not least powerful board members of organizations such as the NED, IRI, or NDI, would defend the need to fund democracy work, but if that legislative fight ever appeared in a more public arena, those voices would have a more difficult time mobilizing popular support for democracy work.

A 2013 Pew study reports that

promoting democracy in other nations in recent decades has not been a top priority for the American public. A new Pew Research Center survey on "America's Place in the World" found that just 18% of those surveyed cited this as a top foreign policy objective, putting it at the bottom of a list of priorities. Since 1993, the share of Americans saying promotion of democracy was a top priority has never topped 29%.[3]

Given this relative lack of public support for democracy promotion, dramatically cutting democracy work appears at first glance to be an easy, if flawed, solution to the democracy promotion paradox. If sufficient political support existed for it, enormous cuts to USAID's democracy and governance division and defunding the NED, NDI, and IRI would kick the legs out from under the stool of U.S. democracy assistance, but it would not, and could not, end the policy entirely. U.S. democracy assistance is, after all, much more than funding to a few offices, programs, and organizations. It is an approach to, and reflection of, foreign policy and the U.S. role in the world, which manifests throughout the foreign policy arena. Simply cutting funding for democracy work would not stop American leaders from speaking about the need for greater democracy and rights or stop the pressure, both internally and externally, on the U.S. government to support various struggles for democracy around the world.

Therefore, meaningfully reducing the U.S. mission of democracy promotion would require rethinking the overall approach to foreign policy in a way that is unlikely to occur and that, if it did, would cause changes in U.S. policy far greater than those directly affecting democracy work.

One of the paradoxes of democracy promotion is that, on one hand, it is a bounded and relatively low-budget set of programs and also, on the other hand, is one of the pillars of American foreign policy. Genuinely cutting democracy promotion requires addressing both these angles. The former is obviously much easier to do, but the latter is probably more important. To remove democracy promotion as a pillar of U.S. foreign policy would require more than just cutting budgets, but also reframing the issue of America's role in the world, disassembling a large and powerful foreign policy establishment, and disrupting U.S. relationships with key, and not so key, allies. This would have global impact, as the United States would be changing its strategy and positioning in almost every region.

For these reasons, this second option is unlikely to fully occur, but it is possible that efforts to at least partially defund parts of direct democracy promotion will succeed, thereby substantially changing the face of democracy work.

BECOMING MORE CONFRONTATIONAL

One of the central paradoxes of democracy promotion, which has become more pronounced in recent years, is that U.S. democracy promotion seeks to peacefully and gradually expand democracy in countries that, as the years go by, look less like transitional governments and more like consolidated authoritarian or semi-authoritarian regimes. The United States has for the most part addressed the paradox by ignoring it. This approach is reasonable in the broader diplomatic and foreign policy context, but it has limited the effectiveness of democracy promotion.

It is possible that the democracy promotion policy community will shift gears in the coming years and adopt a more aggressive, perhaps even confrontational, approach to democracy promotion. This would begin with a recognition that most of the countries where the United States is currently seeking to strengthen, expand, or build democracy are governed by regimes that, regardless of their broader foreign policy orientation, are undemocratic and committed to staying that way. This recognition would lead to two clear policy changes.[4]

First, democracy programs would focus more on making change rather than on modest improvements to existing institutions. For example, fewer resources would be committed to programs helping bureaucracies and legislatures in undemocratic countries function more effectively, while more emphasis would be placed on civil society organizations committed to highlighting the undemocratic nature of the government or working on a more strategic level with democratic-leaning political parties and forces.

This approach would not require an investment of more resources, but a reallocation of existing resources. Programs seeking to partner with government institutions would be eschewed in favor of those working with more radical civil society organizations, independent media outlets, and opposition political parties. The United States has a fair amount of experience with these types of programs, but primarily in undemocratic countries that are also not American allies such as Belarus, Russia, or Cuba, where programs have often been more discreet, and even clandestine, than in most countries. States like Azerbaijan or Vietnam do not have nearly as negative a relationship with the United States as those countries do, but regarding human rights and democracy are not dramatically different from Belarus, Russia, or Cuba.

There might even be a fair amount of support for this type of programming at USAID, the NED, and U.S.-funded NGOs that work on democracy. These organizations (or in the case of USAID, the democracy and governance office) and the people who work for them believe in democracy and the U.S. role in promoting it. They would likely be open to approaches that place democracy more front and center and that lead to more programs likely to have a greater impact on democracy.

Policymakers charged with working on U.S. foreign policy more broadly and with placing democracy promotion in its proper context, however, would likely be less enthused about a more aggressive approach to democracy work. Pursuing such a policy would complicate and even threaten relations with the United States and dozens of valuable, if undemocratic, allies. For this reason, the second policy change for this strategy—being more consistent and confrontational in providing political support for democracy work—is unlikely to happen.

A more confrontational approach to democracy work would require not only a change in democracy programming, but a broader change in the language, rhetoric, and politics surrounding U.S. democracy work. For example, during the last few decades elections in countries with which the United States enjoys a good relationship have been recognized as legitimate regardless of the extent or degree of fraud. Observers have dutifully reported the fraud, at least most of the time, but the results and overall legitimacy of the elections have not been challenged by the United States, and the winners of those elections, regardless of the quality of the election, have been able to assume office without any obstacles presented by the United States or the West. Nor have there been any meaningful consequences for fraudulent elections. Choosing a more confrontational approach would require changing this.

Likewise, diplomats and other representatives of the U.S. government would have to provide support for a more aggressive approach to democracy work by highlighting problems of democracy, making it clear to the relevant governments that it is a top priority for the United States and not asking democracy organizations to tone down or moderate their work.

The advantages of this approach are reasonably clear. First, it would resolve a major paradox that colors and weakens democracy work, thereby freeing democracy promotion to have a significantly greater impact and allowing innovative and effective programs a better chance of flourishing. Second, it would lead to more support for the United States from those currently fighting for democracy who are increasingly aware of the limits of what the United States will do in support of their efforts. Third, and most obvious, it would lead to more effective and, in the long term, more successful programs.

Unfortunately, the problems of this approach are equally apparent. It would require a substantial rethinking of democracy work and indeed much of American foreign policy. Democracy promoters rarely have the upper hand in the U.S. foreign policy community and are unlikely to get it anytime soon. For this reason, it is hard to imagine this scenario coming to pass.

A MORE STRATEGIC APPROACH

The last potential shift in democracy promotion would be to continue to do democracy work, but to approach it more strategically. Rather than applying the same battery of democracy programs in more or less whatever nondemocratic country will allow it, a more strategic approach would entail targeting fewer countries, putting more resources into those countries, and making an effort to craft programs that address the specific needs and political environment in each. This may mean moving away from a methodology that rests heavily on technical support and capacity building. This reform is intuitively appealing, as becoming more strategic always sounds like a wise decision in any endeavor.

The problem with a more strategic approach to democracy promotion is twofold. First, the decisions that would drive strategy are difficult to make. Determining which countries are most likely to have a democratic breakthrough or consolidate democracy, in which countries democracy is most likely to help the United States, and which programs are most likely to help achieve these goals is difficult.

In the last decade or two, democratic breakthroughs have occurred in a range of countries, from weak semi-democratic regimes like Shevardnadze's Georgia to stronger authoritarian regimes like Mubarak's Egypt. Similar regimes, for example Egypt and Azerbaijan under the Aliyevs, have experienced very different fates, as some nondemocratic regimes have collapsed while others that in most key respects appear similar have become stronger. Indeed, the collapse of most nondemocratic regimes usually appears unimaginable only a few months before it happens and inevitable a few short months later—or, less usefully for analysts, most regimes are stable until they are not. Further, democratic breakthroughs have occurred in countries such as Ukraine in 2004 or Georgia in 2003, where democracy promotion organizations were well funded, able to function, and influential, as well as in countries, such as most of the North African states of the Arab Spring, where this has not been the case.

Devising a more strategic approach to democracy work requires information and analysis that does not yet exist and will be hard to develop. Too much is contested: disagreements about the regime types of different countries, the efficacy of various strategies, and, of course, the strategic value of a given country are likely to remain widespread in the future. Building an analytical consensus around which to craft a more strategic policy will therefore be difficult. It might work, however, for the State Department simply to decide priorities and target a few countries, regardless of the absence of good analytical arguments for or against a particular country.

Disputation about regime types, strategic approaches, and the relative importance of countries is exacerbated by the bureaucratic incentives facing not only democracy work, but also foreign policy more broadly. In addition to organizations working in democracy that have incentives to continue working in a large number of countries, each country and region of the world has a battery of experts, think tank personnel, academics, NGO officers, and others who have a stake in assistance programs being implemented in the country or region they study. One of the key ways they generate support is through consistently stressing the strategic importance of whatever part of the world they study. An American approach to democracy assistance that questioned or threatened the existing consensus that every region of the world is strategically vital would meet a great deal of resistance. The resistance would be bureaucratic as well as political. Supporters of both an internationalist foreign policy and a more isolationist one might be able to unify behind this approach—the former because it would provide for continued U.S. involvement in key countries and the latter because it would somewhat limit the scope and breadth of U.S. commitments internationally.

These hurdles are significant, but the upside of a more strategic approach is apparent and substantial. Democracy promotion would be much more effective if it evolved, from a general policy pursued in dozens of countries and aimed at achieving moderate and nonconfrontational goals, into a targeted policy seeking meaningful democratic change in a handful of countries that were either poised for a democratic breakthrough or at a key juncture of democratic consolidation. Democracy promotion would also benefit from moving away from the civil society/legislative support/political party development/election monitoring paradigm currently being applied in virtually every country and toward a framework individually developed for each country based on needs and opportunities.

Democracy promotion can also be made more strategically sophisticated without taking on the very difficult task of restructuring democracy promotion more broadly; for example, democracy programs could be tailored more appropriately to the countries in which they are implemented. This evolution would not necessarily involve stopping democracy work in some countries or cutting funding for programs or organizations too deeply, so it would not encounter as much bureaucratic opposition.

It is striking that even modestly sharpening the strategic framework of democracy work is a challenging task likely to encounter meaningful institutional resistance, but this speaks to the overall state of democracy promotion and the depth of the paradoxes that define it.

CONCLUSION

Democracy promotion remains deeply embedded in paradoxes. The work is both essential and modest. Democracy promoters aim to radically reshape the domestic politics of countries, but seek to do it while working cooperatively with the governments of those countries. Critics see democracy promotion as both undermining sovereignty and as an expression of American imperialism, but sometimes see it as simply ineffective as well. Democracy promotion, in its contemporary form, largely evolved from a moment of unique American hegemony but continues despite an electorate that has lost confidence, a rise in competing powers, and a budgetary situation in the United States that has led many to oppose government spending of any kind. It is that environment in which democracy promotion today attempts to operate.

Democracy promotion has been characterized by impressive if easily overlooked accomplishments; it has contributed to the spread of democracy to parts of the world where democracy would have been completely unimaginable a few decades ago. Democracy promotion continues to provide valuable guidance and oversight to many of the world's remaining nondemocratic countries. However, it is difficult not to recognize that democracy promotion also appears to have stalled in recent years. In some countries democracy itself has stalled. In others, from the former Soviet Union to the Middle East and North Africa, the largest democracy-related gains have occurred without a great deal of involvement from the organs of American democracy promotion. This stagnation is a result of a changing world where democracy, and the West, now have strong ideological and political rivals, but also a result of a set of policies that have not evolved to meet these new challenges.

Addressing the paradoxes that limit the effectiveness of democracy promotion is not easy. These paradoxes have existed, and have been dutifully ignored, for years. Addressing or even recognizing them would force America to have to rethink not only its democracy work, but also its foreign policy more broadly. For example, recognizing that cooperating with consolidated nondemocratic regimes is not an effective strategy for nurturing democracy would logically lead to either questioning that cooperation—and therefore the broader bilateral relationship with that country—or recognizing that democracy is not a sufficient priority to risk jeopardizing a bilateral relationship between governments.

Democracy promotion is both a stand-alone policy and deeply embedded in U.S. foreign and domestic politics. Significantly altering democracy promotion will have an impact on foreign policy in general. Cutting these programs will signal a less engaged United States. Becoming more confrontational will create more rifts between the United States and other countries. Changing little will ensure that democracy work remains ineffective but that the basic orientation of the United States toward the rest of the world does not change.

The paradoxes surrounding democracy promotion should be viewed in this context. Resolving the paradoxes is only possible if they are examined relative to broader American foreign policy. The question of how to make democracy promotion work better cannot be separated from questions of how America sees itself in the world or how important democracy really is to the United States. Unfortunately, these questions too frequently go unaddressed.

NOTES

PREFACE

1. Tsveta Petrova, "The New Role of Central and Eastern Europe in International Democracy Support" (Washington: Carnegie Endowment for International Peace, 2011); Laurynas Jonavicius, "The Democracy Promotion Polices of Central and Eastern European States" (Madrid: Fundación para las Relaciones Internacionales y el Diálogo Exterior, 2008).

2. Gerd Schonwalder, "Promoting Democracy: What Role for Emerging Powers?" (Bonn: German Development Institute, 2014); Sarah Repucci, "The Democracy Promotion Gap," *The American Interest*, December 8, 2014.

3. Andrew Youngs, *Europe's Role in World Politics: A Retreat from Liberal Internationalism* (New York: Routledge, 2010); *International Democracy and the West: The Role of Governments, NGOs and Multinationals* (Oxford University Press, 2004); and *The European Union and the Promotion of Democracy: Europe's Mediterranean and East Asian Policies* (Oxford University Press, 2002). Also Frank Schimmelfennig and Hanno Scholtz, "EU Democracy Promotion in the European Neighbourhood, Political Conditionality, Economic Development, and Transnational Exchange" (European Union Politics, 2008).

4. Peter Burnell cites "a variety of terms to describe the many countries whose transitions from dictatorship toward democracy have only been very partial . . . 'hyphenated democracy' . . . semi-democracy, illiberal democracy, facade democracy, partial democracy, virtual democracy, delegative democracy and so forth" (Peter Burnell, "Promoting Democracy," *Government and Opposition*

48, no. 2 [April 2013], pp. 265–87). Writing more than fifteen years earlier, David Collier and Steven Levitsky describe "a surprising number of (regime) subtypes involving democracy 'with adjectives.' Examples from among the hundreds of subtypes that have appeared include 'authoritarian democracy,' 'neo-patrimonial democracy,' 'military-dominated democracy,' and 'proto-democracy' " (David Collier and Steven Levitsky, "Democracy with Adjectives: Conceptual Innovation in Comparative Research," *World Politics* 49, no. 3 [April 1997], pp. 430–51).

5. Thomas Carothers, "The End of the Transition Paradigm," *Journal of Democracy* 13, no. 1 (January 2002), p. 10.

6. Carothers, "The End of the Transition Paradigm," pp. 11–12.

7. Marina Ottaway, *Democracy Challenged: The Rise of Semi-Authoritarianism* (Washington: Carnegie Endowment for International Peace, 2002), p. 3.

CHAPTER 1

1. Freedom House, "Contending with Putin's Russia: A Call for American Leadership," February 6, 2013, p. 2.

2. Tony Smith, *America's Mission: The United States and the Worldwide Struggle for Democracy in the Twentieth Century* (Princeton University Press, 1994).

3. USAID, "Budget and Spending" (www.usaid.gov/results-and-data/budget -spending).

4. USAID, Azerbaijan Country Development Cooperation Strategy 2011–2016 (http://pdf.usaid.gov/pdf_docs/PDACU274.pdf).

5. See Freedom House, Azerbaijan Country Reports, 2005–2014 (http:// freedomhouse.org/country/azerbaijan#.U1VW9V64nFI).

6. James Sharp, "Egypt: Background and US Relations," Congressional Research Service, March 3, 2015 (www.fas.org/sgp/crs/mideast/RL33003 .pdf).

7. Anne Mariel Peters, "Why Obama Shouldn't Increase Democracy Aid to Egypt," *Foreign Policy*, February 14, 2011 (http://foreignpolicy.com/2011/02/14 /why-obama-shouldnt-increase-democracy-aid-to-egypt/).

8. Foreign Aid Explorer (http://gbk.eads.usaidallnet.gov).

9. International Republican Institute (http://iri.org/learn-more-about-iri-0).

10. Griff Witte, "NGO Workers Convicted in Egypt," *Washington Post*, June 4, 2013.

11. Dan Murphy, "Egypt to Global Democracy NGOs: Drop Dead," *Christian Science Monitor*, June 4, 2013.

12. Freedom House, Annual Report, 2013.

13. Jeffrey Pickering and Mark Peceny, "Forging Democracy at Gunpoint," *International Studies Quarterly* 50, no. 3 (September 2006), pp. 539–60.

14. See "Iraq: Democracy at Gunpoint," *The Economist*, January 27, 2005, or "Gunpoint Democracy," *San Francisco Chronicle*, April 13, 2002.

15. Rahul Mahajan, "Gunpoint Democracy in Iraq," *The Progressive*, August 31, 2003 (www.progressive.org/node/1093).

16. Jesse Jackson Jr., "Iraq: From Gunboat Diplomacy to Gunpoint Democracy," March 28, 2003 (www.commondreams.org).

17. Tom Hayden, "The Cold War that Threatens Democracy," *The Nation*, March 20, 2014.

18. Stephen Gowans, "What's Left: The Role and Aims of US Democracy Promotion in the Attempted Color Revolution in Iran," July 4, 2009 (http://gowans.wordpress.com/2009/07/04/the-role-and-aims-of-us-democracy-promotion-in-the-attempted-color-revolution-in-iran/).

19. U.S. Department of State, "Strategic Plan: Fiscal Years 2007–2012," May 7, 2007, pp. 4, 18.

20. Ibid., "Strategic Plan: 2014–2017," March 17, 2014, p. 30.

21. Amy McDonough, "Human Rights and the Failing of US Public Diplomacy in Eurasia," Policy Brief, Open Society Institute, Washington, February 2013 (www.opensocietyfoundations.org/sites/default/files/Policy%20Brief%20-%20Human%20Rights%20and%20the%20Failings%20of%20US%20Public%20Diplomacy.pdf).

22. David Reiff, "Democracy No!" *Democracy* 24 (Spring 2012) (www.democracyjournal.org/24/democracy-no.php).

23. Nicole Bibbins Sedaca and Nicolas Bouchet, "Holding Steady: US Democracy Promotion in a Changing World," Chatham House, London, February 2014 (www.chathamhouse.org/sites/default/files/home/chatham/public_html/sites/default/files/170214DemocracyPromotion.pdf).

24. Kenneth Wollack, "Democracy Promotion: Serving U.S. Values and Interests," *Northwestern Law Review* (2008) (www.law.northwestern.edu/lawreview/v102/n1/433/LR102n1Wollack.pdf).

25. Cassie Spodak, "McCain Calls US Military Support for Ukraine 'Right and Decent,'" *CNN Politicker*, March 14, 2014 (http://politicalticker.blogs.cnn.com/2014/03/15/mccain-calls-u-s-military-support-for-ukraine-right-and-decent/).

26. Pew Research Center, "Most Say US Should 'Not Get Too Involved' in Ukraine Situation," March 11, 2014 (www.people-press.org/2014/03/11/most-say-u-s-should-not-get-too-involved-in-ukraine-situation/).

27. "Where We Work," National Democratic Institute (www.ndi.org/wherewework).

28. Ibid.

29. See, for example, Immanuel Wallerstein, *Decline of American Power: The U.S. in a Chaotic World* (New York: New Press, 2003); Geir Lundestad, *The Rise and Decline of American "Empire": Power and Its Limits in Comparative Perspective*

(Oxford University Press, 2012); or Charles Kupchan, *No One's World: The West, the Rising West, and the Coming Global Turn* (New York: Council on Foreign Relations, 2012).

30. Noam Chomsky, "Humanitarian Imperialism: The New Doctrine of Imperial Right," *Monthly Review* 60, no. 4 (2008) (http://monthlyreview.org/2008/09/01/humanitarian-imperialism-the-new-doctrine-of-imperial-right).

31. Rand Paul, "Senator Rand Paul: Why I'm Voting No on Syria," *Time*, September 4, 2013.

32. Pat Buchanan, "Outside Agitators," Creators.com, 2013 (www.creators.com/opinion/pat-buchanan/outside-agitators.html). Although it is tempting to dismiss the angry, anti-Semitic, and increasingly marginalized Buchanan, his views on democracy promotion are not unreflective of what many Americans believe.

CHAPTER 2

1. George W. Bush, Second Inaugural Address, January 20, 2005.

2. White House, "A National Security Strategy of Engagement and Enlargement," February 1995, p. 2 (http://nssarchive.us/?page_id=64).

3. Jonathan Monten, "The Roots of the Bush Doctrine: Power, Nationalism and Democracy Promotion in US Strategy," *International Security* 29, no. 4 (Spring 2005), pp. 112–56, p. 113.

4. Tony Smith, *America's Mission: The United States and the Worldwide Struggle for Democracy in the Twentieth Century* (Princeton University Press, 1994), p. 43.

5. Thomas Carothers, *Aiding Democracy Abroad: The Learning Curve* (Washington: Carnegie Endowment for International Peace, 1999), p. 19.

6. Takashi Inoguchi, "Post-Second World War Japan," in *The Edinburgh Companion to the History of Democracy*, ed. Benjamin Isakhan and Stephen Stockwell (Edinburgh University Press, 2012), p. 305.

7. Alexander B. Downes and Jonathan Monten, "Forced to Be Free? Why Foreign-Imposed Regime Change Rarely Leads to Democratization," *International Security* 37, no. 4 (Spring 2013), pp. 90–131, p. 15.

8. Larry Diamond, *Squandered Victory: The American Occupation and the Bungled Effort to Bring Democracy to Iraq* (New York: Times Books), p. 27.

9. Nora Benashel and others, "After Saddam: Prewar Planning and the Postwar Occupation of Iraq," Rand Corporation, p. xvii (www.rand.org/content/dam/rand/pubs/monographs/2008/RAND_MG642.pdf).

10. Stanley Nider Katz, "Democratic Constitutionalism after Military Occupation: Reflections on the United States' Experience in Japan, Germany, Afghanistan and Iraq," *Common Knowledge* 12, no. 2 (Spring 2006), pp. 181–96, p. 186.

11. Lloyd E. Ambrosius, "Woodrow Wilson and George W. Bush: Historical Comparisons of Ends and Means in Their Foreign Policies," *Diplomatic History* 30, no. 3 (2006), pp. 509–43.

12. Smith, *America's Mission*. For more on democratic peace theory, see, for example, Michael Doyle "Kant, Liberal Legacies, and Foreign Affairs: Parts I and II," *Philosophy and Public Affairs* 12, no. 3 (Summer 1983), pp. 205–35.

13. Kenneth McCreedy, "Planning the Peace: Operation Eclipse and the Occupation of Germany," *Journal of Military History* 65 (July 2001), pp. 713–40, p. 714.

14. Ibid., p. 738.

15. See, for example, Jason Brownlee, "Can America Nation-Build?" *World Politics* 59, no. 2 (January 2007), pp. 314–40; or Katz, "Democratic Constitutionalism after Military Occupation," but this view is most noticeable, and least challenged, in the media and among many nonspecialist pundits.

16. Robert Morgenthau, *Germany Is Our Problem* (New York: Harper and Brothers, 1945).

17. Andrei Cherny, *The Candy Bombers* (New York: G. P. Putnam and Sons, 2008), p. 85.

18. Smith, *America's Mission*, pp. 157–58.

19. Thomas Carothers, *Aiding Democracy Abroad*, pp. 19–25.

20. Smith, *America's Mission*, pp. 217–218.

21. Hugh Wilford, *The Mighty Wurlitzer: How the CIA Played America* (Harvard University Press, 2008), p. 7.

22. Sung Bin Ko, "Confucian Leninist State: The People's Republic of China," *Asian Perspective* 23, no. 2 (1999), pp. 225–44.

23. Nick Serafino and others, "US Occupation Assistance: Iraq, Germany and Japan Compared," *Congressional Research Service*, March 23, 2006 (www.fas .org/sgp/crs/natsec/RL33331.pdf). Figures are in 2005 dollars.

24. Smith, *America's Mission*, p. 162.

25. Ibid.

26. Philippe Schmitter, "More Liberal, Preliberal or Postliberal," *Journal of Democracy* 6, no. 1 (January 1995), pp. 15–22.

27. Milja Kurki, "Democracy and Conceptual Contestability: Reconsidering Conceptions of Democracy in Democracy Promotion," *International Studies Review* 12 (2010), pp. 362–86, p. 365.

28. This notion is often associated with Huntington (1996) but since September 11, 2001, this argument has been made in countless editorials, opinion pieces, and blogs, largely but not exclusively from conservative perspectives.

29. See, for example, Noel Ignatiev, *How the Irish Became White* (New York: Routledge, 1996).

30. Ronald Reagan, "Remarks at a White House Ceremony Inaugurating the National Endowment for Democracy," December 16, 1983.

CHAPTER 3

1. "Bush: 'Democracy Will Succeed' in Iraq," CNN.com, November 19, 2003 (www.cnn.com/2003/WORLD/europe/11/19/bush.speech/).

2. Michael McFaul, "Democracy Promotion as a World Value," *Washington Quarterly* 28, no. 1 (2004–05), pp. 147–63, p. 148 (parentheses in original).

3. Mark J. L. McClelland, "Exporting Virtue: Neoconservatism, Democracy Promotion and the End of History," *International Journal of Human Rights* 15, no. 4 (2011), pp. 520–31, p. 520.

4. Thomas Melia, "The Democracy Bureaucracy," *American Interest* 1, no. 4 (2006).

5. Thomas Carothers, *U.S. Democracy Promotion during and after Bush* (Washington: Carnegie Endowment for International Peace, 2007).

6. Thomas Carothers, *Critical Missions: Essays on Democracy Promotion* (Washington: Carnegie Endowment for International Peace, 2004), p. 110.

7. See, for example, Fred Barbash, "Bush: Iraq Part of 'Global Democratic Revolution,'" *Washington Post*, November 6, 2003 (www.washingtonpost.com/wp-dyn/articles/A7991-2003Nov6.html).

8. For more on the Color Revolutions, see Lincoln Mitchell, *The Color Revolutions* (University of Pennsylvania Press, 2012); Lucan Way, "The Real Causes of the Color Revolutions," *Journal of Democracy* 19, no. 3 (July 2008); Valerie Bunce and Sharon Wolchik, "Favorable Conditions and Electoral Revolutions," *Journal of Democracy* 17, no. 4 (October 2006); Donnacha O Beachain and Abel Polese, *The Colour Revolutions in the Former Soviet Republics: Successes and Failures* (New York: Routledge, 2012).

9. See, for example, Edward Lucas, *The New Cold War: Putin's Russia and the Threat to the West* (New York: Palgrave Macmillan, 2009); Dmitri Trenin, "Welcome to Cold War II," *Foreign Policy*, March 4, 2014; and numerous comments by the media and the punditry following the Georgia-Russia war in 2008 and during the Russia-Ukraine conflict of 2014.

10. George W. Bush, "Transcript of Bush's UN Speech," September 19, 2006.

11. For an analysis of Bush's Freedom Agenda, see James Traub, *The Freedom Agenda: Why America Must Spread Democracy (Just Not the Way George Bush Did).* (New York: Picador, 2009).

12. George W. Bush News Conference, November 8, 2006 (www.presidency.ucsb.edu/ws/?pid=24269).

13. Pew Research Center, "Declining Public Support for Global Engagement," September 24, 2008.

14. Pew Research Center, "Historically, Public Has Given Low Priority to Promoting Democracy," February 4, 2011.

15. Alexander Cooley, "These Colors May Run: The Backlash against the US-Backed 'Democratic Revolutions' in Eurasia," *After the Color Revolutions: Political Change and Democracy Promotion in Eurasia* (PONARS, 2010), p. 63.

16. Christopher Walker, "Authoritarian Regimes Are Changing How the World Defines Democracy," *Washington Post*, June 13, 2014.

17. Joseph S. Nye, *Bound to Lead: The Changing Nature of American Power* (New York: Basic Books, 1990).

18. "Singled Out: Russia's Detention and Expulsion of Georgians," *Human Rights Watch* 19, no. 5 (October 2007) (www.hrw.org/reports/2007/russia1007 /5.htm).

19. Larry Diamond, "Promoting Democracy in the 1990s: Actors and Instruments, Issues and Imperatives" (Washington: Carnegie Corporation on Preventing Deadly Conflict, 1995), p. 1.

CHAPTER 4

1. USAID, "Strategy on Democracy, Human Rights and Governance," June 2013.

2. USAID, "Armenia Democracy and Governance" (www.usaid.gov/armenia /democracy-and-governance); "Cambodia Supporting Rule of Law and Human Rights" (www.usaid.gov/cambodia/supporting-rule-law-and-human-rights); "Uzbekistan: Democracy, Human Rights and Governance" (www.usaid.gov /uzbekistan/democracy-human-rights-and-governance).

3. National Democratic Institute, "What We Do" (www.ndi.org/whatwedo).

4. International Republican Institute, "Mission" (http://iri.org/learn-more -about-iri/mission).

5. These claims are largely, but not entirely, true. While most of the work of NDI and IRI reflects the approach suggested by these verbs, there are times when the organizations are more active and more directly involved in trying to sway political outcomes.

6. USAID, "USAID Strategy on Democracy, Human Rights and Governance," June 2013, p. 37.

7. QED Group, Turkmenistan Governance Strengthening Project (www .qedgroupllc.com/project/turkmenistan-governance-strengthening -project).

8. Ibid.

9. Center for International Private Enterprise, "Helping Build Democracy that Delivers" (www.cipe.org/sites/default/files/publication-docs/Democracy Delivers07.pdf), p. 3.

10. See Lincoln Mitchell, *The Color Revolutions* (University of Pennsylvania Press), for a discussion of U.S. efforts to promote Color Revolutions and regime change in Belarus.

11. According to an evaluation of this program by Democracy International, the goals of this program were "(1) develop and strengthen parliamentary capacity, (2) promote greater procedural and legislative transparency, and

(3) enhance the overall effectiveness of the parliament." USAID/Azerbaijian "Parliamentary Program of Azerbaijan Evaluation: Final Report," July 2011.

12. See Sheila Carapico, "NGOs, INGOs, GO-NGOs, and DO-NGOs: Making Sense of Non-Governmental Organizations, *Middle East Research and Information Project* (www.merip.org/mer/mer214/ngos-ingos-go-ngos-do-ngos), for a critical look at the taxonomy of NGOs and their roles, particularly in the Middle East.

13. Mikheil Saakashvili was, at that time, a leader of the Georgian opposition.

14. About three months after that meeting, we were summoned to another meeting with U.S. officials, this time to discuss U.S. support for now president Saakashvili. At that meeting we both expressed our concerns about the constitutional reforms and concentration of power in Saakashvili's hands. We were told that those opinions were not welcome. Thus, my colleague and I were the last Americans to be scolded by our government for being too close to Saakashvili, and the first to be scolded for being critical of Saakashvili.

15. *Bolivia Weekly*, "Morales Accuses NGOs of Spying," January 30, 2010.

16. George Steinbrenner was the owner of New York Yankees for more than three decades. He was famous for his imperial and capricious style of leadership. In a city full of powerful people running major organizations, for a quarter century, Steinbrenner was known as "The Boss."

CHAPTER 5

1. Alexander Hamilton, John Jay, and James Madison, *The Federalist Papers* (New York: Cosimo Classics, 2006).

2. In *Federalist Paper* No. 10, Madison argues that factions are essential to liberty and that a variety of competing factions ensures pluralism and defines democracy. The most significant contribution of Fed 10 to theories of governance is that it moves away from the search for the right system or policies and toward recognition that a process based on contestation is most important. The implication of this for democratizing countries is self-evident.

3. Zeke J. Miller, "Biden Takes Veiled Shot at Clinton, Panetta over 'Inappropriate' Books," *Time*, October 3, 2014.

4. U.S. Department of State, "Experts Discuss Promoting Democracy and Human Rights Worldwide," January 29, 2009 (http://iipdigital.usembassy.gov /st/english/texttrans/2009/01/20090129180446xjsnommis0.8254663.html #axzz3FNylHhKL).

5. Ibid.

6. "Remarks by President George W. Bush at the 20th Anniversary of the National Endowment for Democracy," November 6, 2003 (www.ned.org

/george-w-bush/remarks-by-president-george-w-bush-at-the-20th -anniversary).

7. Campbell, "The Basic Concept for the Democracy Ranking of the Quality of Democracy," *Democracy Ranking* (www.democracyranking.org/downloads /basic_concept_democracy_ranking_2008_A4.pdf).

8. E. B. White, "The Meaning of Democracy," *New Yorker*, July 3, 1943.

9. Elizabeth Cohn, "US Democratization Assistance," *Foreign Policy in Focus*, July 1, 1999.

10. Negar Azimi, "Hard Realities of Soft Power," *New York Times*, June 24, 2007 (www.nytimes.com/2007/06/24/magazine/24ngo-t.html?pagewanted=all&_r=0).

11. "USAID Strategy on Democracy, Human Rights, and Governance," USAID, New York, June 2013.

12. For more on the declining state of democracy during the later years of Saakashvili's presidency, see Lincoln Mitchell, *The Color Revolutions* (University of Pennsylvania Press, 2012); "Georgia: The Issue Is Not Democracy," *Survival* 54, no. 2 (April-May 2012), pp. 97–112; "Faded Colors," *The American Interest* 6, no. 5 (May-June 2011), pp. 22–28; Thomas de Waal, "So Long Saakashvili: The Presidency That Lived by Spin—And Died by It," *Foreign Affairs*, October 29, 2013; or Miriam Lanskoy and Irakli Areshidze, "Georgia's Year of Turmoil," *Journal of Democracy* 19, no. 4 (October 2008).

13. For more on Bakiev's Kyrgyzstan, see Ben Judah, "A Sinking 'Island of Democracy,'" *Transitions Online*, August 26, 2009; or Human Rights Watch, "Kyrgyzstan: Human Rights Watch's Letter to President Bakiev on Freedom of Assembly," January 17, 2008 (www.hrw.org/news/2008/01/16/kyrgyzstan -human-rights-watchs-letter-president-bakiev-freedom-assembly).

14. The White House, "A National Security Strategy for a New Century," October 1998 (http://clinton2.nara.gov/WH/EOP/NSC/html/documents/nssr .pdf).

15. The White House, "The National Security Strategy of the United States of America," March 2006 (http://usa.usembassy.de/etexts/nss2006.pdf).

16. Robert A. Dahl, *Dilemmas of Pluralist Democracy: Autonomy vs. Control* (Yale University Press, 1982), p. 5.

17. Dahl, *Dilemmas of Pluralist Democracy*, p. 40.

18. *Seinfeld* was a situation comedy on NBC during the 1980s and 1990s that was "about nothing" and included this dialogue between two friends trying to decide how to pitch a television show to NBC:

George: Everybody's doing something—we'll do nothing.
Jerry: So, we go into NBC, we tell them we've got an idea for a show about nothing.

19. OSCE, "Election Observation Mission, Georgia, Interim Report No. 2," September 24, 2012 (www.osce.org/odihr/93966?download=true).

20. NDI, "Statement of the National Democratic Institute Pre-Election Delegation to Georgia," June 29, 2012 (www.ndi.org/files/Georgia-PEAM -062912.pdf).

21. Thomas Carothers, "The End of the Transition Paradigm," *Journal of Democracy* 13, no. 1 (January 2002), pp. 5–21.

22. In the United States, for example, some in the Republican Party, particularly at the state and local level, have strong anti-LGBT views that would draw attention from U.S.-funded government watchdogs in NGOs in most countries. Clearly, the Republican Party is an important voice in American politics representing millions of people who have the right to have their voices heard on this and other issues.

23. Carter Center, "Preliminary Report, Study Mission of the Carter Center: Presidential Elections in Venezuela," April 14, 2013 (www.cartercenter.org /resources/pdfs/news/peace_publications/election_reports/venezuela-pre -election-rpt-2013.pdf).

24. Paul Eckert, "US Holds Back Recognition for Venezuela's Maduro," *Reuters*, April 17, 2013 (www.reuters.com/article/2013/04/17/us-venezuela-usa -kerry-idUSBRE93G0MJ20130417).

25. A Condorcet winner is a candidate who in a multi-candidate election would defeat all other candidates in a direct head to head matchup. Although these candidates exist in some elections, no voting system is able to ensure the Condorcet winner always wins.

26. In 2001, President George W. Bush commented after meeting Putin that he had been "able to get a sense of his soul." Carla Anne Robbins, "Mr. Bush Gets Another Look into Mr. Putin's Eyes," *New York Times*, June 30, 2007 (www .nytimes.com/2007/06/30/opinion/30sat3.html).

CHAPTER 6

1. CBS News, "Text of Bush Speech," May 1, 2003 (www.cbsnews.com/news /text-of-bush-speech-01-05-2003/).

2. Rosa Brooks, "Democracy Promotion: Done Right, A Progressive Cause," *Democracy Journal* 23 (Winter 2012) (www.democracyjournal.org/23/democracy -promotion-done-right-a-progressive-cause.php?page=all).

3. Ibid.

4. Omar G. Encarnacion, "The Follies of Democratic Imperialism," *World Policy Journal* 22, no. 1 (Spring 2005) (www.worldpolicy.newschool.edu/wpi /journal/articles/wpj05-sp/encarnacion.html).

5. Shashi Tharoor and Sam Daws, "Humanitarian Intervention: Getting Past the Reefs," *World Policy Journal* 18, no. 2 (Summer 2001).

6. CNN, "Bush: Democracy Will Succeed in Iraq," November 19, 2003 (www.cnn.com/2003/WORLD/europe/11/19/bush.speech/index.html?_s =PM:WORLD).

7. Fred Barbash, "Bush: Iraq Part of 'Global Democratic Revolution,'" *Washington Post*, November 6, 2003 (www.washingtonpost.com/wp-dyn/articles /A7991-2003Nov6.html).

8. George W. Bush, "The Struggle for Democracy in Iraq: Speech to the World Affairs Council of Philadelphia," December 12, 2005 (www.presidential rhetoric.com/speeches/12.12.05.html).

9. Pew Research Center, "Americans Put Low Priority on Promoting Democracy Abroad," December 4, 2013 (www.pewresearch.org/fact-tank/2013/12/04 /americans-put-low-priority-on-promoting-democracy-abroad/).

10. There are many possible good answers to this question, but the case has not been persuasively made to the American public.

11. USAID, USAID/Kyrgyzstan Collaborative Governance Program (www .usaid.gov/kyrgyz-republic/fact-sheets/collaborative-governance-program).

12. Pew, "Americans Put Low Priority on Promoting Democracy Abroad."

13. In fiscal year 2013, 5.4 percent of U.S. foreign assistance was spent on democracy and governance. For FY2014, democracy and governance represented 5.8 percent of obligated funds. Foreign assistance itself typically represents less than 1 percent of the total U.S. budget, so in the big picture, the amount of money used for supporting democracy and governance is clearly quite small. USAID, USAID/Budget and Spending (www.foreignassistance.gov).

14. Thomas Carothers and Saskia Brechenmacher, "Closing Space: Democracy and Human Rights Support Under Fire" (Washington: Carnegie Endowment for International Peace, 2014) (http://carnegieendowment.org/files/closing _space.pdf).

15. Lincoln Mitchell, "The US Should Stop Patting Itself on the Back over the Torture Report," *New York Observer*, December 12, 2014 (http://observer .com/2014/12/the-u-s-should-stop-patting-itself-on-the-back-over-the-torture -report/).

16. See, for example, Benjamin Bidder, "Russia Today: Putin's Weapon in the War of Images," *Spiegel*, August 13, 2013 (www.spiegel.de/international /business/putin-fights-war-of-images-and-propaganda-with-russia-today -channel-a-916162.html); Hadas Gold, "Behind the RT Propaganda Shop," *Politico*, March 14, 2014 (www.politico.com/blogs/media/2014/03/behind-the-rt -propaganda-shop-185138.html); or Felix Gillette, "On the Kremlin's Overseas Propaganda News Channel, Putin Really Rules," *Bloomberg*, March 4, 2014 (www.businessweek.com/articles/2014-03-04/putin-rules-on-rt-russia-s -overseas-propaganda-news-channel).

17. See Lincoln Mitchell, "How Kremlin TV Covers America and Why It Matters," *New York Observer*, February 3, 2015 (http://observer.com/2015/02 /how-kremlin-tv-covers-america-and-why-it-matters/).

18. David W. Brady, "Is the US Government Really Broken?" *Real Clear Politics*, February 2, 2014 (www.realclearpolitics.com/articles/2014/02/02/is_the _us_government_really_broken_121395.html).

19. David Frum, "Why Our Government Is Broken," *CNN*, September 26, 2011 (www.cnn.com/2011/09/26/opinion/frum-broken-government/).

20. Thomas Mann, "Admit It, Political Scientists: Politics Really Is More Broken Than Ever," *The Atlantic*, May 26, 2014 (www.theatlantic.com/politics /archive/2014/05/dysfunction/371544/).

21. John W. Dean, *Broken Government: How Republican Rule Destroyed the Legislative, Executive and Judicial Branches* (New York: Penguin Books, 2007).

22. Elias Isquith, "The System Is Broken: How the Midterms Expose Our Dying Democracy," *Salon*, November 4, 2014 (www.salon.com/2014/11/05/the _system_is_broken_how_the_midterms_expose_our_dying_democracy/).

23. See Latin America Working Group, "USAID's Cuban Twitter: 'Democracy Promotion' Does More Harm Than Good" (www.lawg.org/component /content/article/1315/1315), on U.S. wasting money in Cuba; or *American Interest*, "USAID Shows Commitment to Democracy by Covering Up Failures," October 23, 2014 (www.the-american-interest.com/2014/10/23/usaid-shows -commitment-to-democracy-by-covering-up-failures/), on Pakistan.

24. Left-of-center sites and articles like Adam Hanieh, " 'Democracy Promotion' and Neo-Liberalism in the Middle East," *State of Nature*, March 29, 2006 (www.stateofnature.org/?p=5438); and David Reiff, "Democracy No!" *Democracy: A Journal of Ideas* 24 (Spring 2012) (www.democracyjournal.org/24 /democracy-no.php) make an explicit link between democracy promotion and imperialism.

25. Thomas Carothers, "Why Is the United States Shortchanging Its Commitment to Democracy?" *Washington Post*, December 22, 2014 (www .washingtonpost.com/opinions/falling-usaid-spending-shows-a-lack-of -commitment-to-fostering-democracy/2014/12/22/86b72d58-89f4-11e4-a085 -34e9b9f09a58_story.html).

26. Ibid.

27. Tomas Bridle, "One Size Does Not Fit All," *Foreign Policy*, September 10, 2013.

CHAPTER 7

1. Reuters, "Putin Says Russia Must Guard against 'Color Revolutions,'" November 20, 2014 (www.businessinsider.com/r-putin-says-russia-must-guard -against-color-revolutions-2014-11).

2. Natasha Abbakumova and Kathy Lally, "Russia Boots Out USAID," *Washington Post*, September 18, 2012.

3. USAID, USAID/China (www.usaid.gov/china).

4. USAID, USAID/Budget and Spending (www.foreignassistance.gov/).

5. See, for example, "United States of America General Election, Limited Election Observation Mission Report," February 13, 2013 (www.osce.org/odihr /elections/99573?download=true).

6. Alexander Bolton, "International Monitors at US Polling Spots Draw Criticism from Voter Fraud Groups," *The Hill*, October 20, 2012 (http://thehill .com/homenews/campaign/263141-international-monitors-at-polling-places -draw-criticism-from-voter-fraud-group).

7. Jake Tapper, "The Woman Under Fire," *Salon*, November 13, 2000 (www .salon.com/2000/11/13/harris_7/).

8. Carlos Valdez and Frank Bajak, "Bolivia's Morales Expels USAID for Allegedly Seeking to Undermine Government," *Huffington Post*, May 1, 2013 (www .huffingtonpost.com/2013/05/01/bolivia-morales-expels-usaid_n_3193115.html).

9. William Neuman, "US Agency Is Expelled from Bolivia," *New York Times*, May 1, 2013.

10. Human Rights Watch, "Choking on Bureaucracy: State Curbs on Independent Civic Activism," February 2008 (www.hrw.org/reports/2008/russia0208 /4.htm).

11. International Center for Not-for-Profit Law, "NGO Law Monitor: Russia," February 17, 2005 (www.icnl.org/research/monitor/russia.html).

12. International Helsinki Federation for Human Rights, "Central Asia: Human Rights Groups Facing Increasingly Restrictive Legislation," February 2006 (www.refworld.org/pdfid/46963aec0.pdf).

13. Nick Paton Walsh, "Russia Says 'Spies' Work in Foreign NGOs," *The Guardian*, February 13, 2005 (www.theguardian.com/world/2005/may/13/russia .nickpatonwalsh).

14. Simon Saradzhayan and Carl Schreck, "FSB Chief: NGOs a Cover for Spying," *Moscow Times*, May 13, 2005 (www.themoscowtimes.com/sitemap/free /2005/5/article/fsb-chief-ngos-a-cover-for-spying/223321.html).

15. Peter Finn, "Putin Links Espionage to NGO Funding," *Washington Post*, January 26, 2006 (www.washingtonpost.com/wp-dyn/content/article/2006/01 /25/AR2006012501061.html).

16. John Ikenberry, "Soft Power: The Means to Success in World Politics," *Foreign Affairs*, May/June 2004.

17. Henry Meyer and Ilya Arkhipov, "Putin Bets $15 Billion to Capture Junk-Rated Ukraine Vassal," *Bloomberg*, December 19, 2013 (www.businessweek .com/news/2013-12-18/putin-wagers-15-billion-to-capture-junk-rated -ukrainian-vassal).

18. See, for example, Dorothy-Grace Guerrero and Firoze Manji, eds., *China's New Role in Africa and the South: A Search for a New Perspective* (Nairobi: Pambazuka Press, 2008); Axel Harneit-Sievers, Stephen Marks, and Sanusha Naidu, eds., *Chinese and African Perspectives on China in Africa* (Nairobi: Pambazuka Press, 2010); or Robert Rotberg, *China Into Africa: Trade, Aid and Influence* (Brookings, 2008).

19. IRI, "Best Practices in Democratic Governance: A Guide for Local Governments," 2012 (www.iri.org/sites/default/files/flip_docs/How-To-Manual _FINAL_012213/index.html).

20. NDI, Neil Nevitte, and Melissa Estok, "Tracking Democracy: Benchmark Surveys for Diagnostics, Program Design and Evaluation," July 1, 2009 (www.ndi.org/node/16046).

21. USAID, "Democracy, Human Rights and Governance Assessment of the Democratic Republic of Congo," November 2012 (www.usaid.gov/what-we-do /democracy-human-rights-and-governance/technical-publications).

CHAPTER 8

1. See, for example, Charles W. Dunne, "Democracy Promotion: Obama's Mixed Record," *Middle East Institute*, November 19, 2014 (www.mei.edu/content /article/democracy-promotion-obamas-mixed-record); Thomas Carothers, "Why Is the United States Shortchanging Its Commitment to Democracy?" *Washington Post*, December 22, 2014; or Shadi Hamid and Peter Mandaville, "The US Is Giving Up on Middle East Democracy—And That's a Mistake," *The Atlantic*, January 7, 2014 (www.theatlantic.com/international/archive/2014 /01/the-us-is-giving-up-on-middle-east-democracy-and-thats-a-mistake /282890/).

2. The budget for democracy, human rights, and governance was only $1.02 billion in FY2014 and $1.19 billion in FY2013, down from $2.16 billion in FY2012 and $1.78 billion in FY2011. USAID, USAID/Budget and Spending (www.foreignassistance.gov/web/ObjectiveView.aspx?FY=2011&tabID=tab _sct_Peace_Disbs&budTab=tab_Bud_Spent).

3. Pew Research Center, "Americans Put Low Priority on Promoting Democracy Abroad," December 4, 2013 (www.pewresearch.org/fact-tank/2013/12 /04/americans-put-low-priority-on-promoting-democracy-abroad/).

4. This is what Melinda Haring recommends in "Reforming the Democracy Bureaucracy," *Foreign Policy*, June 3, 2013 (http://foreignpolicy.com/2013/06 /03/reforming-the-democracy-bureaucracy/).

INDEX

ABA (American Bar Association), 99
Abu Ghraib, 147
Ackerman, Peterman, 12
ACLU (American Civil Liberties
Union), 158
Advocacy organizations, 95
Afghanistan: Bush on, 60; democracy
building, need for, 3, 38; democracy
promotion in, 14, 35, 52–53, 59,
131; national security vs. role of
democracy promotion in, 76; U.S.
unpreparedness for regime change
in, 31; war in, 18–19, 163–64
Africa, Chinese activities in, 168
"After Saddam: Prewar Planning and
the Occupation of Iraq"
(Benashel), 30–31
Albright, Madeline, 77, 150
Aliyev family, 180, 189
Al-Jazeera, 145
Allende, Salvador, 48
Alliance for Progress, 37

Al-Maliki, Nouri, 49
Ambassadors (U.S.), 56, 128
Ambrosius, Lloyd E., 32
American Bar Association (ABA), 99
American Civil Liberties Union
(ACLU), 158
American exceptionalism, 76–77
American identity, democracy as part
of, 106
"America's Place in the World" (Pew
Research Center), 185
Ang Son Su Kyi, 127
Anti-Americanism, 2, 58–59, 151–52
Anti-free market authoritarianism, 113
Anti-interventionism, growth of,
22–23
Arab Spring, 1, 63
Armenia: as democracy promotion
funds recipient, 69; democracy
work in, 23–24; Russian influence
in, 168, 180
Asia, Chinese activities in, 168

National security strategy documents, 113
Nation building, definition of, 38
Nations vs. states, 38
Nativist movements, 45
NATO, 11, 56
Natural disasters, 169
NDI. *See* National Democratic Institute
NED. *See* National Endowment for Democracy
Neoconservatives, 43, 52, 61, 132–33, 137
Netherlands, 78
New Deal policies, 43
New democracies, delivery by, 89–90
New Yorker, 110
NGOs. *See* Nongovernmental organizations
Nicaragua, 48
9/11. *See* September 11 terrorist attacks
Noncommunist authoritarian regimes, 70
Nondemocratic countries and regimes: anti-democratic actions of, 68; bilateral relationships with, 192; Cold War policy toward, 44, 49; collapses of, 182, 189; consolidated nature of, 179; democracy promotion programs in, 5–6, 65, 70, 73, 74–75; democratic reform and, 86–94; foreign aid to, 94; foreign policies of, 143; geopolitical orientation of, 112–13; governance of, 89; ineffectiveness of democracy promotion in, 84, 175; legislatures in, 118; overthrow of, democracy building vs., 120; political parties in, 122–23; replacement cycle of, 85–86; Russian support of, 168;

signs of democracy in, 129; transitional countries vs., 66–67; unity, belief in, 116; Western democracy promotion, attitude toward, 160. *See also* Semi-authoritarian countries; Semi-democratic countries
Nongovernmental organizations (NGOs), 94–102; during Cold War, 45; confrontational future scenario, possible support for, 187; foreign governments, relationship to, 96; funding sources for, paradox of, 9–10; GONGOs, 95–96; government, relationship to, 99–101; importance of, 152; INGOs, 97; perceptions of, 94–95; Russian laws against, 2, 161; secret service agencies, supposed links to, 161–62; SGOs, 98; suspicions against, 97–98; USAID and contractors, relationship to, 101–02; varied characteristics of, 95. *See also specific NGOs, e.g., U.S. Agency for International Development*
North Africa: challenge of nondemocratic regimes in, 24–25; democratic breakthroughs in, 189; role of democracy promotion in, 182. *See also individual countries*
NSA surveillance, 145
Nye, Joseph, 68, 164

Obama administration: comparison with Bush administration, 178; democracy promotion, 3, 22, 25, 62, 132; economic outlook, 140; expenditures for democracy promotion, 149; Freedom Agenda and, 61; on Russia's invasion of Crimea, 20; soft power, 144–45